CELEBRITIES OF OUR TIME

CELEBRITIES OF OUR TIME

INTERVIEWS

BY

HERMAN BERNSTEIN

Essay Index Reprint Series

 BOOKS FOR LIBRARIES PRESS
FREEPORT, NEW YORK

First Published 1924
Reprinted 1968

LIBRARY OF CONGRESS CATALOG CARD NUMBER:

68-8438

MANUFACTURED
BY
HALLMARK LITHOGRAPHERS, INC.
IN THE U.S.A.

Acknowledgment is due to The New York Times, The New York Herald, The New York Sun, The New York World, The New York American and Our World for permission to reproduce these interviews which originally appeared in these publications.

A few of my interviews reproduced here appeared also in 1913, in a privately printed little volume entitled "With Master Minds," the entire edition of which has been exhausted since 1914.

H. B.

PREFACE

During the past fifteen years, I have met celebrities under all conditions and in many lands. Some were only get-notorious-quick celebrities, made suddenly by some unusual situation, wearing the garments of momentary grandeur, their glories dimming and their personalities fading in a descent as rapid as their rise.

In contrast to these were other celebrities whom I travelled thousands of miles to meet. These were the men who by their genius for art, science and government, touched close to the springs of life; who were the real, even though sometimes unrecognized, hewers of circumstances.

I have thus met practically every outstanding figure of my time who has influenced thought and shaped important events. I have experienced the stimulating pleasure of discussing with these geniuses in their own work-shops, in the studies where they conceived and executed their great work, those questions which had been raised in their writings, researches, or by their political activities.

Always and everywhere I have gone to the fountainhead. What gratified me most is that acquaintance with a number of these men deepened into friendship, establishing relationships that I treasure with pride.

I do not know how many tens of thousands of miles I have traversed in the course of these journeys, during the past fifteen years. Though at times beset with numerous hardships, it has been in the main a pleasant road. The

days enroute were spiced with incident and color. I have
come to know the sea at all times of the year—the Atlantic
and the Pacific, the Mediterranean, the Black Sea and the
Arctic Ocean. I have seen the little comedies of tourist
and professional travel, as well as the stark tragedies of
the war, which I viewed not only on military and diplomatic
fronts, but also in the homes of the people involved in
the war.

What were the emotions experienced on meeting these
celebrated men? I am often asked. Some of them have
been to the mind what a dip in the surf is to the body on
a hot day, or like the clean, strong, invigorating November
wind. Some—I am thinking principally of Leo Tolstoy—
have been like the calm effulgence of the setting sun, illumi-
nating heaven and earth as the day is dying. A visit to one
was like a day in a fairyland grotto, a place where magic
arts were thriving. With one's intellect and vision I was
millions of miles away from the earth, gazing with a cold,
detached laboratory view upon the vanities of the human
species. Another showed me the world as a circus, of which
he was the clown, the rest of mankind the donkeys in the
show, and the Olympian gods as the laughing audience.
Some of them were electric currents transmitting their high-
powered voltage of revolution through the minds of millions of human beings. Among them were apostles of
peace and leaders of unrest.

I have seen the war at close range—I have seen the
militarist diplomats and politicians, blind with passion,
wild with vengeance, savage from the sight of blood, craving
conquest and power. They turned the world into a madhouse, into a huge cemetery, while all of them were reading
the same Bible, praying to the same God to destroy the

enemy—the people who did not know one another, who had no real grievance against one another, who wanted peace and work and happiness. I have seen the real victims of the war—the children. And I wondered as I looked at them: What will the young generation think of us when it grows up and sees the truth behind the war? What ideals will it have? What standard of morality? What respect for law and order? What sense of sympathy? After the most bloody war in history, in which the very dreams of inventors were harnessed for destruction, what respect will the children have for the life of a human being? The tears and the blood that irrigated the devastated fields, what harvests will they yield?

And I have seen the peace. I have seen the victims of peace in various lands. And though five and a half years have elapsed since the armistice, peace has not yet been restored. The war spirit is not yet demobilized in many lands. New conflicts, new strife and new hatreds have sprung up. Instead of peace without victory, we have victory without peace.

———

The interviews included in this book are perhaps the most characteristic among the hundreds of talks I have had with celebrities in various lands. I have made no attempt at fine writing, but have endeavored to secure from the celebrities their views on problems which interested them and me, and on which they could speak with authority. I have also tried to present their views faithfully.

I have not changed these articles, and have indicated in each instance the time and place of the interview, so that the reader may be able to judge who of these celebrities read the future clearly and who was short-sighted.

The subjects touched in this book are varied and are of necessity treated in a fragmentary manner.   Yet the flashes of thought of the men occupying such conspicuous posts in the activities of the world during the most stirring period in history may prove of peculiar interest to all sorts and conditions of readers.

If the interviews in this collection should lead the reader to a closer study of the work of some of these famous men, I shall feel that this book has served its purpose.

HERMAN BERNSTEIN.

New York, June 21, 1924.

CONTENTS

CONTENTS

CONTENTS

CONTENTS

THE CELEBRITIES OF OUR TIME

LEO TOLSTOY

St. Petersburg, June, 1908.

BEFORE my departure for Yasnaya Polyana, Prof. Maxime Kovalevsky, one of Russia's foremost editors and authorities on international law, said to me:

"You will see the only man in Russia who dares to tell the truth, even to the Tsar, and is not punished for it."

I left St. Petersburg on the day after the first convention of the representatives of the Russian press. The elite of Russian publicists had come together for the purpose of considering the most adequate ways and means of celebrating the eightieth anniversary of Tolstoy's birthday. Young and old, men and women, offered suggestions of how best to honor the man who is at present the Russian people's only pride. They spoke with boundless enthusiasm, with fire, with zeal and earnestness with which an enslaved people, suddenly set free, speaks of freedom.

A young journalist rose and in a forceful speech declared that the most suitable means of honoring Tolstoy would be for the entire Russian press on the 28th day of August, the birthday of Tolstoy, to condemn the wholesale executions that are being committed daily in the Russian Empire and to issue a general appeal that these death sentences be abolished. Then an officer walked over to the chairman and informed him that unless the delegates stopped talking of the executions he would disperse the Convention.

But Russia—all Russia, except the Government, the Holy Synod, and the Black Hundreds—seems to have for-

3

gotten for a while its helplessness and its misery in its preparations to do honor to Tolstoy. The people throughout Russia are infinitely more interested in the Tolstoy celebration than in the work of the Russian "Parliament." Only from time to time the Union of the Real Russian People, composed of bands of dark reactionaries, in their organs, which are patronized by the Government, but which are despised by the people, attack Tolstoy in the vilest terms, branding him as an anti-Christ and a traitor. The Church has done all in its power to hinder the jubilee, and on the day that I started for Yasnaya Polyana I read in the newspapers that the St. Petersburg authorities had refused to legalize a society which was to be formed in honor of Tolstoy and which was to be known as the Leo Tolstoy Society.

On the way to Tula, in the train, a stout, red-faced "man with long hair"—a Russian priest—was seated opposite me. Eager to hear a Russian priest's view concerning conditions in Russia, and particularly his opinion of Tolstoy, I entered into conversation with him. When I told him that I was going to see Tolstoy I noticed how his face suddenly brightened, his red cheeks turned still redder, and bending over to me he said in a low voice, so as not to be overheard by the other passengers:

"You are a lucky man. . . . When you see that saintliest man in Russia, tell him that you met a Russian village priest who sends him greetings from the bottom of his heart. Tell him that the priest you met bowed his head with shame for the manner in which the Church has treated Tolstoy. And tell him that the few peasants who have learned to read, read nothing but the Bible and Tolstoy. They understand his works even better than the Bible."

As we turned past the little blue church at Yasnaya Polyana, I saw five women in bright parti-colored loose dresses, laughing and singing and whirling about as they worked in the field, and the group, as well as the colors of their clothes, reminded me of Malyavin's masterly painting, "The Whirlwind," which is symbolic of chaotic, red Russia. Finally, at about half past nine in the morning, after having passed through numerous labyrinthine roads, I found myself at the door of the little white house where lives and works the greatest artist and the most remarkable man in the world to-day—Leo Tolstoy. I was met by Nicholas Gusev, Tolstoy's secretary, an amiable young gentleman, who took me into his room.

Presently he entered. I cannot recall what I said when I shook hands with Tolstoy, but he put me at my ease immediately, and he strengthened my conviction that the greatest men are the simplest, even as the chief characteristic of the greatest masterpieces is their simplicity. In the corner, like a striking painting by Rembrandt, sat the grand old man, a black, soft silk turban on his head, his wide-open eyes bright with kindness, such as I have never seen in any painting or photograph of Tolstoy.

"You will pardon me if I will drink my coffee as we speak," he said to me in English. Then, changing from English to Russian, he asked me about my impressions of Russia, and particularly about the popularity of Henry George's works in America.

I related to him the incident that occurred at the Convention of the Representatives of the Press.

"Yes," he said, "an appeal by the press for the abolition of executions in Russia would please me better than any other honor." He spoke in a soft, caressing voice, and the peculiar radiance of his face, the far-away look in his eyes—all really gave him the appearance of a saint, "a man not of this world," as Repin had aptly described him.

"Count, I should like to know your views upon the future of Russia," I asked.

"One of the most horrible superstitions," answered Tolstoy, after a minute's pause, "more harmful than all religious superstitions—one which has caused rivers of blood —is that very strange superstition which sprang from the use of violence, and which makes people believe that a small number of men can now establish the social life of the whole community. This activity to transform the present order of things not only fails to help, but actually hinders the course of progress. The activity of revolutionists, like the deeds of violence committed by the Government, will not lead to any improvement in the life of our people. On the contrary, Stolypin, who hangs hundreds of people, and the revolutionists, who are trying to kill Nicholas II, are only interfering with the natural development of events. History is full of examples to prove this. The French Revolution produced Napoleon. The civil war produced the terrible negro problem in America."

Count Tolstoy shook his head, brushed back a tuft of white hair from under his turban, and added, as though to himself:

"Strange—very strange."

"Nearly fifty years ago," he went on slowly, "the great question that occupied all minds in Russia was the emancipation of the serfs. The burning question now is the ownership of land. The peasants never recognized the private ownership of land. They say that the land belongs to God. I am afraid that people will regard what I say as stupid, but I must say it: The leaders of the revolutionary movement, as well as the Government officials, fail to do the only thing that would pacify the people at once. And the only thing that would pacify the people now is the introduction of the system of Henry George. I have outlined a plan according to which the agrarian question can be solved, and have submitted my plan to the Government as well as to the Duma. I have written about it to one who occupies a high post in the official world, and whose family I have known very well. But his hands are tied. His attitude toward the Court and toward his enemies is such that he cannot do anything in this direction. I do not reproach him. I only feel sorry for him. They do not understand that the proper solution of the land question is the only means of pacifying nine-tenths of the Russian population.

"As I have pointed out in my introductory note to the Russian version of 'Social Problems,' Henry George's great idea, outlined so clearly and so thoroughly more than thirty years ago, remains to this day entirely unknown to the great majority of the people. This is quite natural. Henry George's idea, which changes the entire system in the life of nations in favor of the oppressed, voiceless majority, and to the detriment of the ruling minority, is so thoroughly convincing, and, above all, so simple, that it is impossible not to understand it, and, understanding it, it is impossible not to make an effort to introduce it into practice, and, therefore, the only means of fighting this idea is to pervert it, or pass it in silence. And this has been done to the Henry George theory for more than thirty years. It has been perverted or passed in silence, so that it has become difficult to induce people to read his works attentively and to think about it.

"It is true that there are in England, Canada, the United States, and Germany very good little journals devoted to the single tax idea, but they have only an insignificant number of subscribers. Among the majority of the intelligent people throughout the world, the ideas of Henry George are unknown, and the indifference toward them is even increasing. Society does with ideas that disturb its peace exactly what the bee does with the worms which it considers dangerous but which it is powerless to destroy. It covers their nest with paste, so that the worms, even though not destroyed, cannot multiply and do more harm. Just so the European nations act with regard to ideas that are dangerous to their order of things, or rather, to the disorder to which they have grown accustomed. Among these are also the ideas of Henry George. 'But light shines even in the darkness, and the darkness cannot cover it.' A truthful, fruitful idea cannot be destroyed. However you may try to smother it, it will still live, it will be more alive than all the vague, empty, pedantic ideas and words with which people are trying to kill it. Thus it will also be with Henry George's ideal.

"It seems to me that just now is the proper time to introduce this idea—now, and in Russia. This is just the time for it, because in Russia there is a revolution, the serious basis of which is the rejection by the whole people, by the real people, of the ownership of land. In Russia, where nine-tenths of the population are tillers of the soil, and where this theory is merely a conscious expression of that which has always been regarded as right by the entire Russian people—in Russia, I say, especially during this period of reconstruction of social conditions, this idea should now find its application, and thus the revolution, so wrongly and criminally directed, would be crowned by a great act of righteousness. This is my answer to your question about the future of Russia. Unless this idea is introduced into the life of our people Russia's future can never be bright." Thus ended our first conversation. Tolstoy advised me to meet Nikolayev, the translator of 'Henry George, who lives a little distance away from the Tolstoy home.

"Talk this matter over with him and then we will continue our conversation. By the way, you had better finish your breakfast," added Tolstoy with a smile, leading me to the dining room.

In the doorway I met Countess Tolstoy, holding a bunch of fresh white roses, and as she passed she said:

"Leo Nikolayevich is very fond of these flowers."

I came out on the porch, where I met Tolstoy's physician, Dr. Dushan Makowitzky. I inquired about Tolstoy's health.

"Three days ago Count Tolstoy had a hemorrhage, which weakened him very much," he said. "But he is recovering very fast. Until a few days ago he walked a great deal and took long rides on horseback."

We had passed the beautiful flower-bed in front of the porch and turned into the "alley of oaks," a straight, long alley, with spreading century oaks on each side.

"Here Leo Nikolayevich prays every morning," Dr. Makowitzky told me. From the "alley of oaks" we went through the forest, where the physician showed me a beautiful bit of scenery, which Tolstoy described in "Anna Karenina."

After an interesting conversation with M. Nikolayev, with whom I visited the homes of the peasants of Yasnaya Polyana, I returned to Tolstoy's room. He spoke to me of his latest work, "I Cannot be Silent," and of another essay, which is to appear shortly.   I asked him what he regarded as his most important work thus far.

"I consider my artistic works as insignificant.   My most important works are those dealing with religious subjects which I have written during the past ten years," replied Tolstoy.

"And the artistic works which were produced during the past ten years?"

"You refer to such works as 'Resurrection'?   They are important insofar as they treat of religious self-perfection. That which is called artistic is aristocratic art.   Therefore, I am against it.   I should have said that I value greatly all my plain folk stories.   But my very best work is the 'Cycle of Readings.'   Only one-tenth of it is my own work. It is composed of extracts I have made from the writings of the greatest masters of all time.   This I consider as my most important and most useful work.   It is my prayer-book.   I use the selections for every day as my daily prayers.   It is in every respect my favorite work."

In discussing the state of Russian literature at the present time, Tolstoy said:

"I have a very poor opinion of it."   He hesitated for a while, then added: "I am re-reading Pushkin now.   My God, what a downfall, what a terrible downfall, from Pushkin to the present-day writers!   When I think of Russian writers I stop on Dostoyevsky, Turgenev and Ostrovsky. Chekhov?   Chekhov was a graceful writer, a master of great irony, but his work is not sufficiently substantial; it lacks deep feeling."

Tolstoy smiled, halted a while, and said slowly:

"The value of a fraction is determined by the numerator.

The smaller the numerator, the smaller the fraction. If the numerator is zero, no matter what the denominator is, the result will be zero. The decadent school of literature in Russia, as well as in all other countries, is made up of nothing save the greatest self-conceit, and this is the numerator which reduces it to zero. Ibsen, Oscar Wilde, and others (Tolstoy enumerated many well-known French, English, and American writers, but later he asked me not to mention their names in this article), they are all decadents—all full of enormous self-conceit. When I read Pushkin I see modesty and beauty in every line. When I read the English or American writers like William Dean Howells, I involuntarily think of Dickens and Thackeray, and the comparison is fatal to the new writers. In Dickens, as in Pushkin, the shortest piece is carefully conceived, elaborated and polished. There is no greater enemy of aristocracy in art than your humble servant—myself. Yet I must say that when art was supported and patronized by aristocrats the artists made all efforts to appeal to the refined tastes of those patrons of art, but when the masses became the patrons of art the artists, in their desire to appeal to the masses, have lost their refinement.

"There is a saying, 'You must value the opinion of the stupid people, for they are always in the majority.' And this is the rule by which present-day writers are guided. Personally, though I appreciate them, I am against such forms of art as those of Dickens. I believe in art for the masses, but I cannot see even the symptoms of it as yet."

I asked Tolstoy to express his views on the Jewish question in Russia. He said:

"Most of the things ascribed to me as my expressions on this question are exaggerated. To me all questions are solved by my religious view of life. All people are equal. Therefore, there should be no such thing as a Jewish question. It is as if you asked me about the Russian question, the German question, or the Japanese question. There should be no Jewish question, no Polish question, no Russian question—all people are brethren. It is very sad and painful if we must make an effort to realize this. If there are any bad traits in the Russian Jews, they were called forth by the horrible persecutions to which we have subjected them. How do I account for the anti-Jewish feeling in Russia? We often dislike more those whom we harm than those who harm us. This is exactly true of the attitude of the Russians toward the Jews."

At dinner Tolstoy brought up the Jewish question once more. He said:

"Herzen used to tell a story of a dispute he had heard between a Greek Catholic, a Roman Catholic, and a Protestant. The Greek Catholic declared that all the witches came from Kiev. The Roman Catholic said that the witches came not from Kiev, but from Tchernigov. And the Protestant swore he was sure that the witches came neither from Kiev nor from Tchernigov, but from Vologda. Herzen was asked to settle the dispute. His reply was:

" 'I cannot answer your question, for I do not believe in the existence of witches.'

"That is how I look upon the Jewish question. Just as I do not believe in witches, so I do not believe in these various national and political questions."

After dinner Tolstoy played several games of chess with his friend, Dr. Goldenweiser, a young composer, while Countess Tolstoy was telling me of the autobiography she was writing.

"We have been married forty-six years now. Another four years and we shall celebrate our golden wedding," said the Countess. "In my autobiography I am describing only those incidents in my life which have a direct bearing upon Leo Nikolayevich and his work. I have already written two volumes, but am only as far as the year 1890. This work of mine will be published only after my death."

Soon the young composer and M. Tchertkov, Tolstoy's most intimate friend, who lives but a vew versts from Yasnaya Polyana, took their leave. Tolstoy rose, and, looking out of the window for some time, said ecstatically:

"What a wonderful sunset!"

It was indeed the most beautiful sunset I had ever seen. Tolstoy stood for several minutes, absorbed in thought. Then, turning to me, he said, in a low voice:

"Yes—yes, I am growing old and weak. My end is nearing rapidly. But the older I grow the happier I am. You cannot understand it. When I was as young as you, I did not understand it. Yes, the older I grow the happier I am."

Suddenly he asked, in a soft yet searching tone:

"Tell me, what are your religious views on life? But be sincere. Few people are sincere when they answer this question."

I answered sincerely, as well as I could.

"Religion must be the highest form of love," said Tolstoy after a while, "or love is merely a word. All religions are based on love, but Christianity is based on the highest form of love."

"In life as well as in theory?" I asked.

"Meanwhile only in theory. But the world is growing ever more perfect. It cannot become perfect unless our inner religious consciousness is directed toward this highest form of love. With the highest form of love as our law we will be perfect."

During the following half hour Tolstoy commented on several subjects. He spoke of Repin's latest paintings, expressed a lively interest in the coming elections in the United States, and was enthusiastic in his praise of William Jennings Bryan, who had visited him several years before, and whose photograph I noticed in a conspicuous place in Tolstoy's study.

In speaking of the latest books he had read, Tolstoy said: "I have recently read Haeckel on capital punishment. He says that capital punishment is a very good thing, for it coincides with Darwin's theory about the survival of the fittest. It is very strange. Who is to judge as to who is fit and who is unfit? I may think Haeckel is unfit. Haeckel may think that I am unfit. Numerous things which are now regarded as scientifically true seem to me ridiculous. It is my belief that in two or three hundred years from now Darwinism will be laughed at."

I asked Tolstoy about his latest work, and whether it was true that he was writing a new novel, the central figure of which was a priest, "Father Sergius," as the newspapers had reported.

"I am working at present on several things that interest me more—religious treatises. The story mentioned in the newspapers is an old one. I worked on it some ten years ago—and it is still unfinished. I may finish it before I die. I have several works of fiction which will not be published before my death. I have another plot for a novel which I may write soon."

And as Tolstoy spoke his voice rang with notes of youthful vigor and I felt that notwithstanding the long struggle between Tolstoy the preacher and Tolstoy the artist, the artist within Tolstoy often asserted himself strongly and often came out victorious.

I shall never forget the impressions I received that day in Yasnaya Polyana. The wonderful sunset that I was fortunate enough to watch in the presence of the great master is one that can never be effaced from my memory. Nor shall I ever forget the kindly words of encouragement that Tolstoy said to me as I bade him farewell.

On July 20, 1908, I received the following letter from Vladimir Tchertkoff, Leo Tolstoy's most intimate friend:

"Dear Mr. Bernstein:

"Leo Tolstoy has requested me to answer your letter of July 10th.

"He is quite satisfied with the way in which you have reproduced the thoughts he expressed during his interview with you.

"Will you allow me to profit by this occasion in order to ask you whether you could see your way clear to help Tolstoy's friends in your country desirous of expressing their sympathy toward him on the occasion of his forthcoming jubilee by putting before them the suggestions contained in the enclosed article of mine on the subject? In order that the position should be well grasped, and that no misunderstanding should occur, I would be very happy to furnish any further information on the subject or act as intermediary agent in this matter which it would be at present a want of tact to broach again direct to Tolstoy until the final communication to him on the day of his jubilee, for reasons

I have endeavored to state as clearly as possible in my article.

"With best wishes for yourself and your work,

"Yours cordially,

"V. TCHERTKOFF."

"P. S. The last deletion I have made about Tolstoy 'preacher' and Tolstoy 'artist,' struggling between themselves in Tolstoy, is a commonplace error which most critics who do not know and understand Tolstoy sufficiently and closely keep continually repeating. In reality the two elements are so blended in his character as well as in all his writings that you cannot separate them. They do not *struggle*—they *harmonize* in Tolstoy.

"P. P. S. Concerning your request that he should express some thoughts addressed to young writers, Tolstoy wishes me to say that he will bear your desire in mind, but he is now absorbed in other work. Should any thoughts in this connection demand expression in him, he will think of you."

In May, 1909, I received the following note from Leo Tolstoy:

"I received in due time the translation of Leonid Andreyev's book 'The Seven Who Were Hanged,' and thank you very much for it, as well as for the dedication.

"As to the 'Cycle of Readings,' it did not reach me, of which I am very sorry. Of all my books I think that it is the one that is most useful, and I would be most glad to see it translated.

"LEO TOLSTOY."

SERGIUS WITTE

St. Petersburg, June, 1908.

THE man who but a short while ago was the idol of the Russian masses, hailed as the hero of the peace, and the savior of blood- and tear-stained Russia, the man who is more than any other responsible for the change that has come over Russia, for the so-called Constitution and the Duma— Count Sergius Witte—is not only not at the helm of the Russian Government, but he stands almost alone even in the Council of the Empire.

A prominent Russian statesman, in speaking of Witte, said: "A mighty mind like Witte's cannot be downed for a long time, especially amid Russian official mediocrities. Even in falling he never loses himself, and he is bound to rise again."

I met Count Witte at his home on Kamenostrovsky Prospect. His large study, furnished with dark-red, massive furniture, holds a collection of paintings and engravings of the rulers of Europe. A fine print of President Roosevelt occupies a conspicuous position. Above Mr. Roosevelt's picture is an etching of Lord Salisbury. Czar Nicholas II is there in various poses on the right of Witte's desk. A large painting of Alexander III is on the left side, and the wall in front of his desk is almost entirely covered with portraits of the Count's ancestors. His huge desk was heaped with books.

Count Witte has aged considerably since his visit to America, and at first sight he gives the impression of a very old man.   But as he speaks, his eyes brighten up, the presence of a master mind is felt, and only at times, when he spoke of death, was a note of hopelessness faintly heard.

My first question was about the Duma.

"The third Duma is the best we have had thus far," answered Count Witte slowly.   "It is perhaps not intelligent enough, not sufficiently experienced, but it is better to have a Duma like this than to have no Duma at all."

Count Witte paused awhile, and then added:

"The third Duma is also better in another sense.   It is not as revolutionary as the previous Dumas.   But in financial questions the Deputies are like children—they know absolutely nothing."

"Minister of Finance, Kokovtzoff, in a recent speech in the Duma thanked God that there is no Parliament in Russia.   Is there a Parliament in Russia?" I asked.

"Let us better not speak of this," said the Count, as he shrugged his shoulders and smiled.

"In America you are regarded by many as the man who gave the Constitution to Russia.   Would you tell me something about this?"

"That is quite true, I am responsible for it," answered Count Witte.   "This is a matter for the future historian. But let me explain to you what prompted me to decide that such a step was the only adequate one.   Personally, I am opposed to such Parliaments and constitutions.   I do not like all these disputes, these discussions, these arguments. I am not against listening to the opinions of other people, but after I have listened to all the advice and the opinions of others I act according to my own lights.   Look at these," and the Count pointed to the portraits of his ancestors on the wall.   "I have been brought up in environments to which constitutionalism and parliamentarianism were entirely foreign. I served under the most autocratic of recent Russian Emperors, Alexander III.

"I cannot say, therefore, that I love constitutionalism and parliamentarianism. But I urged it as a physician would urge a patient to undergo an operation. I realized that this operation, if it may be called so, was absolutely essential. Without it, the Russian Government was on the point of"—and the Count lowered his hand to the floor—"do you understand? On the point of crumbling away. There are many people who cannot forgive me for having signed the Portsmouth treaty, for they believe that if I had not signed it at that time Russia would have come out victorious in the end. . . . It is their patriotic feeling that speaks in them, although they are convinced that this could never have happened. But I am quite satisfied with these achievements of mine—the signing of the Portsmouth peace treaty and the 'operation' by means of a constitution."

"I understand that there is at present a Pan-Slavic Convention in Prague. What are your views as to the efforts made in the direction of a federation of all Slavic nations?"

"I regard this movement as of very slight importance. All that was characteristically Slavic in our religion and culture has been submerged in Western European culture, so that there is no longer anything distinctly peculiar to Slavic nations. The time when nations were actuated by ideals is past. Now nations are guided solely by their egotistical interests, not by ideals. The tendency among the Poles to join the Slavic federation and cling even to Russia is due simply to the setback they have received in Germany. But I regard this movement on the whole as rather insignificant."

"Could you tell me something about the Amur Railroad affair?"

"You probably know that I have opposed it all along, and that I am in the minority in this matter. But I feel that a tremendous blunder is about to be committed. Here I am looking over the speeches that were made in favor of this road. They have said that unless the Amur Railroad is built Russia would within four years be devoured by Japan, or by England, or by the United States. The only thing they did not say, which would have made their arguments complete, is that within four years the moon will fall down on Russia and destroy it, if the Amur Railroad is not built. The future will show whether I was right or they. We shall see. But it is possible that we shall not be able to tell this very soon, for I understand that it is planned to extend the time for constructing the road from four to fifteen years. That would be more sensible."

Speaking of Russian literature, Count Witte said:

"I am not a specialist in this line. Perhaps it is because I am a little too old, but I cannot adapt myself to the taste of the reading public. To me the younger Russian writers appear like youngsters who daub paintings made-to-order-while-you-wait, which the public likes. These young men are suffering from enormous self-conceit. I am speaking of such writers as Gorky and Andreyev. Of course, Tolstoy is the greatest artist in the world, though his philosophy is absolutely childish. We read his naive treatises on economic questions merely for the flashes of his great genius which penetrates everything he writes. Our younger writers are going through a period of decadence."

"How do you account for the decline of Russian literature during the past few years?" I asked.

"How would you account, for instance, for the fact that the crops in France are sometimes good and sometimes poor? How would you account for the fact that we have no Washington now? If we must account for it, perhaps the decline of Russian literature, even as the decline of the literatures of other countries—for decadence has of late become the characteristic feature of almost every European literature—is due to the fact that this is the age of technical development and growth. In my younger days perhaps eight hundred of every thousand intelligent youths dreamed of becoming poets. Nowadays it is quite different. I have just been playing with my grandson. He is four years old. He does not like story books as the children of our days did. He is interested in automobiles and all sorts of mechanical devices. I can remember—when I was a child in Caucasia—the emotion I experienced when I saw the first telegraph erected there."

A flash of youthfulness brightened up his face for a while.

"No, no," he added after a pause, "you can't account for the decline of our literature, even as you can't account for the failure of crops, even as we do not know why we have no Napoleon, no Washington now."

"What of the future of Russia? Do you think that the present situation will remain unchanged for some time, that there will be no fresh outbreaks?"

"Russia was great and powerful, and I think that in time it will become greater than it ever was. A country that is recovering from such a horrible, disgraceful, stupid, criminal war as we had is a country with a future.   There will, of course, be outbreaks from time to time.   At times the waves of discontent will rise mountain high, and then they will sink again.   For some time to come there will be a periodic rising and falling of the waves.   But this indicates life.   A smooth surface would be a sign of death. I cannot say definitely how soon this bright era will commence.   Nor can I say that it will be during my lifetime. Perhaps in fifteen years.   Perhaps in five years.   Perhaps even sooner."

St. Petersburg, June, 1908.

Last night I had a lengthy conversation about the Jewish question with Count Sergius Witte, the former Premier of Russia.

"The Jewish question is the most acute and painful problem before the Russian people to-day," said he.   "One-third of the population of Russia is composed of non-Russian elements, such as Poles, Jews, Finns, Armenians, Tartars, and others.   Yes, we have more than fifty millions of people whom Russia took unto herself in her eagerness to expand, to enlarge her territory, and yet we are pursuing a narrow Russian nationalist policy.   Empress Catherine II wanted more land, therefore she took the provinces peopled by the Poles and the Jews.   But nothing was done to make their life tolerable.

"Nicholas I started a policy of reform with regard to the Jewish question.   Alexander II carried on the work of reform along this line in a mild and admirable manner and if his policy had been continued we would have had no such thing as a Jewish question to-day.

"But during the past twenty years Russia, instead of going forward in this respect, has made rapid strides backward, so that now the Jews in Russia have no rights whatever.

"I have just recalled a very characteristic incident. When I served under Alexander III, who was the most autocratic of Czars, he said to me one day:

" 'Sergey Yulievich, is it true that you are so fond of the *zhidi* [a degrading name for Jews] ?'

" 'Permit me to answer you by another question,' I said. 'Could you gather all the Jews of Russia, place them in ships on the Black Sea and then sink the ships? You would not do that, would you? The Jews must live among us, with us. Therefore, we must give them the opportunity to live as we do. In my opinion, the only way of solving the Jewish question is to give the Jews equal rights.'

"Alexander III was silent for awhile. Then he remarked:

" 'Perhaps you are right.'

"But as I said before, we have gone backward for the past twenty years, the Jews have no rights of any kind at present, and it is impossible to go farther back than Russia has gone.

"In official spheres I have always been almost alone whenever the Jewish question came up for consideration. The same is true of the situation to-day. There is not a single repulsive thing conceivable that has not been attributed to me. The Union of the Real Russian People, through its organs, has conducted and is still conducting a bitter campaign of slander against me. According to them, I should have been hanged a thousand times. They have sought to discredit me before the Emperor as well as before the people, and in a measure they have perhaps succeeded."

"How can the condition of the Jews in Russia be remedied now?" I asked.

"The Jewish question cannot now be solved at one stroke," answered the Count. "Now that the Jews have been deprived of all rights for twenty years it would be dangerous to give them equal rights at once. Such a step would lead to terrible pogroms."

"Do you regard the Russian masses as anti-Semitic and do you believe that if equal rights were given to the Jews of Russia, the people would start massacres of the Jews of their own accord, without any 'outside' encouragement?" I asked.

"There is no anti-Semitism among the Russian masses. But if the Jews were given the right to buy land, there would be a terrible conflict between the peasant population and the Jews. The agrarian question is a most painful wound in the body politic of Russia. The peasant is reduced to a state of despair because he has not enough land to maintain himself. It is quite easy to foresee what the outcome of such a conflict would be in Russian provinces where Jews are entirely unknown. This, of course, must be averted. When I was in America I explained to Schiff, Seligman, Straus and Kraus that now the Jewish question in Russia must be settled gradually, but they did not agree with me. Not being Russians they could not realize the danger of a hasty solution of the Jewish problem."

"But what is to be done now to ameliorate the condition of the Jews in Russia?" I asked again.

"In my opinion, the Jewish question can be solved entirely within twenty-five years. The first essential thing in the Jewish question, as in the agrarian question, is that the official spheres should begin to realize that these questions must be solved. Thus far there is no such feeling. My project would be to abolish the Jewish Pale of Settlement immediately, but on one condition that the Jews shall not be allowed to buy land in the real Russian provinces, say, for twenty-five years to come, so as not to stir race-hatred in the down-trodden peasantry. At the same time all educational institutions and government positions should be opened to the Jews. In a word, the only way of ameliorating the Jewish question is to give the Jews equal rights with the Russians."

June, 1911.

There are many opinions about Count Sergius Witte in Russia. The Czar, it is known, hates him for having hastened the conclusion of peace with Japan and for having overestimated the strength of the revolutionary forces. The Czar and the reactionaries still believe that but for Witte the Russian army would have defeated Japan, and but for Witte there would have been no Constitution in Russia to-day.

Not that there is a real constitutional Government in Russia now, but there is, after all, a semblance of a Parliament, and the more progressive members of the Duma from time to time criticise the Government in their speeches, and these speeches are published in the newspapers and read by the people. All this is a tremendous step forward for the Russian people and the Czar will not forgive Witte for having curtailed his powers as an autocrat.

The revolutionists have blamed and criticised Witte, believing that if he had not concluded the peace treaty at

Portsmouth the revolution would have triumphed because of the inevitable defeats of the Russian troops in Manchuria.

The Constitutional Democrats, whom Witte summoned to his assistance when he was Premier, did not respond, fearing that he was not sincere in his promises of reform in 1905. Prof. Maxime Kovalevsky, a man of great learning and unblemished repute, in speaking of Count Witte, said to me recently:

"The part he has played in the history of Russia has not yet been properly estimated, nor even realized. I happen to be familiar with certain episodes of his activities in 1905, and I believe him to be one of the best patriots Russia has had, in the best sense of the word."

Whether people believe that Count Witte is an opportunist or a patriot, one thing is certain, the former Premier of Russia, as a statesman, towers head and shoulders above those who are ruling Russia to-day. Whether Witte be called "the father of the Russian Constitution" ironically or in earnest, there is no doubt that it was he who wrung the manifesto of October 17, 1905, from the Czar, and though most of the reforms promised then have not yet been fulfilled, and some of the reforms introduced have since been revoked by Premier Stolypin, Russia is bound to work out its destiny as a liberated people, and, notwithstanding the machinations of the reactionary forces, the Constitution can no longer be revoked completely.

In the course of the numerous conversations I have had with Count Witte, he has made upon me the impression of a man of great imagination, of picturesque viewpoints, wide horizons, deep religious feeling, and remarkable sagacity. Though no longer at the helm of the Russian Government, Count Witte is still regarded as Russia's foremost statesman, and his views on national or international affairs are eagerly sought in Europe as well as in Russia.

I met him again in his house on Kamenostrovsky Prospect, "the White House" of Russia at one time. Count Witte would not discuss the present condition of Russia at home or abroad, but expressed a keen interest in the efforts of President Taft as a peacemaker.

"The proposed arbitration treaty is in principle not a new idea," he said. "The ideal of peace is as old as Christianity, if not older. It is older than nineteen centuries and yet what little progress it has made! The real essence of Christianity is based on peace, on the prohibition of murder. I am with all my heart in favor of arbitration as an idea, but it is difficult to believe that it can now be applied in our life, that it is not merely a vague though beautiful dream."

The Count rose from his armchair and, pacing his spacious study, continued:

"As I study the cost and the tremendous burden of armed peace, to which all nations are striving even more now that arbitration and peace are talked about; as I scrutinize the meaning of armed peace, of standing armies and navies, I am wondering whether armed peace is not much worse than war. This may sound strange, but it is true, if we look into the matter more deeply than the people who talk of peace are usually in the habit of doing.

"Let us examine the budget of the different nations. I believe that from 40 per cent to 50 per cent of all expenditures of Governments are absorbed by the standing armies and navies, by armed peace. I often ask myself whether armed peace is not really worse than war, with all its bloodshed and its horrors and its enormous costs. 40 per cent or 50 per cent of the budget go to cover the expenses of wars in the past and the maintenance of armies and navies for wars in the future.

"Now imagine what mankind would gain if the powerful nations were really in earnest in their professions of peace and would do away with their enormous standing armies and navies, with armed peace. Think of the money, which represents the labor, the brains, the courage of mankind, that would be saved. Imagine to what great purposes such enormous sums of money could be put.

"I shall say nothing of the fashionable words 'education of the masses,' but if these sums of money were used on improving the sanitary and hygienic conditions of the people, mankind would be a hundredfold happier than it is now. The people would live healthier, better, purer lives, and they would live longer, too. Then we should have real progress.

"The best of our people are ruined, the best efforts, the greatest minds, the strongest intellects are now wasted contriving and perfecting new life-destroying instruments. People are learning to fly. What is the first thought of those brave conquerors of the air? Are they inspired by any lofty sentiments? No. These airmen, encouraged by the Governments, at once contrive to turn the airship into a terrible, death-dealing machine.

"We are perfecting ourselves in the art of murder. Compare the wars of to-day with those of yesterday, with those of the remote past. We have fewer wars nowadays, but one modern war is more terrible, more costly in human life, than a score of wars in the past.

"The Russian-Japanese war was, perhaps, the most

brutal war of the nineteenth century, and the next war, when it comes, will far outstrip the preceding wars in cruelty, horrors, bloodshed. For we have made progress in the art of warfare. Now, if one nation gets airships for purposes of war, planning to destroy the enemy by hurling explosives upon his camps and his battleships, the other nations, not to be caught napping, naturally hasten also to provide themselves with similar life-destroying devices.

"We have fewer wars now, it is true. But is it because we have advanced, because we have grown more Christian in spirit, because we realize the brutality of war? Not at all. We are not conscious of any such feelings. We have fewer wars because of our economic and commercial relations. So long as the idea that war is a crime against the best qualities of mankind is not realized by the powers, all these talks about arbitration and peace will remain mere empty words.

"See how a man who preached real peace was looked upon in these days of ours. Take Tolstoy for example. He preached 'Thou shalt not kill.' He advocated peace and good will to all men, but everywhere people regarded his philosophy as unsound, his doctrines as those of an insane man. They all said: 'Oh, Tolstoy is a great artist; he is a wonderful writer of stories and novels; he is a great student of the human soul, but he is not sane in his moral sermons, in his philosophy of life.'

"To me, I must admit, Tolstoy as a preacher seemed quite ordinary. I also admired him as a great artist, but as a teacher of life he gave me nothing new.

"He was paraphrasing Christ. He was repeating the things I first learned as a child. In the course of my first lessons in religion I was taught that man should be kind to his fellow man, I was taught the principles of peace and love. Tolstoy was merely stating in simpler form that which Christ and other religious reformers before had preached thousands of years ago.

"I had learned these things as a child, but I have been spoiled by life. When I grew up I saw that human beings, instead of taking seriously these fundamental truths, deceived and harmed one another in their efforts to achieve what they called success. I was spoiled by life when I realized that none of the lofty ideals, none of the truths which constitute the essence of true religion, were applied in life.

"Therefore, I say, if the United States, or England, or Germany, or any other great power, in coming to an understanding of settling disputes and differences by means of arbitration, would show its sincerity by disarmament, that would be quite another matter. But for a long time to come the nations will not do it, and therefore these peace negotiations are not serious.

"Armed peace is the heaviest burden humanity is carrying on its back. Look at the greatest efforts of the best minds that are wasted on infernal inventions—on the invention of smokeless powder, noiseless guns, and so forth.

"And what is more important than the budget, the heavy cost of standing armies,—millions of people are torn away from agriculture and other useful work. The armies and navies are robbing the nations of their best physical, mental and moral strength, which is, of course, far more important than the budget.

"If a million men, now in the army, were working and earning, say, for instance, 50, or even 30, copecks a day each, what a vast increase in the capital of the land! For the main wealth of a country is its labor, and yet millions of the strongest young men are forced to lead unproductive lives under the present state of affairs."

Count Witte paused at the window of his study, facing the street.

"Look at the people passing there," he said.

"Perhaps if the enormous sums absorbed for armed peace were spent more wisely we should have more happiness everywhere.

"The state of armed peace is also responsible for the growth of Socialism, and even Anarchism, in most countries. These two—armed peace and Anarchism—go hand in hand. The burden of standing armies, the heavy taxes thus imposed upon the people in one form or another, make their life intolerable, and the result must express itself in movements of discontent, protest, and revolution."

I reproduce here a number of letters which I received from Count Witte from time to time and which contain interesting comments on various subjects.

In 1909 Count Witte wrote:

"Dear Mr. Bernstein:

"I will be in St. Petersburg in March and will be extremely glad to see you. I hope that you are feeling well. I envy the peace which is prevailing in your beautiful country.

"Sincerely and respectfully yours,

"COUNT WITTE.

"January 28*–February* 10."

In 1909 Count Witte wrote about the revolution in Turkey as follows:

"Dear Mr. Bernstein:

"I am glad to learn that you arrived in Constantinople at the same conclusions which I reached without my ever having been in Turkey, but only through the logical course of events.

"In general, it seems to me that there can be nothing more dangerous than a military autocracy. It lacks the good qualities of an autocracy of traditions, hereditary culture and complete personal independence, and it has all the defects of such a form of government. The armed forces of modern governments serve as the chief support of their existence (perhaps that is bad, but it is so); therefore the military element is considered the most respected; but heaven defend us if the armed forces of a government should begin to occupy themselves with internal revolutions!

"I hope that you have arrived safely in America and I extend to you my best wishes.

"COUNT WITTE."

"July 3, 1909.

In March, 1911, Count Witte wrote me the following letter, in which he referred to the Russian-American treaty, which had just been abrogated:

"Dear Mr. Bernstein:

"I am sending you my book with pleasure.

"As far as the sad conflict which has occurred between Russia and America, I am inclined to believe that reason will triumph and in the end grounds will be found for an agreement. I am convinced that in this matter passions have played a greater rôle than reason. Because of my position in Russia, I cannot state anything for publication on this subject, but at the same time I cannot share the viewpoint of our official spheres on this question. I would be very glad to have the pleasure of seeing you in St. Petersburg.

"Accept my best wishes. If you should have an occasion to meet Mr. Roosevelt, extend to him my greetings.

"COUNT WITTE."

"*March* 9, 1909.

"Dear Mr. Bernstein:

"I was very pleased to receive your letter of June 24.

"When I am abroad you may write me freely, but when you write to me in Russia you must bear in mind that Stolypin and his pack of hired agents read the entire correspondence. Such is the régime of Stolypin.

"I am writing my memoirs, but I am writing very lazily. My memoirs cannot be published so soon. Under no circumstances can they be published before my death. But if we meet next year in St. Petersburg I can let you have certain important documents.

"As for the cablegram published in one of the New York newspapers to the effect that I have written a pamphlet about Roosevelt, I would ask you to state in the newspapers in my name that the information contained in that cable is false; that I have never written any pamphlets against anybody; that I am not devoting my time to such matters, and that surely I would not have written any pamphlet against Roosevelt, whom I remember with the highest esteem and regard as a man, a public character and as the former President of the great and sympathetic American nation.

"With the very best wishes, devotedly yours,

COUNT WITTE."

"*July* 20 (*August* 2), 1911

"July 20 (August 2).—I am sure that the above-mentioned cablegram emanates from one of the newspaper men in St. Petersburg bribed by Stolypin—there are many of them here. He probably refers to the brochure of Morskoy, which you know, but I learned of this brochure only after it was published."

In October, 1911, Count Witte wrote concerning the conflict in the Balkans:

"Dear Mr. Bernstein:

"I am very grateful to you for your letter.

"Concerning the situation in the Balkans, it is my opinion that this affair will lead to many serious consequences. That which should have happened has happened, otherwise we should have to admit that our divine world was created not by God but by Satan. But more than unexpected is not only the shortsightedness but rather the complete blindness of the official diplomats who failed to foresee and prepare for this affair, and who are even to this day groping in the dark. What a remarkable collapse of talents!

"As far as Japan is concerned, there is not the slightest doubt in my mind that, under the present state of affairs, Japan will always go hand in hand with Russia. America has always proclaimed the principle of the open door in China (in Manchuria and Korea), and now after the Russo-Japanese war these doors have become narrower for America than before the war.

"With regard to the rumor as to my accepting the post of Minister of Foreign Affairs, it is too late for me to start my career anew. I have long ended it. Only extraordinary circumstances could compel me to change my viewpoint on this subject.   With best wishes.

"COUNT WITTE."
"Biarritz, October 22.

"In about fifteen or twenty days I will leave for St. Petersburg."

In October, 1911, Count Witte wrote the following letter containing a remarkable characterization of the Russian Prime Ministers, Stolypin and Kokovtzov:

"Dear Mr. Bernstein:

"I have received your letter.   I may say about your article on Stolypin and Kokovtzov that a better article could not have been written by any one living outside of Russia.

"Kokovtzov is a practical man of affairs, while Stolypin was not.   Kokovtzov has infinitely more knowledge than Stolypin had.   But Kokovtzov is, nevertheless, not a man of big affairs.   If he were to become Premier he would in all probability not raise so many acute and absurd questions as Stolypin raised.   Still he is not in position to block the way of the band which is now leading Russia to grave blunders.   Stolypin submitted to this band; he himself invented problems to please the spirit of this band.   Kokovtzov himself would not raise foolish questions, but he would obey and follow in the direction indicated by this band.

"As far as the Jewish question is concerned, Kokovtzov himself would not devise, for the sake of his prestige, new persecutions against the Jews, but he will never dare, and even if he dared he will never be able to obstruct the course of the now fashionable currents in Russia.

"I shall be very glad to see you when you come to us.

"With best wishes for your health.

"COUNT WITTE."

"*October* 3, 1911.

Other letters from Count Witte are as follows:

"Villa Narichkine, Biarritz,

"*Dear Mr. Bernstein:*

"I received your letter only to-day, as it was addressed to St. Petersburg and I am in Biarritz, where I will stay about two months and then return to Russia.

"Thank you very much for your statement about Mr. Wilson.

"I do not think that in view of the present false 'nationalistic' course of politics in our ruling spheres there will be sufficient common sense to settle the question regarding the commercial treaty with America before January 1. You say that no matter who will be the next President, America will insist upon equal rights for all American citizens with regard to the passport question. It seems to me that in the present frame of mind the Russian government will maintain its point of view—that is, it will not want to equalize Jews with other American citizens.

"I am extremely sorry about this, and I believe that with the slightest mutual prudence it would be altogether possible to find a proper solution of the question.

"Returning to the question concerning Mr. Roosevelt, I think that now America cannot help seeing that it made a mistake by supporting Japan in her conflict with Russia. Japan, instead of being grateful for this favor, has turned

her back to America.   With best wishes, sincerely yours.
"COUNT WITTE."
"October 3 (*new Style*), 1912.

"Dear Mr. Bernstein:
"With regard to your questions, it seems to me that America will make a mistake if it does not find a platform for an agreement with Japan.   It seems to me that America could find important interests in China.   It is much to be regretted that apparently America is not sufficiently energetic in the attention it is paying to China.

"There is no doubt that Mr. Roosevelt at the time of our conflict, before my arrival in America, sympathized more with Japan than with Russia and aided Japan by loans.   Such a state of affairs made my difficult task all the more difficult.   But I do not blame Mr. Roosevelt in the least.   President Roosevelt expressed the frame of mind of the American people at the time.   America furnished Japan with money and America was more inclined toward Japan than toward Russia.

"One of the causes of such a state of affairs in America was the Jewish question.   With best wishes yours,
"COUNT WITTE."

On August 23 Count Witte wrote from Biarritz as follows:

"Dear Mr. Bernstein:
"I am very grateful to you for your statement concerning the insinuation sent out purposely from St. Petersburg that I had written a pamphlet against the esteemed Mr. Roosevelt.

"With regard to your desire to know my opinion about

the present condition of the Jewish question in Russia, I must say that the situation of the Jews is now hopeless. Not only is there no reason to expect any symptoms of amelioration, but quite the contrary, in its efforts to please an insignificant number of people now in favor, the government is devising new forms of persecution and restrictions directed against the Jewish people.   Such a state of affairs may be changed only through certain internal and external catastrophes, which, of course, fill me with fear, for they would be accompanied by the greatest misfortune for my fatherland and the empire.

"As far as the matter regarding passports for foreign Jews is concerned, under certain circumstances which are changing, this question could find a favorable solution, *especially if the claims of the American Government would be supported also by the governments of other countries.* Even then the question would be settled by Russia not very willingly, but under a certain measure of compulsion.

"The abrogation of the treaty of 1832 is not desirable, for it would separate Russia from America still more, and that would be in the interests of Japan.

"I should very much like to visit America again, but for such a visit there would have to be a special reason.   If, for instance, they decided to erect some kind of monument in Portsmouth in front of the palace where the peace conference was held or some other peace monument to commemorate the Portsmouth peace conference, which had such an important influence on the political events of the world, I would be very glad to come to America on such an occasion.

"Of course I would be very glad if I could meet you

during the coming Winter. I could give you some documents and facts of interest.

"Meanwhile accept my best wishes. Sincerely and respectfully yours,

"COUNT WITTE."

On January 15, 1913, Count Witte wrote as follows:

"Dear Mr. Bernstein:

"Concerning the commercial treaty, I think that in the immediate future there is no hope for the possibility of an agreement, because for reasons which are quite clear to me the American Government cannot retreat from its principles and change its point of view, and Russia under the influence of the present ruling spheres will not want to lower its flag, even if it was raised unjustly. Therefore it is necessary to wait, for time is the best means of healing and rectifying blunders and appeasing passions.

"With regard to the Balkan situation, it appears to me that in the near future there will be no general European war as a result of this important world question, because all the great countries, or rather their Governments, are either unprepared for war or afraid of it. But the renewal of military operations in the Balkans is possible, though hardly probable.

"In this way the historical Eastern question will not be settled, and within a few years (a year hence or perhaps ten years or more) this universal question will arise again. Then the question will in all probability be solved through a general European war. At present such a war will probably not break out, not because the nations have come to the conclusion that war is in principle a terrible affair, but merely because the Governments want either to prepare themselves the better, or are waiting for a more favorable juncture for themselves.

"Our fourth Duma will be in essence like the third, but of a lower standard.

"Now I will ask you the following: In the European newspapers there appeared a cablegram from America to the effect that Roosevelt is about to publish a letter by the late Mikado in which the latter asked him to negotiate for peace with Russia because Japan could not continue the war any longer. In other words, that Russia in 1905 was less in need of peace than Japan, who could not go on with the war any longer.

"I know that Roosevelt took upon himself the initiative of peace negotiations at the pressure brought by Japan, but I am convinced that that was done not because Japan could not go on with the war any longer, but because she considered the military successes already achieved as sufficient. Could you perhaps see Mr. Roosevelt and ask him in my name to give a proper explanation, which I would ask you to send me for publication? I think it is not in the interest of Mr. Roosevelt that the *European press* should spread inaccurate reports concerning his great rôle in this great matter which present a historical picture of that time in a wrong light. With best wishes for your health.

"COUNT WITTE."

"*St. Petersburg.*

"*Dear Mr. Bernstein:*

"I received your two letters and your book. I am grateful to you for the interesting information contained in your letter about the invented letter from the late Mikado to Roosevelt. As soon as I read in the newspapers about it I felt certain that the whole story was a fabrication.

"I am leaving for Biarritz (Villa Narichkine) within the next few days, and I intend to remain there until the end of April (May 13).

"If you are in Europe at that time I shall be very glad to see you. With best wishes, devotedly yours.

"COUNT WITTE."

"*March* 3, 1913.

"*Dear Mr. Bernstein:*

"I am very grateful to you for your letter and for the enclosures which I have received here only a few days ago. Your letter has been traveling.

"How the present tragic political conditions of Europe confirm that which I had occasion to tell you quite a long time ago in Petersburg with regard to war by explosives and powder and war by the burden of taxation, that is, by war expenditures in times of seeming peace.

"As for the commercial treaty between Russia and America, I may say that in view of the ever more acute Jewish problem in Russia, in which passion rather than reason plays an enormous rôle, I do not think that this question will be settled so soon.

"Unfortunately the relations between America and Japan are apparently not adjusting themselves. According to the general world position of these nations, they have no particularly strong points of unity, while having several quite powerful points of difference.

"I think that the American people should recognize by this time that they were dragged in by England into a too-prejudiced sympathy in favor of Japan in 1903–5. It is useless to deny now that before my arrival to Portsmouth and during the first weeks of my stay there, the majority of the American people and at any rate official America, sympathized more with Japan than with Russia. And during my negotiations I was treated politely, while Kamura was treated in a spirit of friendship. They would not have hesitated to deceive me if I would allow myself to blunder.

"Seven or eight years have elapsed,—England is a greater friend of ours even than Japan, and America has not seen any gratitude from Japan. But let us hope that everything will adjust itself.

"I am taking the cure here and am not planning to return to Russia before December. When you write you may address your letters either to Petersburg or Biarritz.

"With best wishes,

"COUNT WITTE."

"Bad Salzschlirf, July 10, 1913.

LEONID ANDREYEV

St. Petersburg, June, 1908.

Two weeks after my visit to Count Leo Tolstoy at Yasnaya Polyana, I went from St. Petersburg to Wammelsu, Finland, to see Leonid Andreyev, the most modern of modern writers in Europe, the author of the great war story, "Red Laughter," and of the remarkable morality play entitled "The Life of Man." The most popular writer in Russia to-day, his popularity having outshadowed that of Maxim Gorky, Andreyev is also, next to Tolstoy, the most gifted of all Russian writers. If his work, which is in every respect original, must be likened to the work of another Russian, it would come nearest to that of Dostoyevsky. His keen psychological insight, as revealed in his later productions may be compared with the best work of the author of "Crime and Punishment."

Andreyev's first steps in literature, his first short stories, attracted but little attention at the time of their appearance. It was only when Countess Tolstoy, the wife of Leo Tolstoy, in a letter to the *Novoye Vremya*, came out in "defense of artistic purity and moral power in contemporary literature," declaring that Russian society, instead of buying, reading, and making famous the works of the Andreyevs, should "rise with indignation against such filth," that almost everybody in Russia who can read turned to the little volume of the young writer.

In her attack upon Andreyev, Countess Tolstoy said as follows:

"The poor new writers, like Andreyev, succeeded only in concentrating their attention on the filthy point of human degradation and uttered a cry to the undeveloped, half-intelligent reading public, inviting them to see and to examine the decomposed corpse of human degradation and to close their eyes to God's wonderful, vast world, with the beauties of nature, with the majesty of art, with the lofty yearnings of the human soul, with the religious and moral struggles and the great ideals of goodness—even with the downfall, misfortunes, and weaknesses of such people as Dostoyevsky depicted. . . . In describing all these every true artist should illumine clearly before humanity not the side of filth and vice, but should struggle against them by illumining the highest ideals of good, truth, and the triumph over evil, weakness, and the vices of mankind.

". . . I should like to cry out loudly to the whole world in order to help those unfortunate people whose wings, given to each of them for high flights toward the understanding of the spiritual light, beauty, kindness, and God, are clipped by these Andreyevs."

This letter of Countess Tolstoy called forth a storm of protest in the Russian press, and, strange to say, the representatives of the fair sex were among the warmest defenders of the young author. Answering the attack, many women, in their letters to the press, pointed out that the author of "Anna Karenina" had been abused in almost the same manner for his "Kreutzer Sonata," and that Tolstoy himself had been accused of exerting just such an influence over the youth of Russia as the Countess attributed to Andreyev. Since the publication of Countess Tolstoy's condemnation, Andreyev has produced a series of masterpieces, such as "The Life of Father Vassily," a powerful psycho-

logical study; "Red Laughter," a war story, "written with
the blood of Russia"; "The Life of Man," a striking
morality presentation in five acts, and, finally, his latest,
and perhaps, also, his most artistic work, "The Seven Who
Were Hanged," in which the horrors of contemporary life
in Russia are delineated with such beautiful simplicity and
power that Turgenev, Dostoyevsky, or Tolstoy himself
would have signed his name to this masterpiece.

Thus the first accusations against Andreyev have been
swept aside by his artistic productions, which are permeated
with sincere, profound love for all that is pure in life.
Dostoyevsky and Maupassant depicted more subjects, such
as that treated in "The Abyss," than Andreyev. But with
them, these stories are lost in the great mass of their other
works, while in Andreyev, who at that time had as yet produced but few short stories, works like "The Abyss" stood
out in bold relief.

Andreyev has often been accused of being the advocate
of pessimism, and it has been charged that his influence
upon the Russian youth is pessimistic. Not long ago,
nevertheless, Andreyev, in speaking of his own pessimism,
said: "I never believed in life so much as when I read
the work of the 'father' of pessimism, Schopenhauer.
Since a man could think as he did and live, it is evident
that life is mighty and unconquerable."

In another place he said: "Neither truth nor falsehood
will conquer. That which is united with life itself will
conquer; that which strengthens the roots of life and
justifies it. Only that which is useful to life remains; all
that is harmful to it will sooner or later perish; perish inevitably. Even if it stands to-day as an indestructible
wall against which the heads of the noblest people are

breaking in the struggle, it will fall to-morrow.   It will fall because it tried to impede life itself. . . ."

As I drove from Terioki to Andreyev's house, along the dust-covered road, the stern and taciturn little Finnish driver suddenly broke the silence by saying to me in broken Russian:

"Andreyev is a good writer. . . . Although he is a Russian, he is a very good man.   He is building a beautiful house here in Finland, and he gives employment to many of our people."

We were soon at the gate of Andreyev's beautiful villa —a fantastic structure, weird looking, original in design, something like the conception of the architect in the "Life of Man."

"My son is out rowing with his wife in the Gulf of Finland," Andreyev's mother told me.   "They will be back in half an hour."

As I waited I watched the seething activity everywhere on Andreyev's estate.   In Yasnaya Polyana, the home of Count Tolstoy, everything seemed long established, fixed, well-regulated, serenely beautiful.   Andreyev's estate was astir with vigorous life.   Young, strong men were building the House of Man.   More than thirty of them were working on the roof and in the yard, and a little distance away, in the meadows, young women and girls, bright-eyed and red-faced, were haying.   Youth, strength, vigor everywhere, and above all the ringing laughter of little children at play.   I could see from the window the "Black Little River," which sparkled in the sun hundreds of feet below. The continuous noise of the workmen's axes and hammers was so loud that I did not notice when Leonid Andreyev entered the room where I was waiting for him.

"Pardon my manner of dressing," he said, as we shook hands. "In the summer I lead a lazy life, and do not write a line. I am afraid I am forgetting even to sign my name."

I had seen numerous photographs of Leonid Andreyev, but he does not look like any of them. He has grown much stouter. Instead of the pale-faced, sickly-looking young man, there stood before me a strong, handsome, well-built man, with wonderful eyes. He wore a grayish blouse, black, wide pantaloons up to his knees, and no shoes or stockings.

We soon spoke of Russian literature at the present time, particularly of the drama.

"We have no real drama in Russia," said Andreyev. "Russia has not yet produced anything that could justly be called a great drama. Perhaps 'The Storm' by Ostrovsky is the only Russian play that may be classed as a drama. Tolstoy's plays cannot be placed in this category. Of the later writers, Anton Chekhov came nearest to giving real dramas to Russia, but, unfortunately, he was taken from us in the prime of his life."

"What do you consider your own 'Life of Man' and 'To the Stars'?" I asked.

"They are not dramas; they are merely presentations in so many acts," answered Andreyev, and, after some hesitation, added: "I have not written any dramas, but it is possible that I will write one."

At this point Andreyev's wife, a charming young woman, also dressed in a Russian blouse, came in. The conversation turned to America, and to the treatment accorded to Maxim Gorky in New York.

"When I was a child I loved America," remarked Andreyev. "Perhaps Cooper and Mayne Reid, my favorite authors in my childhood days, were responsible for this. I was always planning to run away to America. I am anxious even now to visit America, but I am afraid—I may get as bad a reception as my friend Gorky got."

He laughed as he glanced at his wife. After a brief pause, he said:

"The most remarkable thing about the Gorky incident is that while in his stories and articles about America Gorky wrote nothing but the very worst that could be said about that country, he never told me anything but the very best about America. Some day he will probably describe his impressions of America as he related them to me. By the way, have you read Gorky's latest work, 'The Confession?' It is a wonderful story. The Russian writers have unlearned to write like that nowadays."

It was a very warm day. The sun was burning mercilessly in the large room. Mme. Andreyev suggested that it would be more pleasant to go down to a shady place near the Black Little River.

On the way down the hill Andreyev inquired about Tolstoy's health and was eager to know his views on contemporary matters.

"If Tolstoy were young now he would have been with us," he said.

We stepped into a boat, Mme. Andreyev took up the oars and began to row. We resumed our conversation.

"The decadent movement in Russian literature," said Andreyev, "started to make itself felt about ten or fifteen years ago. At first it was looked upon as mere child's play, as a curiosity. Now, it is regarded more seriously. Although I do not belong to that school, I do not consider it as worthless. The fault with it is that it has but few talented people in its ranks, and these few direct the criticism of the decadent school. They are the writers and also the critics. And they praise whatever they write. Of the younger men, Alexander Blok is, perhaps, the most gifted. But in Russia our clothes change quickly nowadays, and it is hard to tell what the future will give us— in our literature and our life.

"How do I picture to myself this future?" continued Andreyev, in answer to a question of mine. "I cannot know even the fate and future of my own child, how can I foretell the future of such a great country as Russia? But I believe that the Russian people have a great future before them—in life and in literature—for they are a great people, rich in talents, kind and freedom-loving. Savage as yet, it is true, very ignorant, but on the whole they do not differ so much from other European nations."

Suddenly the author of "Red Laughter" looked upon me intently, and asked: "How is it that the European and the American press has ceased to interest itself in our struggle for emancipation? Is it possible that the reaction in Russia appeals to them more than our people's yearnings for freedom, simply because the reaction happens to be stronger at the present time? In that event, they are probably sympathizing with the Shah of Persia! Russia to-day is a lunatic asylum. The people who are hanged are not the people who should be hanged. Everywhere else honest people are at large and only criminals are in prison. In Russia the honest people are in prison and the criminals are at large. The Russian Government is composed of a band of criminals, and Nicholas II is not the greatest of them. There are still greater ones. I do not hold that the Russian Government alone is guilty of these horrors. The European nations and the Americans are just as much to blame, for they look on in silence while the most despicable crimes are committed. The murderer usually has at least courage, while he who looks on silently when murder is committed is a small, insignificant creature. England and France, who have become so friendly to our Government, are surely watching with compassion the poor Shah, who hangs the constitutional leaders. Perhaps I do not know international law. Perhaps I am not speaking as a practical man. One nation must not interfere with the internal affairs of another nation. But why do they interfere with our movement for freedom? France helped the Russian Government in its war against the people by giving money to Russia. Germany also helped— secretly. In well-regulated countries each individual must behave decently. When a man murders, robs, dishonors women he is thrown into prison. But when the Russian Government is murdering helpless men and women and children the other Governments look on indifferently. And yet they speak of God. If this had happened in the Middle Ages a crusade would have been started by civilized peoples, who would have marched to Russia to free the women and children from the claws of the Government."

Andreyev became silent. His wife kept rowing for some time slowly, without saying a word. We soon reached the shore and returned silently to the house.

Leonid Andreyev's brief autobiographical sketch is characteristic as it is interesting.

"I was born," he said, "in 1871, in Oryol, and studied there at the gymnasium. I studied poorly; while in the seventh class I was for a whole year known as the worst student, and my mark for conduct was never higher than 4, sometimes 3. The most happy time spent at school, which I recall to this day with pleasure, was recess time between the lectures, and also the rare occasions when I was sent out from the classroom. . . . The sunbeams, the free sunbeams, which penetrated some cleft and which played with the dust in the hallway, all this was so mysterious, so interesting, so full of a peculiar, hidden meaning.

"When I studied at the gymnasium, my father, an engineer, died. As a university student, I was in dire need. During my first course in St. Petersburg I even starved—not so much out of real necessity as because of my youth, inexperience, and my inability to utilize the unnecessary parts of my costume. I am to this day ashamed to think that I went two days without food at a time when I had two or three pair of trousers, two overcoats.

"It was then that I wrote my first story—about a starving student. I cried when I wrote it, and the editor, who returned my manuscript, laughed. . . . In 1894, in January, I made an unsuccessful attempt to kill myself by shooting. As a result of this unsuccessful attempt I was forced by the authorities into religious penitence, and I contracted heart trouble, though not of a serious nature, yet very annoying. During this time I made one or two unsuccessful attempts at writing; I devoted myself with greater pleasure and success to painting, which I loved from childhood on. I made portraits to order at 3 and 5 rubles apiece.

"In 1897 I received my diploma and became an assistant attorney, but at the very outset I was sidetracked. I was offered a position on *The Courier*, for which I was to report court proceedings. I did not succeed in getting any practice as a lawyer. I had only one case and lost it at every point.

"In 1898 I wrote my first story—for the Easter number —and since that time I have devoted myself exclusively to literature. Maxim Gorky helped me considerably in my literary work by his always prcatical advice and suggestions."

In 1909 Andreyev wrote me the following letter as an introduction to my translation of "The Seven Who Were Hanged":

"I am very glad that 'The Story of the Seven Who Were Hanged' will be read in English. The misfortune of all is that we know so little, even nothing, about one another —neither about the soul, nor the life, the sufferings, the habits, the inclinations, the aspirations of one another. Literature, which I have the honor to serve, is dear to me just because the noblest task it sets before itself is that of wiping out boundaries and distances.

"As in a hard shell, every human being is enclosed in a cover of body, dress, and life. Who is man? We may only conjecture. What constitutes his joy or his sorrow? We may guess only by his acts, which are ofttimes enigmatic; by his laughter and by his tears, which are often entirely incomprehensible to us. And if we, Russians, who live so closely together in constant misery, understand one another so poorly that we mercilessly put to death those who should be pitied or even rewarded, and reward those who should be punished by contempt and anger—how much more difficult is it for you Americans to understand distant Russia? But then, it is just as difficult for us Russians to understand distant America, of which we dream in our youth and over which we ponder so deeply in our years of maturity.

"The Jewish massacres and famine; a Parliament and executions; pillage and the greatest heroism; 'The Black Hundred,' and Leo Tolstoy—what a mixture of figures and conceptions, what a fruitful source for all kinds of misunderstandings! The truth of life stands aghast in silence, and its brazen falsehood is loudly shouting, uttering pressing, painful questions: 'With whom shall I sympathize? Whom shall I trust? Whom shall I love?'

"In the story of 'The Seven Who Were Hanged' I attempted to give a sincere and unprejudiced answer to some of these questions.

"That I have treated ruling and slaughtering Russia with restraint and mildness may best be gathered from the fact that the Russian censor has permitted my book to circulate. This is sufficient evidence when we recall how many books, brochures and newspapers have found eternal rest in the peaceful shade of the police stations, where they have risen to the patient sky in the smoke and flame of bonfires.

"But I did not attempt to condemn the Government, the fame of whose wisdom and virtues has already spread far beyond the boundaries of our unfortunate fatherland. Modest and bashful far beyond all measure of her virtues, Russia would sincerely wish to forego this honor, but fortunately the free press of America and Europe has not spared her modesty, and has given a sufficiently clear picture of her glorious activities. Perhaps I am wrong in this: it is possible that many honest people in America believe in the purity of the Russian Government's intentions —but this question is of such importance that it requires special treatment, for which it is necessary to have both time and calm of soul.   But there is no calm soul in Russia.

"My task was to point out the horror and the iniquity of capital punishment under any circumstances.   The horror of capital punishment is great when it falls to the lot of courageous and honest people whose only guilt is their excess love and the sense of righteousness—in such instances, conscience revolts.   But the rope is still more horrible when it forms the noose around the necks of weak and ignorant people.   And, however strange it may appear, I look with a lesser grief and suffering upon the execution of the revolutionists, such as Werner and Musya, than upon the strangling of ignorant murderers, miserable in mind and heart, like Yanson and Tsiganok.   Even the last mad horror of inevitably approaching execution Werner can offset by his enlightened mind and his iron will, and Musya, by her purity and her innocence. . . .

"But how are the weak and the sinful to face it if not in madness, with the most violent shock to the very foundation of their souls?   And these people, now that the Government has steadied its hands through its experience with the revolutionists, are being hanged throughout Russia—in some places one at a time, in others, ten at once.   Children at play come upon badly buried bodies, and the crowds which gather look with horror upon the peasants' boots that are sticking out of the ground; prosecutors who have witnessed these executions are becoming insane and are taken away to hospitals—while the people are being hanged—hanged.

"I am deeply grateful to you for the task you have undertaken in translating this sad story.   Knowing the sensitiveness of the American people, who at one time sent across the ocean, steamers full of bread for famine-stricken Russia, I am convinced that in this case our people in their misery and bitterness will also find understanding and sympathy. And if my truthful story about seven of the thousands who were hanged will help toward destroying at least one of the barriers which separate one nation from another, one human being from another, one soul from another soul, I shall consider myself happy."

ELIE METCHNIKOFF

St. Petersburg, June, 1909.

IT was at the dinner table of Count Sergius Witte that I learned that Elie Metchnikoff, the world's foremost biologist, head of the Pasteur Institute, was in Russia. The St. Petersburg newspapers did not mention for three days that Russia's greatest scientist had come to visit Russia after an absence of many years, during which he had become famous throughout the world.

"Metchnikoff came to St. Petersburg quietly, unheralded. He has been in this city three days now, and none but some of his immediate friends know about it. He dined with us yesterday and will be here again this evening," Count Witte said to me.

Countess Witte spoke of Metchnikoff's modesty, of his tenderness, and of the simple life the Metchnikoffs were leading near Paris. The ex-Premier of Russia commented upon the meagre income of the world's greatest scientist, remarking that if Metchnikoff did not have his little estate in Russia, it would have been difficult for him to make ends meet on the salary he was receiving as head of the Pasteur Institute.

"When you meet Metchnikoff, do not speak to him about Russian politics. He has strange views on the subject," Count Witte warned me.

When the newspapers discovered that Metchnikoff was in St. Petersburg, all the news of the day suddenly shrank into insignificance, and from that day until the day of his return to France Metchnikoff held the attention of all Russia. Not even the official reports that flooded the newspapers about the meeting of Kaiser Wilhelm and the Czar in the Finnish waters interested the Russian people so much as the visit of Metchnikoff. When it was learned that the great student of the human body had decided upon a pilgrimage to the great student of the human soul, Tolstoy, the press was occupied almost exclusively with the meeting of the two monarchs of universal literature and science, Leo I, and Elie I, Tolstoy and Metchnikoff. The little village in the Government of Tula, Yasnaya Polyana, and not the *Standart*, the imperial yacht on which the Kaiser and the Czar met, held the center of the stage in chaotic Russia. This was the most effective rebuke to the Russian Government that had forced Tolstoy to seclude himself in Yasnaya Polyana, and Metchnikoff to seek and grace another fatherland.

Prof. Metchnikoff received me in the house of his friends, on Malaya Spasskaya, at 10 o'clock in the morning.

"I have just been tortured by the photographer," Metchnikoff said to me good-naturedly. "I don't like these forced poses."

"This is one of the penalties of fame," I remarked.

"Very true," he said, wiping his glasses and smiling broadly.

Metchnikoff, the man who has devoted his life to studying the problems of how to make mankind happy by combating and wiping out the most dreadful diseases, and who writes his scientific treatises in a simple and vivid style that many a famous novelist might envy, is indeed, in whatever he says and does, so radiant and brimful of the joy of living that he may be styled an apostle of optimism.

Commenting on the changes he found in Russia, Metchnikoff said: "I find the most hopeful signs in the educational institutions. A few years ago the youth of Russia was occupied exclusively with politics. The universities were not institutions of learning, but arenas for political activities. After the storm of 1905 a reaction has set in. The youth of Russia has returned to the more serious problems that confront mankind. It has abandoned politics and is studying human nature and life. The universities and laboratories are again crowded with young people thirsting for knowledge. While I was a student there were two strong currents struggling against each other among the Russian youth. On one side was the educational movement, which forced its way into Russia from Western Europe. Many of us turned to science with enthusiasm, believing that the salvation of Russia lay in that direction.

"On the other side the revolutionary propaganda carried away many of the best young minds, which were thus lost to science. I went through that stage myself. I remember one incident particularly well. When I was a gymnasium student, about 16 or 17 years of age, I received a letter from abroad in which I was urged not to be satisfied under any circumstances with a constitutional monarchy, but to demand immediately and insist that Russia shall be a republic. After the assassination of Alexander II, it was impossible to continue any serious work in the Russian universities, and it was then that I understood that the youth of Russia could do more for Russia by devoting itself to education rather than to politics. I am glad to see that there are at present signs pointing to a normal condition in the educational institutions."

I asked Prof. Metchnikoff about his work.

"First of all," he said, "I am glad to inform you that I have just received a letter from Paris telling me that the Pasteur Institute has come into a fortune which will enable us to carry on our work on a larger scale than before. Osiris, the Jewish banker, who died in February, 1907, left 40,000,000 francs to the Pasteur Institute, and now the formalities connected with the gift are at an end. By this donation Osiris made himself one of the great benefactors of mankind."

"Osiris, as far as is generally known, never took any interest in philanthropic or educational institutions. He had the reputation of a miser. Can you tell me something about the man?" I asked.

"Osiris was indeed a very strange personality. He was a Bordeaux Jew, became a widower early in life, and had very few near relatives. After he had amassed his great fortune he became interested in archaeology. He went to Egypt with an archaeological expedition and brought some valuable objects from there. Osiris was not his real name. His name was Iffla, but he called himself Osiris in honor of the most popular of Egyptian gods—the god of light and health.

"At first he wanted to give his fortune to the French Government. He purchased a large number of Napoleonic relics and the house in which Napoleon lived, and wanted to turn it into a museum. But he met with so many obstacles in the shape of formalities and the attitude of the government toward him was so cold that he became disgusted.

"It was then that some one advised him to donate his fortune to the Pasteur Institute. A few months before his death he became ill and invited Prof. Roux of the Pasteur

Institute.   He then informed him that he was planning to leave his fortune to the Institute, and asked that the interest—600,000 francs annually—be used especially for investigations of tuberculosis and cancer.   One of the conditions was that Prof. Roux and I visit him daily during his illness.   He was a very peculiar man.   His reputation as miser was well deserved.   I recall a little incident during the time that I visited him when he was ill.   The physicians had prescribed for Osiris a portion of ice cream three times daily.   Osiris was greatly disturbed by this prescription and he complained to me.

" 'Where will I get the means for such luxuries?   I can't afford to have ice cream three times a day.'

"He had no electricity in his house, but used candles instead, for the sake of economy.   A niece of his, a very poor girl, came to him one day and asked him to assist her. Though she was penniless, Osiris refused.   But when he learned several months later that she had gone on the stage he sent for her and, praising her for having found work, gave her an allowance of 200 francs a month, and left her a small fortune when he died, in February, 1907, at the age of 82.   He was almost a legendary figure, peculiar in every way.   In our case the formalities connected with his donation were entangled for two years, and I am glad that they are at an end at last.   The Institute has already expanded as a result of his gift.   We have bought another building which is to be used as a department for tropical diseases.   Special investigations will be made of the so-called 'sleeping sickness.' "

"May I know whether you are pleased with the results of your recent investigations concerning premature senility?" I asked.

"We are working all along in this direction in the hope of finding the most effective remedy for premature senility. I am convinced the main cause of our growing old too fast lies in the microbes within the intestinal canal. All our efforts are therefore directed against these microbes which we are endeavoring to fight."

Prof. Metchnikoff touched his gray beard with his fingers and said lightly:

"I am only 64 years old, and yet see how gray my beard is. I look much older than I really am. This should not be. People will attain happiness only when they will grow old naturally, not as they now grow old without years, and when they will be able to use all their faculties, without suffering or pain, until the time sets in for their natural death. As I have pointed out in my introduction to the Russian edition of my 'Studies in Optimism,' science brings happiness to mankind. The relief that medical science brings to suffering humanity should not be regarded as merely a negative ideal. The absence of suffering, which means that man can make use of his perfect health, constitutes a very positive ideal, which is appreciated all the more as the years go by, and which makes it possible for man to avail himself of the other advantages of life.

"The idea, which has become rather popular, that the animal is happier than the human being is erroneous. Of course, it is difficult to solve this question with any degree of certainty, because it is impossible to compare the feelings and the sensations of animals and human beings. But we can compare the different feelings and sensations of man himself. We know that to many people the happiness afforded by science and the solution of scientific problems is undoubtedly higher than the happiness which animals are capable of feeling and which is attained by them through satisfying their hunger or other requirements. The consciousness of inevitable death, which animals have not, and which often makes man so unhappy, is an evil that can be remedied, that will be remedied by science.

"It is more than likely that science will teach us to live in accordance with the principles of orthobiotics, and will lead life to the moment of the approach of the instinct of natural death, when there will be no longer the fear of the inevitability of the end. Science can and must in the future give to mankind a happy existence. When science will have secured for mankind a normal cycle of life, when the people will forget the majority of diseases, even as they need not worry so much about the plague, cholera, diphtheria, rabies, and other scourges that threatened them until recently, then the efforts of gratifying the higher requirements of spiritual life will come to the front even more than now. But together with the quest after knowledge for the sake of the highest pleasure, that is, together with 'science for science's sake,' mankind will then even more than now seek happiness in the pleasure afforded by all kinds of beauty, that is by 'art for art's sake.'"

In speaking of his critics, Prof. Metchnikoff said:

"It may seem strange, but it is a fact, nevertheless. My own countrymen, the Russians, have been my harshest critics. Among others, K. K. Tolstoy, attempted to attack my theories, and especially my statements regarding the use of sour milk bacteria for hindering the decay of the intestines. He keeps repeating that I advise everybody to use sour milk simply because I was attracted by some foodstuff that appealed to me.

"As a matter of fact, I caution people against the constant use of sour milk because, together with the helpful and useful microbes, it frequently contains also undesirable microbes. He argues that instead of the curdled milk other things may be used, such as raw fruits, cider vinegar, and even light wine, and that these would produce the same effect. But I have explained very carefully in my works that it is not merely a question of swallowing acids, for they are absorbed before they reach the heavy intestines. And that is just where they are needed in order to offset the destructive bacteria. That is why I advise the use of live pure sour milk bacteria cultures in boiled milk, which reach the proper place alive and hinder the decay of the intestine. This has been established beyond any doubt."

I asked Prof. Metchnikoff whether progress had been made in the investigation of tuberculosis by the Pasteur Institute.

"The experiments with preventative inoculation have not proved successful. But even the simplest measures adopted in France against the spread of the disease have been very helpful. Thus, such things as isolating the children of tuberculous parents and separating the consumptives in the advanced stages of the disease from those in the less advanced stages, have already shown good results. The number of consumptives is decreasing in France."

"I see that they have started an energetic campaign against tuberculosis in America," Prof. Metchnikoff added after a while.

"What is your opinion of American scientists?" I asked.

"It seems to me that Americans are rather fond of sensationalism even in their science. When my volume 'Studies in Optimism' appeared in English it was called 'The Prolongation of Life.' I cannot understand why the title should have been changed. But that is not important. I have the greatest respect for American scientists.

"America has produced in recent years a number of first-class scientists. Jacques Loeb is perhaps the most important of them. I can foresee the time when America will outshine Europe by her scientists. I believe it is unfair to the American people that they are regarded everywhere in Europe as good business men only. As soon as a man shows any signs of talent here, the Americans try to attract him to America, and as they are richer and have more means for carrying on experimental scientific work, they secure our best men. It will not be long before our best scientists will be in America."

"When are you coming to America, Professor?"

"I am afraid the voyage across the ocean will not agree with me," he answered with a smile.

Prof. Metchnikoff then spoke with great enthusiasm about the "grand old man" of Russia and his prospective visit to Yasnaya Polyana.

"I have always looked forward with the greatest pleasure and reverence to a meeting with Tolstoy, and I am happy that my hope is about to be fulfilled now."

Upon my request for some facts concerning his biography, Prof. Metchnikoff said:

"I was born in 1845, in the Government of Kharkov. I am a Little Russian, a son of the steppe. My father was an officer of the Guards, who later became a general. My mother was a Jewess. I ascribe my love for science to my descent from the Jewish race. I studied natural science at the gymnasium and the university in Russia. Later I studied zoology and biology in Germany and Italy. I was professor in St. Petersburg and Odessa. After the assassination of Alexander II, I found that it was impossible to do any serious work at the university because of the political tendencies that crowded out the desire for study among the youth. Soon the Russian universities had no serious professors, and some of the best men in Russia who could achieve much for their fatherland were lost to Russia. I am speaking of the Russian Jews. The Russians have the mind, but the Russian Jews have in addition to that vivacity and energy to a remarkable degree. Russia has lost many great talents by persecuting the Jews. Prof. Minkowsky, the great mathematician, was a Russian Jew who had to leave Russia simply because he was a Jew. The same was true of the other Minkowsky. My own assistants, Bezredka and Weinberg, are men of great talent, and I am sure that they will be shining lights in the scientific world. But as they are Jews, they could not develop in Russia, and Russia has lost them."

Metchnikoff paused for a while and added optimistically:

"I feel quite certain that there will be a change even in this. The Russian Government will realize its errors and will improve the condition of the Jewish people, for its own sake, if for no other reason."

Paris, 1909.

I met Prof. Metchnikoff again in Paris after his visit to Yasnaya Polyana. He received me in his laboratory at the Pasteur Institute.

"I am delighted with my visit to Tolstoy," he said. "I must confess that I never expected he was such a splendid man. He is really wonderful. His feelings, his heart, are developed to the highest degree of sensitiveness and delicacy."

"Did you discuss his works with him?"

"Yes, I told him that I value his purely literary work more than his philosophical work. Tolstoy replied that he considered his philosophical work of more importance than his artistic work. He said that it was very easy for him to produce his artistic work, while his philosophical work proved more difficult, and it was for this reason that he loved it all the more. We spoke about religion and science. He took a deep interest in my work and was particularly eager to have me tell him what I knew about cancer. We walked in his garden and I picked out some leaves with wart-like growths upon them, and he was very much interested in my explanations of these growths. In speaking of religion and science, he said that people were wrong in believing him to be opposed to religion or science. What he opposed, he said, was the hypocrisy and the falsehood that the Church had introduced into religion. As for science, Tolstoy said that he opposed the narrow-minded so-called scientists who believed that, having made some small discovery, they should be considered as superior people—benefactors and teachers of mankind."

"May I know your own views on religion?"

"I am an atheist, as you will see from my 'Studies in Optimism.' The fact that the majority of the people believe in God and in future-existence is based not upon religious instinct but may be explained by the influence of education. That is why we often see that people who in their childhood believed in what they had been trained to believe, in time lose their faith in those things as their minds develop."

"I understand that you expressed yourself very strongly about the inferiority of women while you were in Russia. May I know your views on this subject?"

"Women are superior to men—in affairs of the heart," said Prof. Metchnikoff, with a smile. "Genius, I believe, is a masculine quality, just as a beard is, for instance, or as strong muscles are. That women are inferior to men they have demonstrated most effectively in the domains where they have always reigned supreme—music and cooking. Women have not produced a single composer of note, and even in the kitchen they have not been able to maintain their supremacy. If they want a good chef they get a man. Of course I am not opposed to women studying the arts and sciences, but I do not believe that women will ever amount to much as scientists. I need hardly say that there are exceptions, just as there are bearded ladies, but at any rate, they are superior to men in affairs of the heart, and that is a great deal. As for women scientists, it is better that they occupy themselves with science than with fashions."

Before leaving, Prof. Metchnikoff presented me with a set of his works in Russian.

"Do you think that a reading of 'Studies in Optimism' will help to prolong life, Professor?" I asked.

"It may shorten your days during your voyage across the Atlantic if you have nothing else to read," he laughed.

When I left the Pasteur Institute I carried away a deep impression of a strong, simple, lovable personality, an apostle of optimism, who has made a religion of science even as Tolstoy has made a science of religion.

MAXIME KOVALEVSKY

St. Petersburg, 1909.

DURING my present visit to Russia I had occasion to discuss
Russian affairs with the leaders of the various parties in the
Duma and with members of the Gosundarstvenny Sovyet
—the Council of the Empire.   I found among them a number of people who are undoubtedly able to accomplish great
things when the psychological moment arrives.   But it
seemed the time for their activity had not yet come.
These people, intellectual giants, equipped with great learning and earnestness of purpose, are architect-builders who
are able to erect structures according to beautiful projects,
but not before the ground has been cleared.

They are as yet surrounded with windfallen trees in a
very thick forest.   The distance is enormous between the
so-called Parliament in St. Petersburg and the millions of
the ignorant masses, who are enmeshed in a dense net of
government organs and agencies, especially created to keep
them in darkness.

As a prominent member of the Duma said to me: "The
Russian Constitution is to be found solely upon a tiny
island—the Tavrichesky Palace—the building where the
Duma holds its sessions.   The autocracy does not allow the
Constitution to go beyond the walls of this palace."   The
conceptions of Czarism and constitutionalism are incompatible.   There are provincial places in Russia, not so very
far from St. Petersburg, where it is still dangerous to speak
of the Duma, for some official might overhear it and ask:

"Are you for the Czar or for the Duma?" But a short time ago in one of the Cossack settlements in the Don region, a crowd listening to the reading of news from the Duma was dispersed with whips.

But the distance between those who worked for the emancipation of Russia and the masses is narrowing—the people have begun to realize who are their enemies and who their friends.

One of the greatest of the architect-builders of the new Russia is Prof. Maxime Kovalevsky, famous historian, authority upon international law, publicist, formerly professor of the University of Paris, now a member of the Council of the Empire. Prof. Kovalevsky is one of the very few great figures in Russia who perceive clearly the actual proportion and importance of events and who analyze them without either going into raptures or falling into despair. A scholar of the highest type, he is at the same time a practical statesman taking an active part in the preparatory work of Russia's reconstruction. His opinions upon the Russian situation are accordingly of the greatest significance. Prof. Kovalevsky presented his views to me as follows:

"The dispersion of the first two Dumas has created a spirit of skepticism among the people. And while the old peasants still remain faithful to God and the Russian Czar, the majority of the young people have come to the conclusion that everything must be taken by force. In fact, they have become a little too violent.

"Looking over the legislation of the Third Duma I must say that it has not shown any necessary economy. The budgets have not been diminished. The Duma, however, was wrong in refusing an appropriation for the four battleships. Our fortresses at Revel and at Kronstadt are not efficient. They could not withstand an attack for more than three weeks. The four men-of-war we are to have now will be of the same type as the Dreadnaughts and will constitute to a certain extent a defense in the event of an invasion by Germany.

"You ask me why has the Russian revolution failed? I begin by denying the fact. My opinion is that it has not failed, but is going on at the present time, and, if some are despairing, it is because they do not realize the real nature of the movement. The movement is far from being only political—it is essentially social. It began years ago, and its chief result will be the creation of a Russian democracy. Centuries ago Harrington, in his 'Oceana,' expressed the idea, new for his time, that power belongs to those who own the land. Now Russian soil is rapidly passing into the hands of the peasants. The first Duma intended to accelerate the movement through legislation. The reaction which followed was chiefly created by the fact that Russian nobility was frightened by the radicalism of the measures proposed.

"But the movement, which has for its ends the transference of the land into the hands of the peasants is none the less going on, perhaps more rapidly than before. The Ministers, with M. Stolypin at their head, are buying the lands of ruined noblemen in order to resell them at lower prices to the peasants. This measure is certainly more ruinous to the Russian treasury than the one we had in view, but it achieves the same end. The dissolution of village communities—another obnoxious measure of the same Ministry—is yet on the whole advancing the day of democratic rising; upon one side it creates a numerous class of peasant proprietors, and upon the other, a much more numerous class of rural proletariats. A collision between them becomes every day more probable.

"Our industries are unable to employ all those who, having no more settled interest in the land, are deserting the villages. And Russian agriculture is not likely to become a secondary branch of our national economy. In such conditions the rising of the country people in the near future seems to me very probable, and all I hear from persons living in the country only confirms my apprehension. The peasant is losing his confidence in the Czar as the natural protector of the country people against the landed squires. The orthodox church is each day losing even more its moral hold upon the people, because of its total lack of independence from civil authority and the nobility. The radical Protestant sects, such as the Dukhobors, the Mennonites, the Stundists (Baptists), are gaining every day new adherents among the peasantry. All this is not calculated to suggest the idea that we have not to fear in the future a new agrarian movement. And for that reason I answer in the affirmative your question. Do I think that the agrarian question will lead to new disturbances in the near future? Yes, I am afraid it will.

"In the spontaneous revolution which shall have for its chief object the creation of a peasant democracy instead of a military empire, reliant upon bureaucracy, nobility and orthodoxy, the Third Duma is likely to play a prominent part, in this way only—it will open the eyes of the peasants to the dependence in which Czardom lives upon bureaucracy, high orthodox clergy and landed gentry. I find no instance in the past of a more cynical pursuit of class interests than the one of which the Third Duma is, and will continue to be, the spectacle. From this point of view it may be compared only with the 'chambre introuvable' of the French restoration. The Ministry is powerless to pursue its own policy. It does what it is ordered to do by the reactionary alliance of 'king, bishop and nobleman.' To give you an instance. We were told (Stakhovitch, Arseniev and myself) by Premier Stolypin that he would do everything he could to render possible a collection of money in the whole empire to be employed for the creation of some memorial associated with the name of Count Leo Tolstoy—and the same Stolypin later took rigorous measures to prevent any demonstration in favor of our 'grand old man.' Of course, he did so against his own will and only because he was ordered to do so by the orthodox clergy and the 'Real Russians,' who find a hearing at the Court.

"I see, therefore, no reason to expect that the 'Government' will do anything in favor of the Jews, except propagating the myth that, once emancipated, the Jews are certain to be exterminated by the peasantry. I call this a myth, because neither at St. Petersburg, Moscow nor in the province of Kharkov, where I own land, have I ever discovered the hatred which the workman and the villager are supposed to entertain against the Jews.

"You ask me what influence the events in Persia and Turkey are likely to exercise upon Russian affairs. I suppose they will induce the governing class—I mean the Court and the high bureaucracy—to maintain the present state of things—I mean a Duma composed of persons devoted to the interests of the minority of noblemen, high churchmen and landed squires.

"The Russian Government is, to say the least, full of the

most amazing inconsistencies. Thus, for instance, the authors of articles distasteful to the Government are not punished—only the publishers of such articles are prosecuted. Leo Tolstoy is not prosecuted for his writings, but his son, who publishes them, is punished. If the Government were consistent the signers of the Viborg manifesto, the Deputies of the First Duma who are now in prison, should not have been prosecuted. They were merely the authors of that document.

"How I regard the condition of Russian literature? This question is more difficult to answer. Periods of transition, such as the one we are experiencing now in Russia, are not as a rule golden ages of literature. Why so? The riddle, if there is one, was disclosed to me at one time by Turgenev. I was insisting upon his writing a new novel, in which the men of my generation would be pictured. 'It cannot be done,' he answered. 'It is impossible to give a definite form in literature to persons and things which have not yet taken a definite form in life.' Applying this aphorism to the present state of our literature I am inclined to think that our young authors do not find it easy to create new types, with two exceptions, that of the 'hooligan,' so admirably represented by Gorky and Arzibashev, and of the social reformer and agitator of whom you will find a less successful picture in Gorky's novel, 'The Mother.'

"It is to the same cause, the want of definite form characterizing our present evolution, that I attribute the great development of lyrics. We have several dozens of young poets who seek new forms and new symbols. Some of them, such as Balmont and Valeri Brussov, have given excellent translations of Shelley, Calderon and Lope de Vega, and have written admirable verses of their own, verses that are comparable with those of our great Pushkin.   In this our revolutionary period reminds me of that of 1789–1800 in France, when the greatest writer (Andre Chenier) was great on account of his lyrical verses and not of his novels. We no doubt possess at this moment young writers who will be highly appreciated in some ten or twenty years, but who so far have not given, as the Frenchmen say, 'toute la mesure de leur talent.' "

SHEIKH-UL-ISLAM

Constantinople, June, 1909.

But a short time ago there existed a saying in Turkey that the Sultan is the shadow of God on earth, and that the shadow of the Sultan is the Sheikh-ul-Islam, the religious head of all the Moslems. When in April, by order of the famous Fetwa, presided over by the Sheikh-ul-Islam, Abdul Hamid was deposed, the new Sultan, though very popular with the people, ceased to be the shadow of God on earth. The circumstances under which he has been proclaimed Khalif of the Ottoman Empire have made him a mere figurehead.

The Parliament, or rather the Union and Progress Committee of the Young Turks, is for the present the almighty power in the land. But there is one man whose authority has increased with the decline of the Sultan's power, and that man is the Sheikh-ul-Islam. Indeed those who know Turkey intimately, are of the opinion that his authority is even greater than that of the Parliament, for while the Parliament has at present the support of the army, the Sheikh-ul-Islam has the masses behind him—the blindly believing, fanatic hordes, headed by the hodjas, the Turkish priests, who exert a tremendous influence upon their followers, and who have on numerous occasions demonstrated their readiness to urge the massacre of those who oppose Islam.

Who knows what would happen, what horrors would be perpetrated, what outrages committed, and what bloodshed caused, if for some reason or another the Parliament and the Sheikh-ul-Islam should clash? The people of Turkey are afraid even to speak of it. But the wisest minds of the Ottoman Empire realize the danger of irritating Islam at the present time, and, therefore, many reforms must wait for the opportune moment, when they may be introduced without shocking the religious sensibilities of the Moslems.

It is for these reasons that of all the Turkish statesmen I was particularly eager to meet the Sheikh-ul-Islam and to learn from his own lips whether a bridge can really be built between Mecca and the Parliament and whether the Constitution does not clash with the Koran.

The opportunity of securing an audience with the Sheikh, the chief of the Moslems, presented itself to me in the Yildiz, the palace of the deposed Sultan, which has now been thrown open to the public. On Friday, after the Selamlik, when the first concert was given for the benefit of the public at the Yildiz, the occasion was turned into a merry festival and a day of great rejoicing. The saviors of the constitution were proudly walking up and down the beautiful alleys of the park, and the people were rowing in the boats which a few months ago had been used by Abdul Hamid. A band was playing and singing patriotic songs, and the words of the songs, as well as the melodies, though old, seemed to carry a new meaning to the people, who cheered and applauded wildly. It was amid these surroundings that I made the acquaintance of the son of the Sheikh-ul-Islam. With him was Col. Galib Bey, the head of the gendarmerie, one of the heroes of the new régime and one of the three men chosen to notify Abdul Hamid that he had been deposed.

Upon my inquiry whether it would be possible for me to

secure an audience with the Sheikh-ul-Islam, his son extended to me an invitation to the Islamate for the following day.

It was about 10 o'clock in the morning when I started in a carriage from Pera to Stambul. The narrow, crooked, filthy streets of Constantinople were crowded with pedestrians in parti-colored gowns and turbans, the women wearing chiefly the charchafs, black dresses, their faces covered with black veils—all walking in the middle of the streets. A jarring noise hung continuously in the air. People were crying their wares in desperate tones, little donkeys carrying heavy and bulky burdens were braying plaintively, and from time to time a dog barked lazily.

We neared the tower of Stambul, and as it was somewhat too early to go over to the Islamate, I entered the Sulieman Mosque nearby. It was a mercilessly hot day, but within the mosque it was very cool. On the floor, in one of the corners, sat a group of four softas, theological students, and, swaying backward and forward, studied the Koran. They were reading softly, in a sing-song, but the extraordinary acoustics carried their voices from one corner of the tremendous building to the other. A little distance away from the students several men lay outstretched on the floor, fast asleep. These were workmen who had come to the Mosque in quest of shelter from the heat. Men in picturesque garb walked in and, turning toward the direction of the sun, knelt, kissed the matted floor, and prayed fervently. Suddenly the shrill voice of a little boy studying the Koran by heart resounded. He swayed backward and forward with dizzying rapidity. Near him a Turkish army officer, his sword, his coat, and shoes removed and placed in a heap at his side, sat on the ground, also studying the Koran. The workmen, some twenty-five or thirty in number, were sleeping, undisturbed by the sing-song of the students. Now and then one of the workmen would stretch himself, rise slowly and walk out, yawning.

I started from the Mosque to the house of the Sheikh-ul-Islam. The square was crowded with beggars, cripples of all kinds side by side with strong, strapping men, seated on the ground with outstretched hands. A woman clad in black, her face veiled, dropped a coin into the hand of one beggar, made a few steps forward, then paused. The happy recipient of the coin bowed his head in gratitude. Suddenly the woman, surrounded by a crowd of beggars, young and old, walked up to the man on the ground and shouted:

"Pray, you rascal! Why don't you pray?"

And he rattled off a prayer mechanically in a tone that sounded like a sob.

Near the beggars lay clusters of yellow dogs—one of the most characteristic features of the streets of Constantinople, the dogs having been aptly styled the Street Cleaning Department of the Capital of Turkey.

The headquarters of the Islamate consists of several large, low, yellow-colored buildings. At the entrance of the yard men are selling beads and cakes. In the hallways of the building where the religious head of the nation attends to the business of Islam, hodjas in fine cloaks and underlings in tattered clothes, and old women in black, chiefly widows of priests, are lounging around the walls, in various positions, waiting for their monthly allowances and pensions.

My companion, a young Turk, a former schoolmate of the Sheikh-ul-Islam's son, led the way to the old Turk who took my card to the Sheikh, eying us suspiciously. In the corridor we had to remove our shoes and put on huge slippers. The priests and the women walked about in their stockings.

Two minutes later I found myself in the presence of the man who guides the destinies of Islam.

The new Sheikh, whose name is Sahib Molla Effendi, and who before his appointment to this highest post had been a member of the Council of the Empire, admired by those who know him for his liberal views, for which he was hated and persecuted by Abdul Hamid, is a tall, white-haired man of about sixty-five. He wore a white turban on his head and a loose brown cloak. His white beard was beautifully shaped, and his remarkably youthful and searching eyes were smiling from under his large jet-black eyebrows. He rose when we entered and stretched out his hand.

"My son spoke to me about you. I am very glad to meet you," he said warmly, pointing to a seat on the lounge opposite him.

My young companion kissed the Sheikh's hand and made a low bow. When we took our seats, the Sheikh bowed to us again, as is the custom in Turkey.

"I am glad to make the acquaintance of the Sheikh-ul-Islam of new Turkey," I said.

The Sheikh smiled, bowed low, and answered:

"Turkey is going through a crisis now. There is a dearth of men—of strong, great men. I realize that this high office needs a greater man than I am."

He paused for awhile. Then he added:

"I know quite well that I have been selected by the Sultan not because I am the right man for the post, but rather because there are so few real men in Turkey at present."

An old Turk entered and whispered something to the Sheikh. The Sheikh then turned to us and said:

"You will forgive me, I hope, if I will receive a few people here and attend to some pressing affairs. It will take but a few minutes, and then we can speak without being disturbed."

The Sheikh rang the bell and ordered that tea be brought in. He poured it into small glasses himself, sweetened it, and handed me one of the glasses.

In the meantime a white-haired hodja entered, kissed the Sheikh's hand and, not daring to sit down in the chair near the Sheikh's low table, bent down toward the Sheikh, speaking softly, in a cringing tone. The burden of his request was that his pension be given to him regularly.

"Allah knows my pension is small enough, and now I am not getting it all," he said tearfully.

The Sheikh lifted his hand to his lips quickly and whispered tenderly:

"Hush! You must not speak of such matters in this way. Everything is being straightened out now. I shall see to it that your pension will be given to you regularly henceforth."

The old priest sank down to the ground, kissed the hem of the Sheikh's cloak, and stepped out of the room backward, bowing reverently.

One after another a half dozen men came in. Some had come to ask the Sheikh to promote them, another begged to be transferred to a district closer to Constantinople. I had seen the priest who wished to be transferred, a while before in the corridor. His black robe was of the finest cloth and on his head was a beautiful turban. In the corridor he stood alone, away from the crowd, his pose bespeaking an air of haughtiness, a look of sternness in his eyes. Now, in the presence of the Sheikh, his tall figure contracted and bent down all the while he spoke, an unnatural smile played in his eyes and on his lips as he cringed and kissed the Sheikh's hand, kneeling before him and kissing the hem of his cloak.

The Sheikh settled the various questions with a smile, a word or two, and a stroke of the pen.

Finally, he turned to me, his face beaming with smiles, as he said:

"Now, we shall not be disturbed. I am glad, indeed, that you have come to see me. There is nothing better on earth than to come and see the truth with one's own eyes, instead of believing in hearsay. Especially is this true of Turkey, now more than ever before.

"Unfortunately so much is being written about us by people who do not know us and who do not take the pains of learning something about us."

The first question I asked was whether it was true that according to the Koran there could not be a constitutional form of government in Turkey, as the Koran prohibited any legislation to emanate from anybody save the Sultan.

"Why, no, that is all wrong," replied the Sheikh-ul-Islam, with a smile. "The Constitution has grown out of our religion. In fact, the Moslem religion orders a constitutional government. The Koran tells us that the wise men of the nation shall come together and decide what is best for all the people. Thus it may be said that the Koran actually gave birth to the Constitution."

He lit a long cigarette and added:

"The Sultan, of course, is our chief, for our religion tells us that a great nation cannot be without a chief."

As I sat there I recalled how the former Sheikh-ul-Islam had defined the importance of the Khalif. It was at the time of the visit of Kaiser Wilhelm to Constantinople and the Holy Land.

"The Sultan is superior to all the other rulers," said the old Sheikh. "The Sultan is God's representative potentate on earth. But as it is impossible for the Sultan to be present everywhere, such rulers as the Kaiser of Germany, the King of England, the President of France, and the President of the United States have been made his assistants. Under such circumstances," declared the Sheikh, "it is not proper for the Sultan to be the first to greet the Kaiser."

When the Sultan and the Kaiser met, and Abdul Hamid stretched out his hand first to greet his royal guest, the Sheikh-ul-Islam, who stood at his side, declared in a burst of anger:

"The Sultan is degrading God by degrading himself!"

The difference in the definitions of the Sultan, as given by the former and the present Sheikhs, mirrors the attitude of the religious Moslems toward their rulers in the past and the present.

In the following question I asked how Islam looked upon people of other faiths and upon non-believers. His answer came slowly, in measured tones:

"There is no difference between Mohammedan, Jew, or Christian in the eyes of a true Moslem. All are equal. The only place where our ways part are at prayer—we go to the mosque, while they go to a synagogue or church. In fact, as far as we are concerned, our ways need not part even then, for we Moslems are at liberty to pray anywhere.

We do not make the slightest discrimination against those who do not believe as we do. We look upon their goods as our goods, and upon their life as our life, and we try to protect them in every way. The Moslem who does not believe in Moses, the founder of Judaism, and Christ, the founder of Christianity, as prophets, is not a true Moslem. Of course, Mohammed, who came later than Moses and Christ, and who found the world in a dreadful state of demoralization, has improved upon their teachings. Otherwise, all the prophets are equal. As for non-believers, we feel sorry for them, we pity them, but we do not persecute them. Our sympathies are naturally with believers, but we are not angry at agnostics. Their conscience is their own affair."

"Have you written any works on religious subjects?" I asked.

"No, I have not written anything. I have never had a moment of unoccupied time. I believe it is a sad waste of time to write, unless one is sure that he can produce a great and useful work."

"May I know who are your favorite writers in Europe?"

The Sheikh-ul-Islam hesitated.

"May I know your opinion of the works of such writers as Goethe, Voltaire, Tolstoy?"

The Sheikh smiled, and it was evident from the expression of his face that he had not heard these names before.

"I have not read their works, for the same reason that I have not written any books myself. I have not had any unoccupied time. But I am, of course, familiar with Arabic literature."

I explained to him Tolstoy's place in modern literature, the nature of his latest writings, and the reason why he had been excommunicated by the Russian Church.

"What would be your attitude toward a Moslem, a man of the calibre of Tolstoy, who would criticise Islam?" I asked.

"Our religion is liberal. Our religion is free. Any one may write whatever he pleases. We are not afraid. We would excommunicate no one for criticising us. We look upon the skeptic and non-believer with a sense of compassion. We feel sorry for our critics, but we have not the slightest fear. And do you know why we have no fear? No one has yet written a better book than the Koran, nor can anybody ever write a better book."

In my next question I asked the Sheikh-ul-Islam to express himself concerning the rights of the various religious heads, such as the Greek and Armenian Patriarchs and the Haham Bashi (Grand Rabbi) under the new régime.

"My position does not permit me to discuss political questions," he said. "Of course, I could enumerate to you their rights under the present régime, not in my official capacity. But I have not yet familiarized myself sufficiently with this subject, and it is my rule never to speak on anything unless I know it thoroughly."

At this point I decided to ask the question to which no Turkish statesman is willing to give a frank answer. The Young Turks are afraid to commit themselves on the subject concerning the amelioration of the condition of women in Turkey, realizing that nothing might so arouse the Turkish masses against the new government as even the mention of reform in this direction.

"Everywhere in Europe and America there are movements for the emancipation of women. Do you intend to introduce in time any reforms which would tend to improve the condition of women in Turkey?" I asked.

The Sheikh's large, dark eyes smiled. Then he lowered his heavy, black eyebrows over his eyes and, after a pause, answered:

"This is a very important question. The emancipation of woman? Ah! that is a most serious problem. But do you know? The idea that such reforms are necessary has not yet been born in Turkey."

"Is it because the men themselves are not yet emancipated?"

"The idea of equalizing the women with the men is not yet born in Turkey and will not be born for a long time to come. At the present time the character, the customs, and habits of our people make it impossible for such ideas to develop in our midst."

"You say, 'at the present time.' Do you believe that the Parliament will take up this question in the near future and introduce reforms in this direction?"

"I am not so sure that this will ever happen in Turkey," replied the Sheikh slowly.

"What is your attitude toward Zionism?" I inquired after a while.

The Sheikh-ul-Islam looked as though he did not understand my question. So I modified it.

"How do you look upon the emigration of Jews from countries where they are persecuted, such as Russia and Roumania, to Palestine?"

"We regard all people as our equals," said the Sheikh. "We make no discrimination against Jew or Gentile. The Jews have always lived comfortably in Turkey, and the

Moslems like them very much. But as much as we sympathise with a suffering race, we Moslems treat all people equally, and if a large emigration of Jews or Gentiles to Palestine would commence, it would become a problem for the Parliament to solve. It is certainly not a religious question."

Suddenly the Sheikh turned the conversation to America and Americans, and spoke with great enthusiasm.

"The Americans are the most progressive people in the world," he said. "They are quick to perceive their opportunities, they possess more initiative and energy than any other people. Let the American capitalists bring their money to Turkey. Turkey is in great need of money just now. They would earn great profits and would at the same time help us to develop along the lines of liberty. They would help us to help ourselves."

Just before I left, the Sheikh-ul-Islam said to me:

"Remember, our religion orders that there shall be a constitution. It does not order this form of constitution or that. Time may change the constitution and improve it. But what is most important, our religion orders liberty, and I assure you that Islam will be the protector of liberty."

After a visit to the various departments of the Islamate and to the room where a few months before the Fetwa had decided to depose Abdul Hamid, I came out on the street. The sun was burning. The beggars and the dogs almost covered the square now. The women with their faces covered, a mass of black from head to foot, walked slowly, and in passing, some of them dropped coins to the beggars and waited for their prayers.

As I passed the Sulieman Mosque on my way from the

Sheikh, I saw new groups of people entering the cool house of prayer—to sleep.

From time to time a wild outcry rent the air, and some phlegmatic Turk would bestir himself about his little shop. In the distance a Muezzin, stationed on the minaret, was calling the faithful Moslems to prayer:

"Allah is great! Allah is most great!"

MAXIMILIAN HARDEN

Berlin, May, 1908.

MAXIMILIAN HARDEN scarcely needs any introduction in America. But it may not be generally known that throughout Germany the name of Harden has become a household word. Among the people at large his name is associated with fearlessness and courage and victory. When, after his second trial, a crowd of about 5,000 people waited for him at the Court House and carried him, amid cheers, on their shoulders, it was but an expression, in a small way, of the feeling of the masses, who everywhere applauded the man who dared to stir up the hornets' nest, to expose the rottenness in the highest places, and who came out triumphant.

Since then the success of Harden and his small but influential weekly journal, *Die Zukunft*, called forth a most bitter animosity among Harden's already numerous enemies, chiefly inspired by a sense of envy. Men like Harden have enthusiastic admirers, but they also make deadly enemies. Thus Harden has been called by some "the savior of Germany," while by others he is styled "the betrayer of the German Empire." Harden has been compared with Couzier and Rochefort, with Girondin and Lasalle, with Sainte-Beuve and Taine; he has been called a harlequin and a prophet, and his speeches as well as his writings have been described as containing "fire and force, thunder and lightning."

But, whatever Harden may be, one thing is certain—he

is the greatest moulder of public opinion in Germany. His intimate friendship with Bismarck gave him a peculiar position as a "private authority" concerning the inner workings of politics and statesmanship in Germany as well as in other European States. Since the passing of Bismarck, Harden has become the centre toward which gravitate all German statesman and high officials who for one cause or another are discontented. To him they unburden themselves, and Harden himself has been called the prophet of discontent.

His fight against "the Knights of the Round Table" has proved successful, even though at the fourth trial, but a little while ago, Harden was found guilty and sentenced to a fine of 600 marks. The men he accused in his articles in *Die Zukunft* are disgraced and dismissed from office. As Harden himself put it:

"The decisive has happened. The German Emperor showed these men the door. Why? This will never be 'established' here. . . . No details are necessary. Can you believe that only the articles in *Die Zukunft* have led to this step? Do we live in an empire where the most favored gentlemen are driven away because a moderately distinguished journal, by no means favored by the Kaiser, contained a few articles against them? Are old, intimate friends simply thrown out on this account? Is this sufficient for the Kaiser to say to the representative of the former President of the Police Department: 'You need not tell me any more about Eulenberg, Moltke, Hohenau, or Lecomte; these are settled. But I want at once a list of the others of the Court and the Guards'?"

In his last speech at the trial just closed Harden wound up with the following words:

". . . When you condemn me, use your judgment, not your right, for you have not proved against me the slightest guilt. Do it! I have nothing against it. Such things must end in this way; such things have always ended thus in history. . . . It must always be thus. Do it again, if you would take the responsibility upon yourself. Let it be known that the Imperial Court has once more tried to disgrace Harden and has convicted him again. I only wish that the sentence be severe (from your viewpoint there can be no question of a fine; such a decision would be incomprehensible) and I am sorry that you cannot go above the four months' limit. Imprison me, brand me, strike me: that's the punishment. . . ."

Next to the Kaiser, Maximilian Harden is perhaps the best known figure in Berlin. If you call up "Wilmensdorf 366" the telephone operator will ask: "Harden?" That is not the number of *Die Zukunft*, it is the telephone number of his house. The German barber, who is quite as talkative as his American colleague, while shaving me noticed that I had with me a copy of *Die Zukunft*, and he immediately went into raptures over Harden. When I hailed a cabman and told him to drive to Wernerstrasse, 16, he looked up importantly and asked: "Herr von Harden?"

As I came to Grunewald, Berlin's most beautiful section, where Harden's villa is located, I noticed the following legend painted on his door: "Walk in lively! You may enter with dust-covered shoes! But if your heart and your mind are covered with dust, leave us alone!"

This legend was not recently inscribed—it showed considerable signs of age.

Mr. Harden received me in the room adjoining his library, and through the open door I could see Franz von Lenbach's famous painting of Bismarck on the wall facing Harden's writing table. From the photographs I had seen of Harden, and from what I knew of his work, I had pictured him as a strong, imposing, rather theatrical figure. Instead, he is small in stature, unassuming, and modest-looking. But when he speaks there is something in his face, in his eyes, that reminds one of the Napoleonic cast of features.

We began to speak about German literature and the drama of to-day.

"I have been ten days in Berlin and have noticed that perhaps nine-tenths of the dramas produced in your theatres are translations or adaptations from other languages. French comedies, farces, and detective plays are in the lead. Shakespeare is given, the Ibsen plays are produced, Goethe's 'Faust' has been revived by Max Reinhardt in a most elaborate form. Occasionally an original, new German play is also produced. What is the state of the drama in Germany to-day?" I asked.

"German literature cannot be said to be in a flourishing condition," said Harden. "Some of our dramatists are writing novels now, but they have not produced anything of importance. Sudermann's 'The Song of Songs' is a fiasco. It was a cheap appeal to the lower tastes of the people, but it failed, nevertheless. As in his dramas, Sudermann was here also striving merely for outward effects. Hauptmann's latest play, 'Griselda,' also failed of success. The trouble with all our dramatists is that as soon as they have met success with one of their plays they set up a high standard of living, and in order to maintain it they must keep on turning out play after play. They must produce even when they have nothing to produce.

"Take Hauptmann, for instance. He has bought eight villas and has grown accustomed to a luxurious life. He is thus compelled to produce unripe work upon the stage. German literature would be in a better state if our novelists and dramatists would rest more than they do. In France Rostand, the most gifted of all French poets and dramatists, produced only one drama after his great success, 'L'Aiglon.' In Germany all—Halbe, Hauptmann, Sudermann, and others—have been writing too fast. Only a genius can produce a drama at one stroke. No other form of literature requires so much careful work as the drama. The great Ibsen always worked intensively; he re-wrote every dialogue three or four times; he reconstructed his scenes until they were dramatically perfect.

"This dearth of good dramas and novels is all the more to be regretted because there is at present a great interest in the drama and in literature in general to be noticed among the people. Many books are bought now and the theatres are thriving."

"Are there any new tendencies, new currents, in German literature? I see that Russian pornographic literature is finding its way into Germany in translations. Do you think this will exert some influence upon the modern German literature?" I asked.

"Unfortunately, too much space and importance are given to eroticism, to sexualism, in our literature. I am not a preacher of prudery. But I detest a work whose success is attained through pornography. Eroticism does not play so important a part in the life of the people as may be gathered from this sort of literature.

"The fault of modern literature is that it mirrors real life too little.   After all the power and efforts spent by the German people on inventions and the development of our industries, the future historian will not find anything in the books written during the past ten years that would give him even the slightest idea of what the people have really been doing. He will find only conflicts of Bohemians; stories of little girls and artists and literary folk. The treatment of real life, in artistic form, has been sadly neglected.

"There is a strong movement now for 'native literature,' for typically German literature.   I regard this movement as worthless.   Who wants to resist outside influences upon art to-day?   Assimilation is felt in all arts at present, and narrow nationalism is becoming impossible.   People of different nations and countries are growing ever more similar to one another.   The national differences are less pronounced than the social differences.   People of the same economic conditions living in different countries understand one another better than the people who live in luxury understand those who live in the cellars of the same houses."

"Which literature do you regard at present as one that is likely to exert a determining influence upon other literatures?"

"Certainly not current German literature.   It is an individual who looms up and introduces a new note.   Hauptmann cannot influence others.   He is himself a conglomeration of other literatures.   You will find in him the influences of French and Russian literatures.   Heine was a strong influence, especially on the young French lyrical poets. Now Nietzche is influencing the minds of young writers. Victor Hugo and Ibsen have had powerful influence everywhere. With Dostoyevsky and Tolstoy came the great Slavic wave over European literature."

"And now?"

"Now we are waiting for the American wave. It will surely come. It must come. It is with literature as with life and with politics," said Mr. Harden. "The influence of America is beginning to be felt in Europe. A great deal is being said about the Americanization of Europe, but the accusation that the Americans are money-mad, that they are nothing but dollar people is but a vulgar prejudice which is rapidly disappearing. There are dollar people everywhere. Nine-tenths of the efforts of all people everywhere are bent on moneymaking, and it is childish to speak of Americans as introducing commercialism into the arts.

"Paul Bourget was the first to weaken the prejudice that the Americans are merely business people. I know several American business men myself, and I am astounded at the interest they take in art. The higher spheres, the nobility, in Germany are not interested in art or literature; they have no libraries and they buy no paintings. If not for the wealthy Jews almost all our artists would have to starve. This abnormal state, caused by the indifference of our upper classes, has certainly had a retrogressive effect upon our art."

Finally our conversation turned from literature to politics. I asked him for his views on the future of Germany.

"It is hard to foretell the future of Germany," replied Mr. Harden. "Germany is strong, colossal, and it is growing ever stronger. But the population of Germany is growing, and it is becoming necessary for Germany to expand. Germany must have colonies, it needs colonies for its natural development, and it will make an effort to acquire them. When? Not immediately, but in the near future."

Mr. Harden paused awhile, and then went on:

"The best and most natural thing would be for the Germanic nations, the Anglo-Saxons and Americans, to unite and go hand in hand together. But England is opposed to such a union because of her antipathy for Germany. Therefore, it is probable that England will form a close friendship with the Slavs and the Japanese.

"With a view to the future, if America is sufficiently far-sighted, it should reflect and consider carefully as to what would be best for herself. It would be best for America to look to her own interests, and therefore not go with England and thus help her carry out her policies, which would work to the detriment of the United States.

"If there is mutual good-will between England, America, and Germany, these three great industrial nations will find the possibility for natural and pacific development. But I fear that it will be impossible to avoid a war. The situation will not be straightened out without a war. It must come to it, because Englishmen are not yet accustomed, they have not yet learned from history to divide power; they are determined at any cost to hold by force and violence that which they regard as theirs.

"The English statesman, who could see clearly the relations between Germany and England, must ponder carefully over everything that England has experienced with both South African republics since 1900 till the present time, and then reproduce this experience in world politics.

Then he would see that it is better to come to an agreement with a great power in the beginning instead of waging war in an effort to kill it off.

"As to Japan, I believe that the United States has made the gravest mistake by allowing it to become so great and powerful. Roosevelt was a very able and energetic President, but I do not think that he had very keen political foresight.

"It was the natural antipathy for Russia that allowed Japan to become great. But the Americans rejoiced altogether too much over Japan's victory.

"I think that America, which has settled the negro problem, will also manage to settle the yellow race problem. The great difficulty for America is how to check pacifically the invasion of the yellow races. But the danger of the yellow-race problems will lose its acuteness as soon as the Panama Canal is ready. Then America will be able to resist Japan. Until then America will have to be careful."

I asked Mr. Harden to express himself concerning the Turkish situation.

"I do not regard this liberalism in Turkey as definitely settled. It was said of the Jesuits that they either remain as they are or they can't exist at all. The same is true of Islam. The liberalism in Turkey is not liberalism in the American or English sense. Turkey is a religious State. It is impossible to make such an important change as has been made in Turkey so quickly. It was brought about by officers and journalists, and the people had no hand in it. I believe there will soon be another uprising and the old Sultanate will reinstate itself. The Turks gravitate to Asia. In European Turkey the Turks are in the minority. The officers furnish the sinews, and the journalists, schooled for years in London, Paris, and Brussels, furnish the brains of the new system in Turkey. But the people have played no part in the revolution. Mohammed and Robespierre, the Koran and Contrat Social—these do not rhyme well. I fear that reaction and revolution will alternate for some time to come.

"The situation in Turkey shows the weakness of Europe. Turkey belongs in Asia. Islam either remains as it is or it can't exist at all. Turkey is in Europe because of the rivalry among the European powers, because of their weakness. It is just the same as if Japan would be tolerated by America to settle down along the Pacific. Americans, because of this example, may be counseled against permitting the Japanese invasion in the very beginning."

"Do you think that the recent change in Turkey will serve as an impetus to a change in Russia?" I asked.

"I do not believe that anything will come about in Russia," answered Harden. "The Russian people, all classes of the Russian people, want peace and rest. Only a war can bring Russia to a new uprising. Russia, too, is an Islam. Nothing save a change in the inner life of the Russian masses will lead to the reconstruction of Russia. There must first be an awakening of their inner consciousness, there must first be an inner revolution. But this, I fear, is a long, hard road. The Russian masses have still to learn the difference between the life of the Czar and the life of an apostle."

Berlin, 1916.

In these days even the great and independent and courageous men of the countries involved in the war, the master minds of the various nations are not at liberty to speak the truth as they see it. They dare not comment on facts as they desire, they must not find fault even when they feel that their criticism might help their own countries, which they love passionately.

When the voice of cannon speaks the voice of reason must be silent. Silent now are the truly great men who are the conscience of the nations at war, and those who speak often distort the truth, believing that they are thereby helping their fatherlands.

When the machine guns are kept in action, mowing down the strongest and the weakest alike, when Zeppelins come in the stillness of the night over unfortified cities and hurl bombs upon women and children, the voices of the thinkers and the creative genius of the nations must be muffled, and it is regarded almost as high treason to utter words and express sentiments that might lead the maddened world back to sanity.

In the course of my journeys through Europe, in England, France, Italy, Germany and Austria I noticed that the people everywhere are thirsting for peace and for the restoration of order and reason in blood-drenched Europe. And even those who are blinded by their sympathies for this nation or that are agreed that the European catastrophe is the most ghastly nightmare of madness and blood and horrors in history.

The military parties of the Governments at war have started a diabolical game which they do not know how to stop. So the slaughter goes on.

The people of all the warring nations believe that they are shedding their blood for humanity, and they sincerely expect the aid of God for their arms, and when the people of one nation pray for their men in the trenches, on sea and in the air, the prayers of the other nations go up in the

same terms to the same God, and if God should heed all
their prayers He would have to destroy them all.

The passions of the people are fanned by falsehoods so
that their hatred and spirit of vengeance might grow.

A German statesman spoke to me about the enthusiasm with which his people went to the trenches to certain
death. I remarked:

"In your country the people seem to hate by order and
to love by order. Now their hatred is directed against this
nation. Suddenly it is directed against another nation.
The Government gives the order and the people hate
accordingly.

"And yet the statesmen themselves do not seem to hate
the statesmen of the nations they are fighting."

"Yes," replied the statesman, "it is quite true. But
how could you expect the people to fight, to sacrifice their
lives, if they were not made to hate the enemy?"

Under such circumstances the real representatives of the
people, the thinkers and the scientists, cannot make their
voices heard, and many of them have even been so carried
away by their chauvinism that they too spur on this spirit
of hatred and violence among the people.

But in all the countries at war there are a few brave men
among the great leaders of public opinion who dare to speak
the truth because they love humanity as well as their own
countries.

Among these few men is Maximilian Harden, the famous
and courageous German editor and publicist.

During my stay in Berlin I had the keen pleasure of a
few interesting meetings with Maximilian Harden in his
home in Grunewald, where we discussed various phases of
the war and the prospects for peace. On the night before

I left Berlin, on my way back to America, I visited him again.

"I envy you because you are returning to America," he said when he learned that I was to start for New York the following day. "I have always longed to visit America. I wanted to familiarize myself more closely with the life of the American people, of the young, growing nation. I believe that America is misunderstood and misinterpreted in Europe.

"I am always disgusted with attacks on the 'Yankees' and on 'Dollarland' that people so delight in making in various European countries. I can see in the American people a strong will for good and a great idealism. It is a younger state and thus it has all the faults and all the virtues of youth. Even in the question of ammunition, which has been in this country very acute, and which has made the Americans extremely unpopular in Germany, I feel that if it were wrong for America to sell ammunition to the Allies, the American Government would not have permitted it.

"The real cause of the differences between the Americans and the Germans has been the lack of knowledge of the facts concerning the attitude of these countries toward each other. There has been so much misinformation in Germany concerning America, and I dare say there has been so much distorted information in America about Germany, that it was extremely difficult for these nations to check the growing irritation, and serious consequences might spring from misinformation.

"The American note to Austria regarding the question of ammunition was an admirable document, which presented the attitude of America in this matter with splendid clearness. This point of view should have been presented in some form or another in Germany long ago and much of the hatred that has developed for America in Germany would not have taken root.

"The military authorities are incensed at America over the question of ammunition and the people at large, fed on newspaper accounts inflaming the passions of the mob against Americans on this point are, of course, also aroused. Only this evening as I came in from the city one of the railroad guards remarked to me: 'Those cursed Americans are again supplying ammunition to the French and the British, with which thousands of our men are killed. But we will teach them a lesson for this. We will give them the whipping they deserve.'

"This is the attitude of the ignorant people. But if the Germans here knew a little more of the truth about America, and if Americans knew a little more of the truth about Germany, I feel certain that such a state of public opinion could not prevail."

"But this view is shared not only by the people who are not familiar with the facts," I remarked. "I understand that in high political spheres in Germany such views have been expressed openly. I have learned from a most reliable source that a well-known German diplomatist said to a prominent American several months ago: 'It would be well for America to realize that there are 500,000 German-Americans in the United States who would rise at a moment's notice from the German Government. The sooner America realizes this the better for America.'

"The American replied to the German statesman: 'You are mistaken. There are no German-Americans, or any other hyphenated Americans who would rise against Amer-

ica by order of another Government.   And I can assure
you that if there were, if so-called Americans would rise
against America by order of another Government, there
are enough lampposts in America on which to hang them
all.' "

Harden shrugged his shoulders and said:

"I am astounded to hear that a statesman should have
dared to make such a statement.   But then in these days
of madness people seem to have forgotten how to speak and
think rationally.   My feeling concerning the German-
Americans is this: If the Germans in America want to
be so thoroughly German that they are displeased and
openly discontented with America, they should have remained in Germany.

"There is no denying that the Germans in America constitute one of the best elements of the American people,
and I know that most of them are patriotic Americans.   It
is quite natural that their sympathies should be on the side
of their old home.   It is human.   But the German-
Americans should employ in a crisis of this magnitude all
the tact and good judgment at their command, and they
ought to realize that the best way in which they can serve
their old home is by showing that they are good Americans,
by actually being and acting as good Americans to-day.

"If they have gone to America they must have come there
to find something which they could not find in their old
homes, and if they stay there they must have found there
what they sought.   They are guests in America.   They
have been welcome guests there before the war and they
will be welcome after the war is ended, but they should be
tactful."

Of the European catastrophe, he said:

"What can a man say at this time of all the unspeakable horrors that have come upon Europe? I had expected that a war would break out before long, but not a war of such magnitude.

"As far as Germany is concerned, whatever may be said of our success on the battlefield, the Allies have had practically no success at all. They are still compelled to fall back on the Marne battle when they speak of their successes. But from whatever point we may view this war I feel that if it will not bring about a change in Europe it is madness, nothing but criminal madness. This should be the last war. Nothing else would justify the millions of human lives and the billions that have been sacrificed."

"May I know upon what terms you believe Germany would agree to stop this war?" I asked.

"The German people are not an impatient people, and this war is unlike any of the previous wars. There is no definite aim for which any of the nations is fighting. Usually there was a definite purpose and aim. When that was attained the war was practically ended. In this war it is altogether different. None of the nations knows just what it is striving to attain through this war. The Germans can fight on. Of course the German people cannot be expected to return home without gaining any advantage after such enormous loss of life, after such extraordinary sacrifices.

"But it is a misfortune that all the Powers consider peace talk as a sign of weakness. Peace negotiations should be started at once. Peace talk, or rather the desire for peace, is not a sign of weakness but rather a sign of strength, of the restoration of sanity, a sign that madness has reached a point beyond which it ought not to be permitted to go.

"I believe that all thinking people of every country are in favor of peace. How can any sensible and honest man be in favor of this hate? How is war started? How is this hate brought into being and forced onto the people? The people wake up one beautiful morning and find that their honor has been assaulted, that their country is in danger, that a cruel enemy has designed to annihilate them. The patriotism of the people suddenly begins to manifest itself in various forms of passionate hatred and violence.

"In time of war everybody is suspected of desiring to betray his country. Even the most devoted sons and the leading thinkers are suspected of treason if they dare to speak calmly and reasonably. There should not be any doubt but that every thinking man loves his country and wishes it to succeed and to grow in power and influence.

"Patriotism is a matter of fact, it is a natural feeling; but in our patriotism we must not forget that in addition to our love for our country there is mankind to which all countries should be responsible. This is the higher patriotism. And this higher patriotism makes the thinking realize all the more keenly that this war is sheer madness, and if there will be no change for the better, if as a result of this slaughter war will not be made impossible within at least the average lifetime of a man, it is the most ghastly and inconceivable madness.

"People have considered me a militarist, an advocate of war. But I am not. I always thought that another great war was inevitable, on account of the wrong ways and methods of the diplomatists, but I never expected that we should be the witnesses of such a terrible war as this, of such downright madness. It is absurd to speak of bringing the great nations to their knees, of crushing this great Power or that. It cannot be done. Neither Germany, nor England, nor France, nor even Russia, can be crushed.

"The people who speak of destroying nations are not taking history into consideration. A great nation cannot be destroyed by war. And even if it could be ruined it is absurd for the other nations to try to do it. It is as though I would destroy everything in the house in which I expected to live simply because I was angry at one of the neighbors living in the same house, The nations now at war will have to live as neighbors in the house which they are now destroying, and the more terrible the hatred and the more extensive the destruction, the worse for all of them.

"I want to see the factors of culture in every nation maintained and not destroyed. The nations, the people, have within them the qualities of right and justice and love; but this zoological war, this atavistic slaughter, has been brought about by elements unfortunately represented in the spheres of diplomacy everywhere. The passions that have been aroused, the hatred that has been spread, have poisoned the people everywhere. The French are as unreasonable against Germany as Germany is unreasonable against France.

"After all it cannot be denied that Germany has certain virtues. Nor can it be denied that France has certain virtues. The same is true of England. Although there are some foolish people among us who still say 'Gott strafe England' (God punish England), we must not forget that after all we have emulated England in many ways. It is ridiculous to speak of cultured nations as savages, to close our eyes to the achievements of the various nations, to their contributions in different ways to the welfare of mankind, but the people everywhere seem to be acting and speaking as though they were all intoxicated. We are destroying the house in which we expect to live in peace.

"I find that the time has come when this terrible catastrophe must make similar catastrophes impossible. It seems to me that mankind should no longer permit such catastrophes to be brought about by the mistakes of the politicians. All great Powers must get together in order to make an end to this unparalleled crime.

"History will some day fix the responsibility and record the truth as to the real criminals who have started this war. But now the great minds of all the countries at war, and especially of the neutral Powers, ought to make every effort to set aright this calamity which has befallen Europe Do not try to go into details as to who started the war, for if you do you will not have peace for a long time to come.

"As to the terms of peace, no one can tell whether a nation has concluded peace upon satisfactory terms or not for at least twenty years. The terms of peace that may seem satisfactory at the time of their conclusion may prove very unsatisfactory.

"The politicians and statesmen who sit in their nooks and intrigue and plot see only one side of the big questions, and it is high time for mankind to guard itself against calamities resulting from the machinations of such politicians and diplomatists.

"The great minds of the countries at war instead of fighting with their pens, instead of emulating their brethren who are fighting with guns, should employ their intellectual weapons to restore order and peace rather than to stir up new hatreds and to encourage violence. It is easy for them to be heroes by shouting and clamoring for vengeance. Blind passion may be a blessing in the trenches, but not in the study. The great sacrifices of human life on both sides of the Powers at war are in vain, for no purpose will be achieved by them. And those of us who are too old or too weak to go in defense of our country on the battlefield, and those of us who can exert influence upon the world, must strive to restore peace as speedily as possible.

"Unfortunately this is the age of small statesmen. The nations are guided by mediocre men. In Europe I regard Sir Edward Grey as one of the saner and better minds among the statesmen."

I pointed to the portrait of Bismarck over Maximilian Harden's desk and said: "Do you think we would have had this war if we had a Bismarck to-day among the diplomatists of Europe?"

"I am convinced that we should have had no war if Bismarck were alive," declared Harden. "The secret of lasting peace is that the power of might shall after this war be curbed. This cannot be done in war but in peace. It is against the genius of the times."

I asked Mr. Harden about the efforts in behalf of peace by neutral countries. He answered:

"The Pope's plans for peace, his impassioned appeals for peace, are fine, but they are largely of a decorative nature. I believe that the United States, that President Wilson, can do more for the peace of the world than any other power. Of course many people everywhere are displeased with America's attitude in this war, but you cannot please all the people with any policy, however just and righteous it may be.   I believe America's attitude has been correct, and that is why America can help in bringing about peace.

"America will be the mistress of the world after the war. Europe will be bankrupt, ruined.   America will be in supreme command in commerce as well as in other matters. It is most important for the world that such a young, powerful part of it has kept out of this war."

In answer to the question regarding the Polish provinces now occupied by Germany, Mr. Harden said:

"The Polish provinces are for us perhaps the most difficult problem.   We must settle it in such a manner as to assure peace in our eastern provinces.   I personally would be opposed to a Polish state under Austrian sovereignty, as has been contemplated.   I hope that we may make no mistake in this direction.   We must make the life of the nationalities in Germany so agreeable that they should not long for the old mode of life in the countries where they lived before.   We cannot make them German by force. We must not repeat the same mistake that England made with regard to the Irish.

"The Poles have disgraced themselves during this war by the wholesale acts of treason, especially in Austria, where numerous Polish leaders betrayed their country.   The cowardly way in which they accused the Jews of the crimes they themselves had committed makes their crimes all the graver."

Before I left his home he remarked once more:

"If this war will not be the last great war, it is nothing else than criminal madness.   Europe will be absolutely bankrupt if the war continues until April.   I believe that if the question concerning Belgium could be settled now, the war would be at an end.   As for indemnities, it should be quite clear that if the war is ended three months earlier all the Powers would save sums constituting large indemnities."

BERNARD SHAW

London, 1911.

OF all the English writers, I was particularly eager to meet Bernard Shaw, the man who was hated or admired; regarded either as a great genius in advance of his time, or as a brilliant literary buffoon; either as a great reformer employing startling methods of expression to attract attention to what he had to say, or an insincere scoffer, jester, cynic and destroyer.

I visited him at his home, at Adelphi Terrace, London. As I walked up the staircase, I saw a sign over the small gate on the first story, bearing the name of "Mrs. Bernard Shaw." His own name was not there. I rang the bell and a rather pretty maid opened the door. As Mr. Shaw was expecting me at the appointed hour, the maid ushered me into his study—a spacious, bright, cheerful room. Mr. Shaw was seated on a couch, and near him, on a low stool, sat his secretary, a young woman, taking dictation. When I entered, the secretary rose and walked out, and I remained alone with Mr. Shaw.

Bernard Shaw is a rather tall, well-built, kindly-looking man; gray yet youthful, almost always smiling. He wore a neat brown suit of the latest cut, which gave him quite a dashing appearance.

He commenced by asking me questions about Russia. Then he spoke of Tolstoy, and finally gave vent to his feelings about America. He still seemed to feel the sting

110

caused him by the suppression of "Mrs. Warren's Profession" in New York several years before.

In the course of our conversation I asked him what he thought of Tolstoy's essay on Shakespeare in which the great Russian tried to prove that Shakespeare was not only not a great dramatist but even a mediocre writer.

"That was a silly little book," replied Shaw. "Tolstoy took one of Shakespeare's very best plays and tried very hard to prove that it was worse than the play from which he had drawn his theme. As a matter of fact, 'King Lear' is an excellent play, and Tolstoy was entirely wrong in his analysis of Shakespeare.

"Tolstoy was a prodigious genius," he went on as he reclined on his couch, with a smile. "But he was devoid of any humor or fun. That's why he could not understand me. He was too dead serious and he was almost childish in the philosophy he evolved and the doctrines he preached.

"I cannot understand how so profound a student of human nature and close an observer as Tolstoy was could expect people to follow his rules of life which even a child would at once recognize as impractical, as hopelessly infeasible. Yet he went on with his theories notwithstanding that his followers suffered disaster.

"But as an artist he was wonderful. With one stroke he knew how to make certain things appear ridiculous. He made no comments. He simply pointed at some thing in passing, as it were, and the effect was tremendous.

"I shall never forget the reference to the manner of exercises made by one of the jurors in the jury room in 'Resurrection.' Without the slightest comment he made the thing thoroughly ridiculous. Or, in his story, 'The Death of Ivan Ilyich,' where he describes the blue velvet thrown over the coffin—he makes no comment whatever, but somehow after reading it you feel how ridiculous funeral ceremonies are."

Much interest was centered on Bernard Shaw on account of the authorized critical biography of him that had appeared a short time before. In referring to it, Mr. Shaw said with an air of great seriousness:

"This is a very good book. One can really get an excellent idea of myself and my works by reading this book, but there is not a single accurate statement in it.

"Dr. Henderson has published in this volume pictures of houses in which I had never lived, and if he mentions a newspaper in connection with some of my work, he invariably mentions the wrong one. He often gets me into trouble by quoting things which I had never said.

"In one place, for instance, he refers to a statement which I am supposed to have made about my unfriendly relations to women. Now, even I would hesitate to say that I had unfriendly relations with women. On the whole, however, the book is very good, but it has what I would call the inaccuracies of higher mathematics. Dr. Henderson, you know, is a mathematician."

When our conversation turned to America and things American, I asked Mr. Shaw why he has never visited the country where some of his plays were so successful.

"Why should I go to America?" wondered Mr. Shaw. "There is nothing there that can interest me. When America will be a real American nation, when the American type becomes fixed, when the American's skin turns red and his forehead recedes, then it will be interesting to go to America. But at the present time, what are the Americans? An appalling, narrow lot.

"Take such a small detail as the incident with the women who wore 'harem' skirts in New York. They were jeered at and had to run for their lives. Now, the 'harem' skirt is really a splendid thing, and there is not the slightest cause for jeering those who wear them. But America is a land of unthinking, bigoted persecution.

"Take another incident, the Gorky affair. Even if Gorky had come from a country where divorces are easily granted, the treatment he received at the hands of Americans was brutal. But Gorky came from Russia, the land of barbaric laws. Therefore, I say America's outrageous treatment of Gorky put her outside the pale of civilization, if she ever was within the pale. This should be said to America. It may do her some good."

"Are you not interested in the development of the American people—in their achievements?" I asked.

"But they are not developing," he answered. "That is why they don't interest me. I am sure they would not be interested in me if I came there. I am not an elephant, so I would not arouse their curiosity. They have much untrained religious enthusiasm, and the trouble with Americans is that each one is working out his own ideals individually instead of having one common religion or ideal for all."

"Are you opposed to individualism, to individual self-perfection?" I asked.

"We must be guided by certain standards. Anything silly or rotten that I write is smashed by public opinion and done for. If I lived on a desert island I would perhaps be writing silly and sentimental romances which are of no use to anybody. But I am working hard. I argue and debate and weigh every phrase, and work on it and reconstruct it; it is quite simple.   It is absolutely true that easy writing is hard reading and hard writing is easy reading.

"Now to return to America, I believe she ought to have a religion of her own.   The Pilgrims took the Bible along with them when they emigrated to America.   The Christian religion was a real religion in the Middle Ages; then a state of skepticism set in at the time of Shakespeare.

"Since the Pilgrims left their countries because of religious persecution, it was quite natural that they should take their religion along with them.   But it would have been much better for them if they had taken the religion of the Indians and developed it.   At the present time we all wear clothes that do not fit us.   We have the Christian religion, which is the Jewish religion, an Oriental religion—and it does not fit us.   It was good for us when we were Orientals, when Judaism and later Christianity came into the world.

"America is overridden with old-fashioned creeds and a capitalist religion.   Mr. Roosevelt is a typical expression of what I mean.

"There is not a single credible religion in the world to-day.   No educated man in Germany or here, or even in America, believes in the things our religions would have us believe.   A new religion is necessary."

Mr. Shaw spoke with apparent seriousness, but there was a peculiar smile in his eyes.

I asked him for his views on the peace movement which was then also attracting considerable attention everywhere, particularly in England and the United States.   He burst into laughter.

"Do you take this seriously?   I am fifty-five years old now, and I have passed through this peace wave several times.   I recall one peace meeting in particular.   It was several years ago. I believe Sir Arthur Conan Doyle presided at that meeting. I was an invalid and came to the meeting on crutches. They spoke of peace there. Everybody was in a peaceful frame of mind. People were sending Christmas cards to one another. Though I was on crutches, I believe I smashed that meeting. You see, we were building torpedo boats at the time, and anyone who would have dared to be opposed to our building those torpedo boats would have been mobbed.

"International war will be stopped some day as duels have been stopped. All countries should combine, and the one that fires the first shot should be dealt with severely. But all this talk at present is nonsense. We talk of our command of the sea. This is ridiculous. We may as well talk of our command of the sun and the moon."

Mr. Shaw leaned back comfortably on the couch and, after a brief pause, went on with a smile:

"But you must not think that we don't like the Americans who come over here. We like them very much—that is, our hotelkeepers and shopkeepers do. The Americans come over here and spend so freely the money made for them by the unfortunate people of America. We live on your earnings, on the sweat of your people, of the little children out in South Carolina and other states. That is all very nice for our hotelkeepers and shopkeepers. Also for France and Germany. We do like the Americans very much."

Mr. Shaw spoke for some time in this strain. Then our conversation turned to the drama in England.

"The drama in England is hopeless," he said. "I should have said the drama in England is hopeless just now. You see, I was born at an extremely unfortunate moment for myself.   I came to England when I was twenty years old, in 1876.   Compulsory education was introduced in England in 1870.   The newly literate needed and bought the same kind of literature we used to buy in the penny numbers—sentimental novels dealing with criminal heroes. The serious works of the dramatist and the novelist appeal only to a very few.

"That is why Stevenson's 'Treasure Island' was successful—he gave the newly literate a story of the type they liked in their penny thrillers, but of course it was beautifully written.   He had to stoop to the masses.   There are several really fine writers in England to-day who are compelled to write sentimental stuff to keep from starving.

"The same is true of the drama to-day.   The old sentimental novels are turned into dramas, and these popular dramas drive out the higher drama.   The only difference between the drama of to-day and the drama of yesterday is that the criminal heroes are somewhat better to-day.   It is quite natural that these plays as well as the silly society plays are successful.   If you or I go to see such a play we may find it dull, and would be bored by it, but the large mass of the people do not want to think; the intellectual play drives them away.   The clerks, the hard-working people like to see fine clothes and elegant manners and society life portrayed on the stage.   They find pleasure in such plays and therefore go to see them.   That is why I told Frohman when he planned to give serious dramas here, that he would not succeed.   Such plays should be given in an endowed theatre."

"What of your own plays, Mr. Shaw?   Are you pleased with the reception they are getting?" I asked.

"Germany, Sweden, Austria—these are the countries that stand by me. France, the most backward country, and Paris, which is a hundred years behind other capitals of Europe, may soon see one of my plays produced there. A French manager has made a contract with me for the production of my play, but I shall not believe that they will produce it until I see it.

" 'Mrs. Warren's Profession' is being produced in Vienna. They are also producing some of my plays in Russia, particularly 'Mrs. Warren's Profession.' This is a good old-fashioned play to bring children to see.

"When 'Mrs. Warren's Profession' was published in book form, I was afraid that some stupid people might buy the book and, without reading it, send it to the children as a Christmas present. People are generally in the habit of doing such things. So I called the volume 'unpleasant plays' to prevent adults from giving it to children. In the following edition I marked it still more strongly by a quotation on the title page which I felt sure would make cautious mothers hide the book from their children.

"Imagine my surprise when one day a lady I know said to me: 'Mr. Shaw, your book is a great favorite with my children.' 'What book is that?' I asked. 'Mrs. Warren's Profession,' she answered.

"I asked her to tell me why the book was such a favorite with her children. She said they liked the story, particularly the love scenes, and they were especially happy when it turned out that the lovers were sister and brother. When I asked what they thought of Mrs. Warren, she told me that they considered her a very funny and amusing person who kept a fried fish shop. Thus you see they found nothing but purity in the play. You must be careful as to what books you give to adults, for they may be corrupted, but children may read anything."

In discussing the drama abroad Shaw touched upon the anti-Semitic demonstration that took place at that time in Paris in connection with Henri Bernstein's play. And then he talked of the Jewish question in general.

"I could never understand what they call the Jewish question. I think the Jewish question everywhere is due to the Jew's business ability and honesty. If a Jew makes a bargain with you he means to keep it, and means you to keep it, too. The Englishman will sign away everything when he needs money, but he does not mean to keep his promise when he makes the bargain.

"Of course, there is no special antipathy against the Jew in England, but whatever there is simply comes from the Jew's straightforward business integrity, which infuriates some of the thick-headed Englishmen. I think that Shakespeare sized up the situation to a nicety in 'The Merchant of Venice.' Shylock made a bargain with Antonio, kept it, and meant that Antonio should keep it. Antonio, who is really a sentimental Englishman, was ready to sign away everything in order to get the money from the Jew, without the slightest intention of ever returning it. When the Jew wanted Antonio to fulfil his end of the contract, the mob jeered and mocked him.

"This, I believe, is true everywhere. The Jew is intelligent, industrious and hard-working, and when he makes a bargain he knows exactly what he is doing.

"The prejudice against the Jewish race is still deep-rooted because people do not pause to analyze the prejudice. I think Macaulay was right when he said that if you start a prejudice against red-headed people there would soon develop a general hatred of them, and they might be massacred.

"The massacres of the Jews in Russia was managed exactly as the massacres of the Armenians in Turkey. The Sultan gave the order in Turkey and the Tsar gave the order in Russia."

Mr. Shaw then reverted to the New Religion in his whimsical manner and wound up by saying:

"I say that Life Force is God. But the Englishman objects to this. He says that Life Force is a foreigner, while God is an Englishman. That is where we disagree."

AUGUSTE RODIN

Paris, May, 1911.

AUGUSTE RODIN, the world's foremost sculptor to-day, the
energetic Rembrandt in sculpture, who but yesterday had
to struggle like a novice and defend his art against the
prejudice of his colleagues and those people who always
condemn the man who dares to speak his own word, is
seventy one years young. Some people are always young.
They have no time to grow old. They do their work, they
say their word in literature or in life, in sculpture, in painting, or in music, regardless of the censure and condemnation of the few or the multitude; they work even
more energetically in the face of such hardships, and
their efforts are always identified with youthfulness. Such
a man is Auguste Rodin, the French sculptor.

The famous painter, Paul Laurens, said of Rodin:

"He belongs to the race of those men who march alone."

Rodin has not only marched alone, but has made the
multitudes, even his former enemies, march behind him.
He has created an art epoch that will, in the future, charac-
terize the nineteenth and the beginning of the twentieth
centuries. In the words of a very gifted painter, Rodin,
in his living creations of bronze and marble, has produced
a natural and moving race of people.

A poet of passion, an interpreter of the human, Rodin
is young in his intense admiration of the old, the undying
art of the Greeks, which was also human. Rodin has made
his life one long, continuous effort to attain the ideal of

art. Though a Frenchman, Rodin is universal in his art. His power and immensity spring from his individuality, rather than from his surroundings.

A keen art critic, Gustave Kahn, has said:

"All great sculptors seek to reproduce life, but not all do it in the same spirit. Some pay more attention to the clearness of expression than to exactness. Michael Angelo is great, mighty and exact; others, like Carpeaux, for instance, are great and elegant; Rude and Rodin are great and pathetic. French sculpture, which together with Italian sculpture of the Renaissance, represented works of the greatest beauty, declined in the beginning of the nineteenth century, until Rodin appeared as an artist. He made motion the chief characteristic of his works."

From his very first productions, beginning with "The Man with the Broken Nose," to his very latest, which is not yet completed, and which is to be dedicated by Rodin to the "Martyrs of the Air," he kept on shocking the placid academicians and conventional judges of art. His "John the Baptist" and his statue of Balzac roused storms of indignation against Rodin in his own country as well as in other lands.

Nevertheless, Rodin forged ahead, creating masterpiece after masterpiece, until he has made a place for himself as the foremost among the sculptors of the age.

Several weeks ago I had the pleasure of meeting Rodin in Paris. I was invited to his studio at a quarter past five in the afternoon, when his day's work is ended. The spacious yard in front of his studio looked rather like the yard of a busy warehouse, with heavy trucks and many workmen going quickly about their work. Within, many artists, young and old, were waiting for the master.

Passing through a number of enormous rooms, containing statuary of various sizes, antique and modern, I was met by the Duchess de Choiseul, a great admirer of Rodin, who informed me that Rodin would see me in a little while.

I had heard that the Duchess de Choiseul, regarded by prominent French people as one of the most brilliant women in France, was called "Rodin's Muse." Also that she was an American. So I asked her:

"Is it true that you are known as Monsieur Rodin's Muse and that you are an American?"

"Yes, I am proud to be both—the Muse of the greatest sculptor in the world and a daughter of the greatest country in the world."

"May I know your maiden name?"

"When I was a little girl I used to say that I was the daughter of the Coudert Brothers of New York," replied the Duchess with a smile.

"I said that I am proud that I am an American. I am also proud that I persuaded an American millionaire, Thomas F. Ryan, to do something really worth while for his country. I am referring to his gift of Rodin works to the New York Metropolitan Museum of Art.

"Mr. Ryan had his bust made by Rodin. Then an inspiration came to me. I said to him one day: 'Mr. Ryan, don't be a dead man forever. You are a millionaire, but your millions will be of no avail when you die. Why shouldn't you do something that will help your country?'

"I talked and talked to him in this strain until I succeeded. Mr. French and Mr. Robinson, on the committee of the Metropolitan Museum, were the judges, and they purchased for Mr. Ryan the works of Rodin which now form the Rodin gallery in New York.

"This collection of Rodin masterpieces in America is of the utmost importance to young American artists. For I believe, just as Monsieur Rodin does, that we have more real artists in America, more talent, more genius, than other countries have.

"Here in Europe we have dried fruit, while in America we have vigorous, young talents—but they are spoiled when they come over here, amidst these surroundings, away from the environments under which they could develop naturally. America is the greatest country in the world, but if every rich American were really interested in the development of his country, America could be made still greater.

"America could be made greater than Greece and Rome ever were; we have enough millions there—now we want artists. By bringing over such works as those of Rodin or of other masters the young American artists could have the best examples of Europe's greatest works amidst their own surroundings, and this would tend to build up a great American art."

At this point the door opened and Rodin walked in. With his long gray beard and gray hair, with his fine penetrating eyes, a dark velvet cap on his head, and in a brown velvet jacket, he looked like a Rembrandt painting, striking and picturesque. As he seated himself upon a sofa, there stood behind him his latest work, as yet unfinished, which he is dedicating to the martyrs of the air,

After some preliminary conversation, I asked Rodin for his views as to the future of sculpture.

"Sculpture is an eternal art," he said, speaking slowly. "At some periods it will assert itself more strongly than at others, but it will exist forever.

"The art of sculpture was perfected by the Egyptians,

the Assyrians, and the Greeks, who brought it to its highest point.   In modern times different styles have been introduced in this art, and different names given to them, but these styles have deviated from the school of the Egyptians, the Greeks, and the Romans.   Therefore, our works are inferior, for the antique art is nearly perfect."

Rodin paused awhile, then continued, speaking more quickly:

"The sculpture of our day is approaching a terrible crisis.   Modern sculpture is losing all the best qualities of the art in the past.   It is also separated from that which belonged to it when it was a perfect art.

"In these days of ours there is a new manner of placing works of sculpture in public buildings called museums. This is a grave mistake.   The works of art thus placed there are only fragments, and art, to be perfect, must be complete.

"Sculpture and architecture belong together, and the deterioration of the one art affects the other.   I believe that sculpture will rise again to its former position only after our architecture has regained its equilibrium.   It seems to be a peculiarity of our time to put works of sculpture in the wrong place.

"In France there is a movement at present striving to restore this art to its former state and to free it from these new tendencies of our age, which have been instrumental in its decline.   The very fact that we have commenced to realize this error leads me to believe that there is hope for progress—by going back to the older conception of this art."

"May I know what you regard as the mission of the sculptor and his art, if there is any such mission?"

"The mission of art is morality, religion.   It is the finest expression of human intelligence, the noblest expression of the thought of the whole of humanity. The epochs that preceded the eighteenth century brought beauty into the world, into life. The confusion of the nineteenth century, which upset everything, which overthrew old standards and created no new standards, entered also into art.

"Confusion reigned supreme in all the arts. The nineteenth century was the epoch of but a few individualities. It was an epoch without any particular style, without any characteristic standard, either in sculpture or in architecture.

"But I feel optimistic as to the future. For I see signs pointing to new and better ways."

"What is your opinion of American sculptors?" I asked.

"American sculpture is still French," replied M. Rodin. "But it is making great progress. America has produced a number of very remarkable artists, such as Sargent, Saint-Gaudens, Whistler.

"There is no doubt in my mind that America has a great future as an art center. There are many fine artists there, artists of unusual qualities, and American art, in all forms, will surely grow ever greater and greater—if it does not become commercialized. There lies the great danger.

"The commercialism of our age, especially in America, is ruining the best talents that would have made this age an art epoch. The commercial spirit, characteristic of this period, is the tomb-stone over the noblest strivings of the artists."

Our conversation turned to his own works, and I asked what he considered his most important production.

"The most difficult thing in the world is to judge your own self and your own works. All my life has been devoted to a continual study of the human body and the soul.

Therefore, each one of my works represents something that is part of all my work, and I cannot say which is better and which is worse.

"There are people who consider 'The Kiss' as my masterpiece; there are others who regard 'The Thinker' as my most important work; still others believe 'Victor Hugo' to be the best thing I have done. To me it is simply a different name, for all these works, as I said, are only a part of my studies of humanity, of passion, and thought."

Speaking of types of women and models, M. Rodin said:

"The type of woman has not changed since the days of the ancient sculptors. It remains always the same—always beautiful. In general the women of the Mediterranean were preferred by the artists as models, but women of the North are just as perfect.

"For what is art? Always the great truth of nature seen by a human mind. Photographs are not art, because they do not pass through a human brain.

"Everything in nature is beautiful for the real artist, for the man of imagination. Nothing is more ridiculous than the effort of an artist to produce something beautiful, something perfect, by combining perfect parts of different models into one. Thus the artist who reproduces the eyes of one model, the hands of another, the feet of a third, the neck of a fourth, produces perhaps a beautiful doll, but it is lifeless and worthless.

"There is no such thing as ugliness in nature, in life. Everything is beautiful if seen through the artist's mind. The imperfections become perfect. There is nothing more wonderful than life."

M. Rodin was fatigued after a hard day's work. The Duchess de Choiseul suggested that we look over some of the sculptures in the studio. There was "The Benediction." Two women, with wings, rising out of the waves of the ocean, their heads bent in prayer. This is Rodin's latest work, intended as a memorial for dead aviators who sacrificed their lives as martyrs to the great future of aviation.

Another statue represents "Psyche et l'Amour." Near it was a striking figure of a girl, seated upon a rock, listening. This was entitled "The Echo."

Another work that attracts much attention in Rodin's studio is "The Mystery." Two hands, a man's and a woman's, clasping each other, form a sort of dome, and represent the mystery of life.

M. Rodin always interested himself deeply with studies of the expression of the hand. He produced hands that seemed to clutch at space, ready to hurl it somewhere; he produced terrible hands that seemed to commit acts of violence; he formed fingers that groped greedily yet hopelessly under the burden of Fate; he produced hands that appear to be clutching at the shadow of mystery. At one period of his life, Rodin attached special significance to these studies of the human hands, but while Rodin never neglects details, his art strives above all for harmony, and these studies formed but part of his complete works.

The Duchess de Choiseul then removed the cloth from an unfinished bust of herself which Rodin is working on.

"The master really regards this bust as his masterpiece," said the Duchess.

It is indeed a most wonderful work, representing laughter.

Rodin's Muse laughed. The great sculptor came into the room, looked at the uncovered bust, and smiled.

"It is not yet finished, but I expect to complete it before long," he said.

Many students, artists, and other visitors were waiting for Rodin in the adjoining room. He went out to see them.

Duchess de Choiseul covered the bust and said:

"We have only one Rodin. He is old. We cannot afford to lose him. We must have him, we must have as much of his work as possible. Therefore, when he is tired or indisposed, I keep on urging him: 'Work! Work! Work!' "

And Rodin's Muse laughed.

Paris, May, 1912.

Just as I was leaving Paris the postman handed me a letter from Auguste Rodin, containing an invitation to visit him in his studio on the following afternoon. My grips were in the automobile and I was on my way to the railroad station.

A gifted painter and keen art critic who was with me said:

"I hope you are not hesitating. I would give up a dozen other important engagements for a meeting with the Michel Angelo of modern times. Besides Rodin is 72, and there is only one Rodin."

I was not hesitating. I remembered the great pleasure I had derived from my meeting with the vigorous, intellectual seventy-one-year young genius of France.

At 2 o'clock I came to the studio where the greatest masterpieces of the famous French sculptor have been produced and where they are still produced.

Before meeting the master I met his "Muse."

"Has M. Rodin completed the bust of his Muse?" I asked the Duchess as she came out and assured me that M. Rodin would soon return to the studio.

"That was a most unfortunate affair. A number of accidents happened to that bust before it was completed and finally when it was ready and was to be shipped to the exhibition another accident occurred and the work was destroyed. That bust was one of the very finest works of the master. But he is working on a new bust."

Saying this she removed the cloth from an incomplete bust of herself, her face laughing broadly.

"I am afraid that this one is not such a happy likeness of me," she added with a smile. "I am almost sure that no accidents will happen to this bust."

The "Muse" commenced to speak with enthusiasm about Rodin's great success everywhere in Europe, in America, and especially in France.

"Rodin has just returned from Lyons," she said. "He has loaned to the city of Lyons his private collection of about two hundred and fifty of his favorite drawings for the exhibition. All the rooms and the salon are brilliantly illuminated and the impression made by the Rodin exhibition there is one that can never be forgotten. The surroundings and the atmosphere are so delightful, and the works of the master seem to be moving and going around. It is a gigantic exhibition."

Then she spoke about the numerous people who are disturbing Rodin with various requests, and robbing him of his precious time.

"There are some who come here in the hope of getting souvenirs," she said, "and if they do not get any they are quite ready to steal them. Sometimes I fear that a crank might attack the master. I have been planning how to guard M. Rodin against such people. Now we have solved this question. I have secured a wonderful police dog to watch Rodin. People with criminal tendencies had better beware of that dog. And now that we have that dog here I feel that the master is safe. There was never a more intelligent bodyguard nor a more loyal one."

Finally Rodin came in. His short stature, his left shoulder somewhat lower than the right, the deep furrows on his face might disillusion his admirer at the first glance, but as soon as Rodin begins to speak and his eyes brighten you see before yourself the genius. You realize that the enormous struggles and hardships and disappointments he had experienced before he could gain recognition had imprinted those deep wrinkles on his face. You feel the deep, sincere note in all he says. And you also feel that, unlike many great artists, he knows how to say things effectively.

Rodin is very modest. Several years ago, when he visited England for the first time, the modesty of the famous French sculptor assumed an amusing aspect. He was invited to London. A deputation of prominent artists and a representative of the King went out to meet him in Dover and to greet him as he stepped on English soil. A special car was in readiness to take the master to London; but the deputation failed to find Rodin. Finally, they noticed him seated in a third class car with his huge valise.

He was taken to the special car. In London a banquet was given in his honor. A great number of celebrities were present. One of them delivered a speech in English which seemed to make a profound impression. Rodin did not understand a word of it. As the speaker referred to the greatest sculptor in the world, who was among them, all applauded enthusiastically. Rodin also applauded, for he did not know whom the people were applauding.

I asked M. Rodin whether he would not care to say something to the American people, among whom his works are beginning to attract so much attention.

The great sculptor answered:

"The American nation has created a Rodin Museum at the Metropolitan Museum of Art. Being now a part of the Metropolitan Museum it may increase and grow in time. The Rodin Museum, I understand, is now visited by many working people, by artisans and students. This pleases me immensely. I think that such museums render great services and are very useful, for I notice that in all countries in Europe and in America efforts are now being made to restore art to its former place. Until recently art has been declining.

"The trouble is that among the students of art there are many who are not seriously devoting themselves to the study of art; there are so many idlers and nobles who pose as art students. I, therefore, have more confidence, and I expect real results from the actual apprentices. These have more courage, more perseverance; they make more serious efforts, and they want to make progress and accomplish ever better results. And this is what we need nowadays. We must try to find again the energy that art students had in former days. Such energy is still to be found in those working for the progress of science. But among the students of art this energy has been declining.

"The fine arts must go on developing with the greatest sincerity. Sincerity should always be the keynote of all works of art.   Art brings happiness into life, for it is for the most part a rational admiration of nature.

"Art is like religion.   And the best religion is that which gives happiness at the smallest cost, almost without money, for after all the different ways of happiness are chiefly intellectual.

"It is upon such principles as this that one realizes the beautiful productions of art which have come down to us from the great epochs in the past.   Sincerity in the admiration of nature has brought us all great masterpieces of all times.   The finest architectural works, the finest sculptures are those suggested by beauties of nature, and the finest adornments of architecture are made of the graceful body of woman.   This I have been trying to explain in my works."

Speaking of his own methods of work, M. Rodin said:

"As I have stated before, I believe that art requires first of all patience and perseverance.   Nowadays the young people want to make progress in the arts too quickly.   They do not even find the time for learning to know themselves. The young people are striving for originality, or what they believe to be originality, and they hasten to imitate it. Forced originality, like the bizarre, has no reason for existence.

"A real artist builds his artistic work upon nature.   Only after he has done that can he infuse his own temperament into the work.   Many young artists will go to a museum and examine quickly a number of works of art, and then they will say to themselves, 'Now we have found ourselves, we have discovered our souls, we will create something new.' It may be that they really have souls, but these souls are the souls of thieves.

"We must try to do the very best we are able to do. We cannot become perfect artists within a few days. Artists need an enormous deal of patience. And they must work hard. Nothing can be achieved without hard work. If an artist is hasty, if he is hurrying to accomplish something, if he does not regard his work as its own end, if he thinks only of the success that will come to him as a result of his work, if he thinks only of the money he will get for his work, of the honors that may be showered upon him, of the orders he will secure, the artist is at an end, he will never accomplish anything really worthy.

"Such people will never be artists. They may make things that will appeal to the masses because these things will be mediocre, they will stoop to the lower taste of the masses and to their short-sighted intelligence. But they will never be real artists. And how easy it is for the artist to go astray! The artist who loves women too passionately is lost.

"You cannot serve two passions at the same time; you cannot serve art and woman at the same time. And yet it has always been the opinion that artists derive their inspiration from the fire of life. Inspiration! Oh, that is an old, romantic idea which is devoid of any meaning. According to that old idea a youth of twenty is smitten with an inspiration to create a marble statue, to build it out of the delirium of his imagination at night. This is nonsense.

"Artists do not love their work if they do not understand it. All that is done in haste and in a state of excessive exaltation should be destroyed. Lombroso and others who imagine that genius borders on insanity are absolutely wrong. Genius is order personified, the concentration of the abilities and level-mindedness of the masses. My work has often been styled the product of inspiration and exalted enthusiasm. I am just the opposite of an enthusiast.

"My temperament is even. I am not a dreamer. I am rather a mathematician. My sculpture is good because it is geometrically correct. I do not deny that I am emotional in my work, but that is only because my emotion is aroused by the beauties of nature which I am reproducing. I admire nature and I find it so perfect that if God called me and asked me to suggest a change I would answer: 'All is perfect. Nothing should be changed.'

"People have often accused me of having made erotic sculptures. I have never made any erotic works. I have never made a sculpture for the sake of the erotic element. Most of the people cannot conceive this because they are forever looking for literary and philosophical ideas in sculpture. Sculpture is the art of forms.

"I have created human bodies in various forms, in various natural forms. Nature is always beautiful. If nature sometimes appears too ugly it is simply because we do not understand it. And what a great number of artists are deforming nature by trying to interpret it!"

"Have you noticed any new tendencies in art that show any promise?" I asked.

"I think that we are becoming more sincere and I hope that our epoch will be marked by a growing sincerity, for all our hope and the future of art depend upon sincerity.

"Much is being said about various new schools in art, about the 'Futurists' and others. But these do not exist. All these new styles and fads are devoid of any power. They are paradoxes."

"If you were asked to give a few rules of advice to young sculptors, what would you suggest to them?" I asked.

"First of all, I must recommend study. We must study hard and be sincere. We must learn to admire nature, and admire the Greeks, who were in this respect sincerer than all of us. We must copy them—or rather no, not copy them, that would be bad. We should introduce the sincerity and the methods of the Greeks into the different arts. In modelling a Dutch woman we can employ the methods of the Greek. The Greek power of modelling must be successful even if the subject be an American woman. It is the form and the sincerity and the power of modelling that have made Greek art so perfect."

I asked Rodin to mention the names of his favorite authors who influenced his life.

"The Romans, the Greeks, Dante and Shakespeare," replied the French sculptor.

Toward the end of the interview, Mr. Rodin said of the feminist movement:

"There is something very good in that campaign. They want to have men understand and appreciate that they possess a value. They want to demonstrate to men that there is some value in women which men lose by not understanding them. The suffragettes are only trying to prove their value. Man has weakened in the course of his work of research and eager quest for money, while women have in the meantime become superior to men in their love."

HAVELOCK ELLIS

London, 1912.

HAVELOCK ELLIS has long been recognized as an authority on woman. His works on "Man and Woman," "The Psychology of Sex," his scientific studies in the psychology of women are widely known throughout the world and have been translated into almost all languages used by civilized peoples. Aside from these important works, he depicted in masterly manner more than twenty years ago the new spirit of literature as voiced by Diderot, Heine, Whitman and Tolstoy. He was also the first to direct the attention of English reading people to the philosophy of Friedrich Nietzsche.

I met Mr. Havelock Ellis in his Brixton home. He looks a little older than he really is. He is only fifty-three years of age. But he is youthful and vigorous in spirit and he speaks with the simplicity and modesty characteristic of really great men.

"Fortunately for America and for American women, you have not the same problems to contend with, and American women do not employ the methods that are used by the leaders of the woman's movement in England," said Mr. Ellis. "There is not the slightest doubt in my mind that these methods are causing a great deal of injury to woman's cause. Personally I have great admiration for the women, but I believe that their tactics of concentrating on the vote as the only solution of their problem and their use of violence are not calculated to help them."

"What methods would you suggest that would help their cause?" I asked.

"Wherever women have secured their rights, as in Finland, for instance, they have attained their aims because they stood beside the men, not against them. Besides, they should not try to emulate men in their methods, but should rather go along their own lines, and they would be much more successful. I quite agree with Olive Schreiner, who believes that women should not concentrate on the suffrage."

"What, then, are the ends women ought to work for instead of concentrating on the suffrage?"

"I regard economic independence as far more fundamental than the franchise," replied Mr. Ellis. "Women ought to do everything instead of doing one thing, harping on the right to vote. They ought to be active in the arts, in literature, in social work, and they will also get the suffrage in the right way.

"England is a very old country, we are old fashioned here, in a good sense, and everything moves slowly. This is why the methods of the suffragettes do more harm than good to the cause of woman. It is, of course, different in new countries, such as America, for instance. There you may attain results more rapidly, because you are accustomed to doing new things. It is hard to understand why the leading suffragettes in England are forever attacking the politicians. As a matter of fact the politicians have always been in favor of woman suffrage more than any other portion of the community.

"The chief point against the movement demanding votes for women is that the majority of women in England do not want the franchise. Therefore, I think it will be much better when the desire on the part of the women to vote comes naturally, and I feel sure that when the majority of English women really want the suffrage they will certainly get it."

Mr. Ellis said that people are in most cases wrong in their estimates of women and their views.

"I have observed that women will sometimes do exactly the opposite of what they are expected to do. The women whose views were asked at a large meeting with regard to divorce proved quite a revelation to those who consider themselves judges of women's ways and thoughts. The majority of the women present at that large gathering expressed themselves in favor of divorce by mutual agreement. At another congress the majority of women declared against the religious education of children. And the women in the Finnish Parliament surprised the male representatives of the people by talking about 50 per cent. less than the men.

"Thus you can never tell what women will do, but in my opinion they are making a grave mistake by morbidly concentrating on the point of the vote, caring for nothing else. The longest way around is very often the shortest way home. Mill said many years ago that women have to educate themselves. This is true to-day as well.

"After all, it is only a small section of women that cares for politics. Women who have had the municipal vote have not used it. The vote is only of minor importance. In Germany the woman's movement is conducted along different lines—there it is a movement for giving women emotional rights. And the list of names of representative people all over the world, indorsing the methods and aims of the German woman's movement, is one that the

English suffragettes could hardly secure for their cause."

"What do you think of the work of women in art and literature in recent years?" I asked.

"I think that a good drama written by a woman or an important novel produced by a woman does more good for the woman's cause than any of the militant methods of the suffragettes. But I must say that too many women who have no business to devote their time to writing are giving themselves to what they call the artistic life. They are thus wasting their lives and doing things that are useless.

"I do not think women have any special aptitude for the arts, though they have produced some good novels. But there is such a great field for women in which they really excel—I mean social work. They are specially gifted for this sphere of activity and such work is much more important than art. Art is after all merely a luxury."

"Would you call the great artistic masterpieces merely a luxury?" I asked.

"No, I would not go as far as that. But it is more important to have a healthy home than to write a novel. Real art, as I pointed out years ago, as a many-sided and active delight in the wholeness of things, is the great restorer of health and rest to the energies distracted by our turbulent modern movements. Thus understood it has the firmest scientific foundations. Its satisfaction means the presence of joy in our daily life, and joy is the prime tonic of life.

"It is the gratification of the art instinct that makes the wholesome stimulation of labor joyous. It is in the gratification of the art instinct that repose becomes joyous. We have already an art in which our desires and struggles and ideals are faithfully mirrored for the great mass of people. But nowadays too many women, for that matter too many men, are devoting themselves to what they call art without having the slighest aptitude for it and they are merely wasting their energy."

Mr. Ellis spoke of the influence of Nietzsche and Tolstoy upon life and literature and then related how he had planned to visit the great Russian at Yasnaya Polyana fifteen years ago.

"Of all your meetings with distinguished men I envy you your meeting with Tolstoy," said Mr. Ellis. "Tolstoy was the only man of letters I was really eager to meet. He was not only the greatest writer of his time, but also the greatest personality. And that is even more important than to be a great writer.

"I was in Moscow about fifteen years ago and was to leave for Yasnaya Polyana when I received word from Tolstoy that one of his children was taken ill with typhoid and, therefore, he could not receive me. I visited Russia and I visited Spain a number of times and I admire both the Russian and the Spanish peoples—they are both unfortunate."

"Perhaps that is the reason why you admire them above others?" I suggested.

"Perhaps. Some of their best qualities are thus brought out. They are of course not perfect from a political viewpoint. I certainly do not admire the politics of these countries. But the political activities of a nation do not always mar it or make it perfect. The trouble is that people speaking of Russia often confound the people with the

Government.   There the line between the Government and the people is drawn very distinctly."

Mr. Ellis referred to Mr. Roosevelt's views on race suicide.   He said:

"We have bishops in England—unmarried, of course,—who are preaching large families.   Mr. Roosevelt ought to go to Russia and to China, the countries with an enormously high birth rate and all its dreadful results.   To my mind civilization, progress and a low birth rate go together."

"There has been progress in China of late."

"Yes, and in connection with this let me tell you what a lady who recently returned from China has told me.   The English lady visited a Chinese school.   She asked the children what they wanted to know about her country.   The children begged her to tell them all about the suffragettes. Now, little girls that want to hear mainly about suffragettes are not likely to have large families when they grow up."

Of the unrest among the working people of England, Mr. Ellis said:

"The wave of unrest here as well as elsewhere is the result of prosperity.   It is only when working people are better off that they can better afford to strike.   I am, of course, in sympathy with bettering the condition of the working people, but I believe they are like the suffragettes, especially in England, where things move so slowly.   They should also go more slowly and they will attain their aims naturally."

Speaking of American literature, Mr. Ellis said:

"I cannot say who is my favorite American author.   The writers in America are not keeping pace with the greatness of their country.   America produced one supreme artist—

Poe.   The other great writers produced by America were Whitman, Emerson, Thoreau.   But the Americans are too busy to produce a real literature.   You must not be too busy, you must have more dreamers if you would produce a literature of importance.   The atmosphere of America does not seem to be favorable to literature to-day.   It was more so half a century ago.   The conditions of New England were certainly favorable in this sense, but those conditions have now almost disappeared."

HENRI BERGSON

Paris, May, 1912.

DURING my stay in Paris I was delighted to receive an invitation to meet the man who is regarded as the profoundest and most original thinker in France to-day, Prof. Henri Bergson.

Bergson's works, "Time and Free Will," "Matter and Memory," "Creative Evolution," and his essay on "Laughter," have been translated into many languages and his influence is making itself felt in many lands. In England Bergson is well known and well liked and the English claim a special share in him, for they believe that Bergson's mode of thinking was determined by his close study of the English philosophers, by the influence of Herbert Spencer and John Stuart Mill, of Locke, Berkeley and Hume.

In Germany Bergson's works are attracting much attention. Hermann Graf Keyserling, the distinguished German writer, says of Bergson's work: "His philosophy is perhaps the most original work since the days of Immanuel Kant." In Russia various editions of his works have appeared and numerous studies by the foremost Russian publicists are published from time to time. In France Prof. Bergson is extremely popular. Unlike most philosophers that preceded him he is a prophet honored in his own land. He is the most popular of lecturers and his lecture room is always crowded with students as well as with women of fashionable society. The Bergson school of philosophy is in great vogue.   It appeals alike to the deep student and to the faddist.

An acute thinker, Prof. Bergson possesses a masterly, clear and direct style.   He presents his views on most difficult themes with fascinating clearness.   Every great thinker treats the eternal problems in some new way, and though so many influences are claimed to have shaped the thoughts and philosophy of Bergson, he is original, for he has treated the great problems of life in an entirely new way.

Bergson does not give us a definite system.   But he opens wide the door of the future and shows us a great variety of new ways and new aims and new possibilities.

Mr. Carr, in his able little work on Bergson's "Philosophy of Change," which was revised by Bergson himself, has summarized the philosophy of Bergson in the following terms:

"Philosophy reveals to us a reality that is consistent with the satisfaction of our highest ideals.   It discloses the life of the spirit.   It may give us neither God nor immortality in the old theological meaning of these terms and it does not show us human life and individual conduct as the chief end, purpose and center of interest.   But the reality of life is essentially freedom.   Philosophy delivers us from the crushing feeling of necessity that the scientific conception of a closed mechanical universe has imposed on modern thought.   Life is a free activity in the open universe.   We may be of little account in the great whole.   Humanity itself and the planet on which it has won its success may be an infinitesimal part of the universal life, but it is one and identical with that life and our struggle and striving is the impetus of life.   And this, above all, our spiritual life means to us, the past has not perished, the future is being made."

I met Prof. Bergson in his home, in Villa Montmorency, in Auteil, Paris. He spoke with enthusiasm about America and American thinkers and never tired of expressing his admiration for the late William James. Prof. Bergson is looking forward with great interest to his first visit to America, next January, when he will come both to teach and to study us.

"You are doing such an immense deal of work in philosophy and psychology in America, and such splendid work," began the French philosopher. "The quality of the work done by American philosophers and psychologists is really remarkable. I consider William James one of the greatest men America has produced. I may even say, one of the great men of all countries and all times. I knew him well. I met him and spoke with him a number of times and I corresponded with him considerably. He was a wonderful man. But there are a number of other great psychologists in America. You have Muensterberg, Royle and many others."

"I understand that you are engaged upon a new volume in the form of dialogues. May I know with what subject you are dealing in your forthcoming work?" I asked.

"I have a special way of working," replied M. Bergson. "I may call it an anarchistic way. When I take up a new subject I just work it out in my own way. I take several avenues in my efforts to attain results. Very often I gain much information in the course of my work upon certain subjects, but no precise work comes out of it. So I really cannot say whether the book upon which I am engaged now will come out or not, for I am only in the process of building it.   As yet I cannot say whether I shall succeed in building it up or not.

"I have no system in philosophy.   I have no simple set of rules from which I could evolve my philosophy.   In philosophy there are different problems and each problem must be solved by special methods.   The methods employed in solving one problem will not do when you attempt to solve another problem.   I cannot always deduce from answers I have already given the answers to other problems.   There must be a new answer to every new question.

"I was once interviewed by a correspondent who wanted me to answer a number of questions.   I told him that I had no opinion on those questions.   I said that each of those questions would take from ten to fifteen years to answer, and if he would come back fifteen years later I might be able to give him the answer."

"But there are general questions on which you have formed opinions, and I would like to know your views on some of these questions," I remarked.

"Oh, yes, there are provisional answers.   But an opinion is of no great importance if it is given in an offhand manner.   One must be impregnated with the subject; one must study and analyze it thoroughly and have intuition.   Now, intuition is not at all guess work.   Many mistakes have been made by those who speak of my theory of 'intuition' as guess work.   I believe it is necessary to be impregnated with the subject if we would find a solution to it.   We must constantly learn.   We must become students again.   We must start the subject anew.   And that may lead us to a new science.   I have several times become a student again.   I have several times taken up a new subject. My present work will deal with ethics and aesthetics, with the principles of morals and the principles of art.

"I have been greatly impressed with a work on ethics written by Prof. Dewey. I find the book very interesting, very original and quite new."

Prof. Bergson paused a while. Then he added:

"I am interested in the various religious movements in America, as far as they touch upon the ethical questions. I am interested in the ethical culture movement. I have met Prof. Felix Adler and am greatly interested in his work. He impressed me as a very penetrating and earnest man, and I think he will succeed, for I believe that his movement has a future.

"I am interested in the religious movements in America because it strikes me that there is more life in America in this direction. In America religious and ethical questions are becoming a living study, while with us in Europe they remain theoretical questions. But to my great regret I shall have no time during my brief stay in America to study closely any of these movements."

"What accounts for this difference in religious movements between America and Europe?"

"First of all the Americans are practical people. They are supposed to be the most practical people in the world to-day. They want definite rules for conduct and ethics. It is a curious fact that modern philosophers have neglected this. Leibnitz and others have given us systems of ethics, but their systems are too general. Even Kant in his great work on ethics, in his masterpiece on practical reason, laid down formulas that are far too vague to be of any use in practical life. Kant said: 'Always act so that your action may become a universal law.'

"This is not quite easy to apply in practical life. Try to apply this formula to the problem of capital and labor, to the differences between employer and workman. Each one would attempt to act so that his action might become a universal law. How are we to judge who of the two is right? Each of them would claim that his action should be the universal law. And there is no real ethics without real answers to these most difficult questions. Of course, a philosopher's answers cannot be as precise as the answers of a mathematician.

"America seems to realize that the philosophers have not given the real answers to the vital questions. And, therefore, there is a great feeling for these religious and ethical movements in America. I am deeply interested in this relation between religion and ethics."

"You have written in some of your works about the immortality of the soul," I said. "Have you made any further investigations into this subject?"

"I have studied the diseases of the mind and the diseases of memory and of certain cases in which I could see the precise relation between mind and memory. I have come to the conclusion that it is a mistake to think that the work of the mind and of the brain is identical. Only a small part of the work done by the mind is done by the brain. The brain is only a province of the mind. The mind represents a country and the brain is only one of its provinces. The work done by the country is immensely wider in scope than that done by the province. The death of the brain is a probability. But I have found that the mind goes on living after the brain has died. From this I concluded that the mind survives the body. I cannot say definitely that the mind is immortal, but there is a strong probability that it is.

"Modern philosophy is a study that can go on doing further work in this direction. Philosophy, like science, can make progress. There is still progress to be made in science; there is still some distance to go in that domain."

"Are you interested in any of the new movements in art and in literature?"

"I am interested in anything that shows talent," replied M. Bergson, with a smile. "Any school is interesting if it shows talent. I do not believe in any special schools of art, in any special methods. In literature and in art schools, methods are nothing. Genius is everything.

"I recall one day a correspondent came to interview me about the original exhibition of the 'Cubists.' Their idea was that any painting must be made of squares. He wanted to know my opinion about the 'Cubists.' My answer was that I preferred genius. The same I may say about the 'Futurists.' As far as I know, the fashion has been to have genius first. Then a system and methods were evolved. I believe that real genius creates its own methods. So with regard to all new movements and new schools, I must say that they must first have genius."

"Who are your favorite authors of to-day?" I asked.

"We have quite a number of geniuses in our literature. Maeterlinck, Pierre Loti, Bourget. But perhaps the most remarkable writer, who is not exactly as good a novelist as a musician in words, is Maurice Barrès. In this respect, as a prose poet, he can rank with the greatest. But his style is so unique that it would be difficult to translate him without losing much of the beauty of his work.

"Then there is, of course, Anatole France.   I have mentioned chiefly French writers, for I understand French literature best.   I am not very familiar with Anglo-American literature.   You see, it is impossible to do two things well at the same time, and I must choose between one and the other—between my work and the reading of foreign literature.   I consider Tolstoy and Dostoyevsky the greatest masters of fiction.   Dostoyevsky was almost unconscious in his art.   He did not describe things but he somehow made you see and feel them.   His works are most important to psychologists.   Tolstoy and Dostoyevsky have seen the human soul naked and they have seen it in action and have reproduced it.   Of the two Tolstoy was the more many-sided genius.

"I have great admiration for Emerson and Poe.   The work of Poe is so vivid and his poetry is so musical, and it is charged with such deep feeling, that I remember it distinctly although I read it many years ago.   Emerson I have re-read recently.   I am not familiar with the works of Henry James, but his brother told me that Henry re-wrote his prefaces and parts of his works for his new edition.   To me this is a sign of a great writer.   Only great artists go to the trouble of doing this.   They are moved by really artistic feelings.   Shaw?   Yes, I certainly admire him.   I have not read all his works, but I have laid them aside and intend to take them up upon the first occasion."

"What are your views on the feministic movement in Europe and America?"

"I have not found any difference of level between the male and female mind," replied Bergson.   "Women have not yet had the chance to produce philosophic work.   But judging by the average aptitude, men and women are equal.

When I lectured to male and female students I experimented by giving the same subject for compositions to men and women. The results were that the papers could be mixed up and it would have been difficult to tell which were written by the men and which by the women. There is no real difference. The question whether women could give as many philosophers as men have given will be seen in time. I see absolutely no reason why women could not produce work of the same quality. Only now we shall see what they can accomplish, now that they are getting the same education. We shall be the witnesses of a great experiment.

"Half of mankind is now submitting to the same education that the other half has been getting. The growth of the woman's movement, the rapidity of its development socially and politically, is astounding. When I was a young man I could not even conceive that such a movement could grow so rapidly. Therefore, when you ask me about the woman's movement, I say I am for experimenting, but I must add that it is a dangerous experiment; since half of the people would suddenly get votes. I think it should be done gradually. Women have thus far not had the interest in politics and could not be expected to have the aptitude for it. I certainly do not approve of the militant methods of the suffragettes. I know that wherever there is enthusiasm there is violence, but the women are injuring their own cause."

In speaking of the many races emigrating to the United States and the effect of immigrants upon the American type the great French philosopher said:

"I have been much struck by the fact that though different races have come to America there is an original type there; though so many elements go to shape the population of your great centers there is a distinct American type. Since there is no tendency on the part of the immigrants to remain separate I feel that much good will come from this mixture of the races. You have more reading of newspapers, current literature, and you have more schools.

"To my mind, the richer a temperament the better. The more elements constitute the population of America the more privileged America will be, the richer and the stronger. I am greatly struck by the generosity and broad-mindedness of the American people. It is certainly a great moral lesson to Europe."

Concerning the Jewish question and the Zionist movement Prof. Bergson, who is himself a Jew, said:

"To us French people this question seems paradoxical. We are so assimilated. If there were a new Zion I do not think many Jews would go there. A prominent Jewish statesman when asked in 1848 what he thought of Zionism replied that he would be in favor of Zionism if he were given the post of Jewish Ambassador to Paris."

"But for the oppressed and the persecuted?" I asked.

"That is another question. Oppressed people must look for ways and they are justified in seeking a home. Whether it would be possible to solve the Jewish question in that way I cannot answer. Russia may become more tolerant. The Jews of other countries have attained equal rights. After equal rights have been secured by the Jews I believe the Jewish question will be solved. I do not much believe in permanent special qualities of races. Nature is very often nothing else than habit and education.

"There are racial differences between the white, yellow and black races, but there is no difference in the white races.

People can adopt the qualities, the defects and the habits of the people among whom they live. In Europe we see that the difference in races is nothing but habit, education and the degree of living together. It is a mistake in psychology that much is ascribed to nature which should be ascribed to habit.

"I doubt whether the Jews have any special hereditary defects or qualities, considering that their blood has been so mixed—very much more than is believed. Whole tribes in Russia were converted to Judaism. I believe the Jewish question will be solved when the Jewish people will have attained equal rights in the countries where they are being persecuted. And the sooner that is attained the better for the Jews of course, and also for the countries where they live."

POPE BENEDICT XV

Rome, 1915.

DURING my visit to London in 1915 I made the acquaintance of a French statesman who informed me of the deep interest the Vatican was taking in the plight of the Jewish people in the war zone. I was investigating for my newspaper the condition of the Jews in the war-stricken countries and was naturally eager to ascertain at first hand the views of the Holy See on this subject and to obtain, if possible, the information the Vatican had received concerning the Jews in Poland and the provinces occupied by Russia, Germany and Austria.

I was also eager to learn the circumstances under which the Pope had made his forceful appeal to the rulers of the belligerent nations in July, 1915.

The French statesman, to whom I was introduced by a friend of mine, a prominent London editor, expressed his readiness to arrange for me an audience with the Pope. On my arrival in Paris several days afterward I found a telegraphic communication informing me that the Pope would receive me in private audience.

I started for Rome immediately. Before my audience with Pope Benedict I had several interviews with Cardinal Gasparri, the Papal Secretary of State, who impressed me as a brilliant statesman, closely familiar with international affairs, and as a man of deep sympathies.

On August 21, 1915, at eight o'clock in the morning, I

had the good fortune of a private audience with Pope Benedict which lasted one hour and a quarter.

Pope Benedict received me most cordially in his large and beautiful library. Through the courtesy of Cardinal Gasparri, an exception was made in my case, and I did not have to go through the ceremonies with which an audience with the Pope is usually surrounded. It was a simple yet most impressive meeting. The Pope, dressed in a white robe, was at his writing desk when Cardinal Gasparri introduced me. The French statesman was also with us. After an exchange of greetings the Pope inquired first about conditions in America, about the attitude of the American people toward the war and then he asked about the Jews in the war zone.

I gave him my views on the subjects in which he was interested. I also called his attention to the fact that under the influence of the Russian autocracy, which always sought to incite one portion of the population against another, the Poles conducted an intense anti-Jewish campaign, which was cruel and far reaching in its effects upon Jewish life in Poland, and which also alienated the sympathy of many friends of Polish independence and freedom.

I pointed out that the militant anti-Jewish campaign in Poland helped only the Russian autocracy, while injuring both the Jews and the Poles themselves.

The Pope displayed a keen interest in the subject and a familiarity with conditions in Russia that was amazing. He said in a soft tone, apparently deeply moved:—

"I know about the tragedy of the Jewish people in Russia. Their sufferings have touched my heart. I have received reports from my bishops about the persecution of the Jewish people in Russia. I know about the wholesale expulsions of entire communities, about the wholesale unfounded accusations against the Jewish people, about their great sacrifices and their terrible sufferings.

"I am aware of the fact that this anti-Jewish manifestation has been stimulated in Poland by the Russian government. The Polish people are themselves suffering untold hardships, my heart is bleeding for their sorrows in this war, and my own bishops have been treated cruelly and mercilessly by the government of the Tsar."

The Pope then referred to several petitions he had received from Galician Jews and to letters he had received from distinguished Jews in various belligerent countries depicting the plight of the Jewish people in the war zone. He declared that if the American Jews, representatives of the Jewish community of the greatest neutral Power, would present some of the facts in the form of an address he would be glad to answer by a public letter and send a circular letter to various countries stating that it was un-Christian to be anti-Jewish. He said he was an energetic enemy of anti-Semitism and would denounce it upon every occasion.

"I am, and we all are—always—for liberty. I am a power for liberty," he said. "Also a power for peace."

It was at this point that I mentioned the remarkable appeal of Pope Benedict addressed to the nations then at war and to their rulers, in July, 1915.

"Yes," he repeated, "we must remember that nations do not die. Humbled and oppressed, they chafe under the yoke imposed upon them, preparing a renewal of the combat and passing down from generation to generation a mournful heritage of hatred and revenge."

The Pope expressed his great admiration for President Wilson as a brilliant statesman, as a great leader and power for peace.   He declared that he had watched his efforts in behalf of peace and that he himself would continue his work for peace.

He said he understood the Kaiser was at that time ready to propose peace to France upon the following conditions:—

1. The evacuation of Belgium and France.
2. The reconstruction of Poland as an independent State.
3. The cession of Alsace-Lorraine in exchange for a French colony.
4. The internationalization of Constantinople.

The French statesman who was present at the audience declared it as his opinion that France would not accept peace in any case admitting the cession of Alsace-Lorraine in exchange for a French colony.

"I believe," remarked Cardinal Gasparri, "Germany would not insist upon the colony."

"The arrangements made by the French government with England and Russia will not allow a separate peace, such as these terms would seem to indicate," said the French statesman.

The Pope then spoke again of his absolute neutrality.

"We reprove injustice, on whatever side it may have been committed," he said.   "I love all the children of God equally and I suffer when they suffer.   I have pointed out in my recent letter to the rulers of the nations at war that it is high time to weigh with a serene mind the rights and aspirations of the peoples, to initiate an exchange of views with the object of holding in due account, within the limits of possibility, those rights and aspirations, and thus succeed in putting an end to the monstrous struggle.

"The equilibrium of the world, and the prosperity and assured tranquillity of nations rests upon mutual benevolence and respect for the rights and dignity of others much more than upon hosts of armed men and a ring of formidable fortresses."

The Pope then wished me success in my investigations concerning the condition of the Jews in the war-stricken countries and said that he would do everything within his power to aid in ameliorating their condition.

"But I know it is a difficult task to ascertain the facts just now," he remarked. "With all my Catholic agents I have not been able to learn what has become of the archbishop of Lemberg, who was seized by the Russian troops."

"You really do not know at this moment where he is?" I inquired.

"No," replied the Pope, "I do not even know whether he is alive."

Then he told the story of the unfortunate archbishop of Lemberg and also that of Cardinal Mercier. He pointed out how the Vatican was affected by the war both by the Allies and the Central Powers, which made his neutrality imperative.

I asked the Pope whether he believed the end of the war would see the fulfilment of the prophecy of Isaiah of universal and lasting peace.

"It is hard to prophesy," said the Pope.

"Under these august vaults prophecy is a tradition," remarked the French statesman.

"Not now," said the Pope with a smile. "Not now."

The Pope then inquired about conditions in Mexico.

"In Mexico, as elsewhere, all we want is liberty," he said slowly. "Liberty and justice."

In answer to my question about his views regarding the aspirations of the Zionists the Pope said:—

"I am in sympathy with the Jewish national aspirations in Palestine. We want liberty and justice, just as the Jews want liberty and justice everywhere."

After a cordial handshake the pontifical audience ended. Cardinal Gasparri told me he was greatly interested in the United States. He spoke in terms of great admiration for President Wilson and expressed a profound sympathy for the Jewish people whose plight in the war zone was tragic.

I remarked that the Pope had rendered a great humane service by calling attention to the terrible persecutions of the Jews in Russia during the war, especially by making known the fact that fifteen hundred Jews, men, women and children had been placed in front of the Russian armies on one occasion and fired upon by the troops of the Central Powers.

Cardinal Gasparri said the Vatican had received information from its own Catholic correspondents concerning the horrors perpetrated by the Russian government. He declared that the Vatican had endeavored through those correspondents to do everything possible to end the atrocities, but all efforts proved futile. Cardinal Gasparri said the Jewish persecutions in Russia were part of a governmental policy and that the Catholics also suffered severely at the hands of the Russian government shortly after the outbreak of the war, particularly in the provinces occupied by the Russian troops in Galicia. He then spoke of the Catholic archbishop of Lemberg, who, without the slightest cause, was brutally removed from his home and banished, together with five hundred Catholic priests.

"We cannot make any official protest out of courtesy to France and England, the allies of Russia," said the Cardinal

Secretary of State. "At the same time, we were reproached by the governments of those two nations for not having registered a more vigorous protest against the German government for the imprisonment of Cardinal Mercier, archbishop of Malines."

Cardinal Gasparri added that it was very difficult for the Vatican to receive complete reports from Russian territory and that the Minister of Russia at the Vatican had evidently been instructed by his government to deny everything. He again expressed a deep interest in my own investigation of the condition of the Jews.

"The Vatican will be glad to help any such investigation to the limits of its neutrality," said the Cardinal. "His Holiness has been accused on several occasions, by one side or the other, of having violated such neutrality, just as President Wilson has been accused of being unneutral, but I can assure you His Holiness has pursued a policy of absolute neutrality in every respect, and I am pleased to observe that in such cases as the sinking of the *Lusitania*, both President Wilson and the Pope acted along the same lines.

"As for the Jews," remarked Cardinal Gasparri, "the Papacy has not changed its views and its attitude toward them. The Old Testament is the father of the New. Whenever an appeal came to the Vatican from persecuted Jews, especially in recent years, the Popes never failed to speak in their defense. You doubtless recall the statement of the Holy See in the outrageous Beilis affair, in which the Vatican denounced the ritual murder accusation against the Jews."

I asked about the reports to the effect that the Pope desired to be a member of the peace congress at the close of the war. Cardinal Gasparri's answer was:—

"It should be clearly understood in the United States and elsewhere that there is no truth at all in any reports that the Pope wishes to go to the peace congress to restore temporal power. His Holiness declares solemnly that if he should go to the congress, nobody will raise the question of temporal power. If he were not to go there, there would be at least two belligerent nations, one of them Germany, who will ask for the restoration of that power.

"His Holiness would like to see the United States act as the peace mediator."

Then he added:—

"I have no doubt that you could do me a service. You have read the pontifical letter on peace. We sent that letter to the rulers of the belligerent nations. We have not yet sent it to the neutral Powers. I am authorized by His Holiness to hand you a copy of that letter with a personal dedication to His Excellency, President Wilson, and I would be grateful to you if you would present it to him when you return to America."

I declared that I would be glad to do this.

Pope Benedict left with me the impression not only of a great religious and moral leader, but also of a brilliant statesman. It was evident that he was suffering because of the horrors of the war and his efforts for peace seemed to me prompted by a wholehearted desire to see a just and durable peace on earth and real good will to men.

Upon my return to America, I presented the autographed letter to the President, who expressed his appreciation and thanks to the Pope.

I also informed The American Jewish Committee that the Pope was willing to issue a declaration regarding anti-

Semitism, denouncing anti-Jewish persecutions as un-Christian, if he received an official request from a representative Jewish organization. I arranged for a meeting of members of the executive committee of the American Jewish Committee with Monsignor Bonzano, then papal delegate to the United States, and the matter of anti-Jewish persecution was discussed.

The following letter was forwarded to Pope Benedict XV by the American Jewish Committee:

"*New York, December 30, 1915.*

"YOUR HOLINESS:

"The petitioners, who are citizens of the United States of America and adherents of the Jewish faith, have learned with increasing horror of the unspeakable cruelties and hardships visited upon their co-religionists in various belligerent lands since the outbreak of the present world-conflict. Far beyond the sufferings which this calamity has inflicted upon those of other faiths, and in addition to the ravages and destruction occasioned by the clash of the contending armies to all who come within the sphere of their hostilities, the Jews have been marked for special persecution and have been subjected to oppressive measures not borne by their compatriots of other creeds. Passion and prejudice have been fomented against our unhappy brethren, frequently by those who bear the same political allegiance, until their lot has ceased to be endurable. In some of the lands where they have long resided their neighbors are bent upon their annihilation, practicing against them the most refined cruelty, and in many instances by means of an economic boycott condemning them to literal starvation. We submit herewith ascertained facts which tell but in small part the hideous truth.

"Fully persuaded that had Your Holiness been acquainted with these facts the Holy See would at once have exercised the profound moral, ethical and religious influence with which the Roman Catholic Church is endowed, upon those who regard Your Holiness as their Shepherd, but who have unfortunately participated in this persecution, with all due veneration we now approach the Supreme Pontiff for succor in this the bitter hour of our need, knowing the exemplary humanity for which Your Holiness is justly distinguished. It is our sincere prayer that the occasion may be deemed a fitting one for resort to the authority vested in the Sovereign of the great Roman Catholic Hierarchy, to urge his Cardinals, Archbishops, Bishops, and Priests to admonish their flocks to hold in abhorrence these acts of persecution, of prejudice and of cruelty, which have overwhelmed our unfortunate brethren.

"We recall with admiration and gratitude that on many occasions in the past some of the revered predecessors of Your Holiness have under like conditions extended protection to those of the Jewish faith, in the interest of right and justice. Appreciating the transcendent importance which the entire civilized world attaches to any utterance from so exalted a source of morality and wisdom as that which Your Holiness represents, we confidently express the hope that timely action will be taken by the Vatican, to the end that the sufferings under which millions of our brethren in faith are now weighed down may be terminated by an act of that humanity to which Your Holiness is so passionately devoted, and that the cruel intolerance and the unjust prejudice which have been aroused against them may forever vanish before this glorious exercise of Your Supreme Moral and Spiritual Power.

"We beg Your Holiness to believe us to be,

"Your most respectful petitioners,

"THE AMERICAN JEWISH COMMITTEE.

"LOUIS MARSHALL, President.

"JACOB H. SCHIFF, CYRUS ADLER, JULIUS ROSENWALD, JACOB H. HOLLANDER, A. LEO WEIL, OSCAR S. STRAUS, J. L. MAGNES, ISAAC W. BERNHEIM, SAMUEL DORF, ISADORE SOBEL, MAYER SULZBERGER, JULIAN W. MACK, HARRY CULTER, CYRUS L. SULZBERGER.

"Executive Committee."

This petition called forth a reply from the Holy See, which was a virtual encyclical, and was followed by directions to the Catholic clergy of Poland, admonishing them to use their best endeavors to put an end to the persecution which prevailed.

Among all the papal bulls ever issued with regard to Jews throughout the history of the Vatican, there is no statement that equals this direct, unmistakable plea for equality for the Jews, and against prejudice upon religious grounds. The bull issued by Innocent IV declaring the Jews innocent of the charge of using Christian blood for ritual purposes, while a striking document, was after all merely a statement of fact, whereas this declaration by Pope Benedict XV was a plea against religious prejudice and persecution.

Thus Pope Benedict XV displayed a deep concern in the tragedy of the Jews in the war. Passionately striving to bring peace to the bleeding nations, he also spoke for the Jews, for the most wronged and most violated of peoples in the war zone.

The remarkable document follows:

"SECRETARY OF STATE TO HIS HOLINESS.

"THE VATICAN

"*No. 13, 726*   *February 9th, 1916.*

"The Supreme Pontiff has with interest taken notice of the letter bearing date of December 30, 1915, which you have been pleased to address to him in the name of the three million Jewish citizens of the United States of America, in order to communicate to him generally the treatment to which your co-religionists complain that they have been exposed in various regions, and at the same time you have requested him to interpose the weight of his supreme moral and spiritual power in order that these sufferings may be terminated by an act of that humanity to which the Holy Father is so passionately devoted.

"The Supreme Pontiff is unable to express himself concerning the special facts referred to in the memorandum submitted with your letter, but in principle, as the head of the Catholic Church, which, faithful to its divine doctrine and to its most glorious traditions, considers all men as brethren and teaches them to love one another, he will not cease to inculcate the observance among individuals as among nations the principles of human right, and to reprove every violation of them. This right should be observed and respected in relation to the children of Israel as it should be to all men, for it would not conform to justice and to religion itself to derogate therefrom solely because of a difference of religious faith.

"Moreover, in his paternal heart, pained by the spectacle of the existing horrible war, the Supreme Pontiff feels in this moment, more deeply than ever, the necessity that all men shall recollect that they are brothers and that their salvation lies in the return to the law of love, which is the law of the Gospels.   He also desires to interest to this noble end all who, especially by reason of the sacred attributes of their pastoral ministrations, are able to bring efficient aid to this important result.

"In the meantime His Holiness rejoices in the unity which in civil matters exists in the United States of America among the members of the different faiths and which contributes so powerfully to the peaceful prosperity of your great country.   He prays to God that peace may at length appear for the happiness of that humanity of which you truly say the Holy Father is the guardian.

"Accept, gentlemen, the assurances of my most distinguished and devoted sentiments.

(Signed) "P. Cardinal Gasparri.

"To Mr. Louis Marshall, President,
       and to the Members of the Executive Committee
       of The American Jewish Committee."

HANS DELBRUECK

Berlin, 1915.

PROF. HANS DELBRUECK, the famous German historian and the tutor of the Kaiser in his youth, was one of the few statesmen in Germany who correctly foretold the present war.

In interviews and statements which I made public at the time Professor Delbrueck declared that while other Powers were dividing the world among themselves, taking all available colonies, Germany, the growing German nation, was asked to stand by and remain a mere unconcerned on-looker. He said that to grow in peace and develop Germany must have colonial possessions like the other great Powers.

Prof. Delbrueck has written extensively on this subject in the "Preussiche Jahrbuecher." He is one of the important moulders of public opinion in Germany.

I sought his views on war and peace, for his views are representative of a great element of the thinking German people. He is a conservative, progressive force, not a "militarist."

I said to him: "So many books have been published—books of all colors, red, white, blue, green, in fact, all the colors of the rainbow—concerning the outbreak of the war, that I should like to know from you the real cause of the war."

"It is very simple," he replied. "Russia's desire to secure Constantinople, to destroy Austria and to conquer the northern part of Sweden led to this European conflict. This was Russia's purpose, and Germany simply would not let her accomplish it. England desired to maintain the Entente, *and by the 'mechanism' of the Entente she is in this war.*

"To put it briefly, the war was started by Patchitch in Belgrade, through Russian machinations. Then Russia came in. Then France and England joined.

"Germany could neither permit the destruction of Austria nor the growth of Russia, particularly at the expense of the Turkish Empire.

"Aside from these causes we are really in this war helping to bring liberty not only to the Poles and the other peoples inhabiting the provinces we have conquered, but we shall also bring liberty to Russia herself, to the Russian people. See what Russia is doing at this moment with the Duma, with the chosen representatives of the Russian people, strangling every effort at reform in that country!

"But the German victories in the Russian provinces, or rather the defeat of the Russian system, will open the eyes of the Russian people and cause their awakening and perhaps also their emancipation. Thus we shall bring liberty to Russia even as we liberated France from Bonapartism in 1870."

"Do you think German militarism will become stronger after this war, or will this grave human crisis, with millions of human lives lost, tend to check the spirit of militarism?" I asked.

"German militarism?" he repeated. "Militarism, as far as it does exist in Germany, has come to us from Russia, and for that matter, militarism has come everywhere from

Russia. Russia's enormous army has been the cause of militarism in Europe. The Russian army was much greater than the German, Italian and Austrian armies combined.

"In order to be able to defend ourselves and Europe against the tremendous Russian army and the domination of the Cossacks, we were compelled to have a great army. And since we had a large army, France followed suit, and then England wanted to protect France.

"If Russia is curbed, if Russian greed for territory is checked, if Russia is dissolved and the smaller nationalities in Russia liberated, then the danger of militarism will have been removed. It may be that then it would be possible to have armaments reduced in every country. Russia has been the real military menace, responsible for the great burden of armaments everywhere."

I mentioned to Prof. Delbrueck that three years ago he practically foretold the present catastrophe in his interview on Germany's aims. He said:

"As I told you then, the natural aims of Germany are to have colonial possessions as the other great nations, for instance, in Central Africa. It is my personal opinion that the moment the other powers realize this and are willing to make reasonable arrangements with Germany in this direction the war will end.

"As I have pointed out, of all the armies in the world, the German army is the best trained and most powerful instrument of war, and yet, at the same time, the least available for mere political ambition and lust for power. Our army is strong only in a political defensive movement, when the existence and honor of the Empire must be defended against an enemy's attacks.

"When they speak abroad so much about the German aggressiveness and refer to German military writers, they mean aggressiveness in a strategical and tactical sense. But for political aggressiveness which would lead to such a war as this, for the purpose of attaining world supremacy, our people could never be used. And of what avail would have been all our technical skill and all the discipline of our army without the spirit which must come of the people's own free will and which cannot be anything but the expression of the whole nation?

"Not more than 15 per cent. of the army in the field now had uniforms on the day of mobilization. The other 85 per cent. are peasants and workmen and scholars, for the most part heads of families. Would such people be prepared to be led to death for the sake of mere plans of political ambition?

"The charge of 'militarism' applies least of all to Germany, unless you refer to the fact that every German subject is a born defender of his Fatherland. It was this spirit that made it possible for Prussia to guard Europe against the universal supremacy of Napoleon and then against the domination of the Czar.

"When we take into consideration the fact that during the past 100 years Germany (Prussia) has had an army constituting only one per cent. of the population, the charge of the growth of militarism in Germany can hardly be substantiated.

"In order that Germany should not be excluded from international affairs, in order that Germany should not have to remain a mere onlooker while the other great powers are dividing Africa and Asia among themselves, and in order to protect our growing oversea commerce, Germany commenced to build her navy in 1888 and thereby aroused England's jealousy in the highest degree.

"During the last 150 years the English people have lived in constant dread of an invasion. At one time it was the Spaniards, then the French, then the Russians, and now it is the Germans who have disturbed the peaceful slumbers of the British. They could not understand why Germany was building a large navy, unless she had intentions of attacking England. In their opinion the German navy would have been merely a luxury if Germany had no intentions of such an attack on England.

"There may have been dreamers in Germany who dreamed of an immediate landing in England, but in responsible quarters Germans have thought much more soberly. It is true, we wanted more than merely to defend our own coasts with our large fleet, but there was never any intention on our part to attack England. What we wanted to impress upon England, as well as upon the other powers, was that Germany must have her proper place among the great nations, in accordance with her greatness and power.

"New colonial possessions have been acquired in Africa and in Asia by the English and the French, the Russians, the Americans and the Japanese. Germany did not want to be excluded from this division of the world forever. If Germany had built no navy she could not have prevented the division of Turkey."

"I understand that you were one of the signers of the petition to the Imperial Chancellor recently, in which the idea of the annexation of Belgium by Germany was opposed. May I know what the attitude of the German people toward this question is at the present time?" I asked.

"The men who signed that petition belonged to the

minority," said Dr. Delbrueck.   "The majority of the German people desire the annexation of Belgium by Germany. At all events the war must go on till Poland and the Baltic provinces are liberated and the freedom of the sea is secured.

"Then the cause of militarism will have been removed, and armaments could be reduced everywhere at the close of this war.   It is quite possible that peace could be secured by ceding to Germany such colonies as Uganda and Nigeria by England and the French and Belgian Congoes, as a ransom for the evacuation by Germany of northern France and Belgium.

"Then there would probably have to be an indemnity to Germany, and I think England ought to pay it, for the cost of another year of war would be far greater than the price of peace to-day."

"You speak of the liberation of Poland.   May I know what, in your opinion, the German Government intends to do with the newly acquired Polish provinces?" I asked.

"So far as Poland is concerned," replied Professor Delbrueck, "you may be quite sure that these provinces will never belong to Russia again.   They have been liberated. It is, of course, one of the most difficult tasks to handle the new Polish problem adequately.   Poland either will be autonomous, or, which is more probable, it will be an independent State, under the sovereignty of Austria.   I hardly believe that Germany will want to take up this new problem herself.   Personally, I should not like to see Germany take upon herself this burden.

"Of course, the Baltic provinces where the population is to a great extent German will remain in the hands of Germany.   They will not be dominated by Russia any more.

As I have stated before, Germany is going to liberate the smaller nationalities in this war.

"The Jews will, of course, see their condition greatly improved after this war in the Polish provinces. Their position in Russia was intolerable. The horrors perpetrated upon them were inhuman. I do not say that all anti-Semitism will be eradicated in Germany after the war, but I can state definitely that it is diminishing now, and that it will continue to diminish in the German Empire."

"What do you think of the likelihood of a separate peace with Russia? Do you believe that now that the Grand Duke has been eliminated from the Russian sphere of influence, the Czar, who has been inclined from the start in favor of a separate peace with Germany, may commence negotiations for peace with Germany?" I asked.

"A separate peace with Russia would mean the end of the war. England would be forced, and so would France be forced, to conclude peace within four weeks after a separate peace with Russia."

"What is your view with regard to the German-American misunderstandings?" I asked.

"I am glad to see that these misunderstandings are being cleared up and that the irritation on either side is subsiding. I must say that there has been a strong anti-American feeling in a certain class of this country on account of the question of ammunition. I belong to that class myself," replied Professor Delbrueck with a smile.

I remarked that the feeling of President Wilson is, in all likelihood, that since the Germans believe the American government to be pro-Allies, and the Allies believe America to be pro-German, he is pursuing the right course.

"I know that America is acting in accord with international law in this matter," said Professor Delbrueck. "I know that legally the United States is in the right. But I cannot understand how the sale of ammunition, even though legally sanctioned, could be reconciled with the lofty ideals embodied in the American notes, in which the American government speaks of humanity, Christianity, of moral rights and the glory of peace.

"If international law permits the sale of ammunition—and this is the only thing that prolongs the war—then America should simply stand upon her legal rights, but should not preach idealism and lofty sentiments. If, however, President Wilson is really in favor of an international policy of idealism—and I have no doubt that he is sincere—he surely must have the right to substitute American law for international law."

"But this would be interpreted as a violation of neutrality, if changed during the war," I said.

"Legally, America is in the right," he repeated. "My complaint is only upon moral grounds."

"How soon do you think peace negotiations will begin?" I asked.

"I believe that peace could be had within a very short time, peace under reasonable terms. In fact, the German Chancellor declared recently that Germany is ready at any time for peace upon reasonable terms. I believe that President Wilson and the Pope could be the peace mediators and practically bring about a speedy peace."

ISVOLSKY

Paris, 1915.

THERE is a man in Paris who may justly say to himself: "This war is mine!"

In the stillness of the night, in the great city that a little more than a year ago harbored within itself so much care-free gayety, frivolity, playfulness and brilliancy, now wrapped in mourning, a veritable graveyard, that man may be rejoicing over the "victory" he has achieved by the realization of his dream and ambition, and if his nerves have not been shattered by the phantoms of the millions of men, dead or crippled, of millions of bereaved and heart-broken mothers and wives and children, he may be repeating to himself, with a diabolical smile: "It is my war!"

For years he has planned it. For years he has craved it. For years he has schemed to provoke it. Spiderlike he kept weaving incessantly his network of intrigues, the moving spirit of the machinations and schemes and cunning devices contrived to make this war.

And now he can say to himself: "I have made this war. It is my war."

Perhaps it has turned out not as he conceived it. He had hoped for victories, but has found defeats, reverses, humiliations instead—an almost complete collapse of his plans, but nevertheless he may boast in his own heart: "It is my war!"

He is not a great statesman, nor is he a great warrior. He is not a Napoleon in any sense. This is the age of mediocrities and of machines.

A small man, the son of a priest, moved by selfish ambitions, persevering, unscrupulous and unhesitating in his methods—he has succeeded, strangely enough, in drawing the great powers into the network of his "diplomatic" intrigues, and now there is flowing upon the fields of battle the blood of millions of human beings, representative of the most civilized nations.

Humanity is destroying itself, devastating all it has been creating—cities, towns, and villages, fields and shops and factories, commerce and industry—spreading hatred and bitterness and cruelty, killing the human in man.   And behind the scenes of this awful calamity there is one man, a so-called diplomat, who can laugh at the whole world and say:

"Yes, it is my war!   I have called it into being!"

That man's name is Alexander Isvolsky.   He is the Russian Ambassador to France.

When I arrived in Dieppe from London I stood in line at the railroad station for some time before I reached the officers examining the passports.   Around a long table sat six men, three in French uniforms.   But the Englishmen, in plain clothes, seemed to be in authority.   They cross-examined the passengers.   Their manner was rude, insulting and their questions were often silly.

When they looked at my passport the officers passed it on to a red-headed Englishman, who made a significant grimace, scrutinized me and demanded to know the purpose of my trip to Europe, especially to France.   I told him the purpose of my journey to Europe, named the newspaper I represented and added that I was particularly interested in ascertaining the facts concerning the condition of the Jews in the various countries at war.

He looked at me askance, stood up officiously and led me by the arm to a small back room in the railway station. He locked the door and whispered something in the ear of the French officer, who sat there at a small desk.

Then he commenced to ask a number of questions, and from time to time again whispered something in the officer's ear.

Several times the door was opened and a soldier was admitted, bringing reports. As the door opened I saw several soldiers stationed outside.

The mysterious air and the rude manner in which they conducted their cross-examination were, to say the least, quite embarrassing. They disregarded the letters of introduction I carried, declaring sneeringly they knew how much it was necessary to pay for letters of introduction in America.

Though I had, in addition to the American passport, the special French passport issued to me by the French Consul General in London, after a most minute examination of my papers, I was kept for an hour in suspense, locked in a little room, guarded by French soldiers.

Finally the Englishman asked me brusquely:

"Where do you intend to stop in Paris?"

"In the Grand Hotel," I replied.

"See that you stop there," he threatened. "If you don't report to the police to-morrow, or if you don't stop at the Grand Hotel, you will be taken back to-morrow on this same boat."

Then the French officer added:

"You must not go near any of the places of military operations under any circumstances."

The British officer opened the door and said:

"You may go now, but remember what I've told you."

In the train waiting at the station for more than two hours I met several Americans who had come from London on the same boat.   There was an American newspaper man, with his family, and three apparently wealthy American women, who were going to France as volunteer Red Cross nurses.   They asked me about my experience, for they had seen the officer leading me away.   They told me they also had been treated rudely.

I was wondering at the threshold of the great French Republic whether I was in France or in Russia.

After a brief stay in Paris I knew what influences were dominating the Republic of France, and I was no longer surprised at the rudeness and stupidity of the officers examining the passports in Dieppe.   It was uncharacteristic of the French.

During my stay in France I met a prominent French diplomatist with whom I discussed the war.   He spoke of France with deep emotion, with tears in his voice, for he loved his fatherland passionately.

In a quivering voice he said:

"My unfortunate country is almost prostrate.   Hundreds of thousands of our best people, of our youngest and strongest men have already laid down their lives, have become disfigured, crippled, maimed; have shed their own blood and that of the enemy, all on account of an intrigue."

"An intrigue?" I asked.

"Yes, a Russian intrigue," he answered.   He paused a while, and then added:

"France is not free now; it is dominated by Russia—the press, the Government and all."

"Do you really mean to say that a Russian intrigue has led to this universal slaughter, to this most terrible tragedy?" I asked.

The Frenchman answered:

"It may seem strange and incredible, but it is true. It is so simple that people would hardly believe it possible, but it is a fact, nevertheless."

He paused again, as though hesitating to speak frankly on a subject that was painful to him. Then he went on:

"If it is possible to fix the responsibility for so horrible a catastrophe upon one man, that man is Isvolsky. He is now the Tsar's Ambassador to France. But the idea of this war was born in his mind when he was Russia's Minister of Foreign Affairs. He commenced to plan this war on the day Bosnia and Herzegovina were annexed by Austria. He then made up his mind to avenge himself on Austria. Not that he was so sorry for the smaller States, or that the Russian government felt sorry for them, but he saw his opportunity of furthering his pet Pan-Slavist movement.

"The first part of his plot was to become the Russian Ambassador to France, so that his activities might generate from that country. As soon as he became Ambassador to Paris he started to organize the French press for Russia's purposes. Within a very short time he succeeded in muzzling it, in making it servile to Russian interests. He had large sums of money for this purpose at his command.

"To further his ambition of vengeance against Austria, Isvolsky formed a secret alliance with Titoni, the Italian Ambassador to France, who was always known as distinctly anti-Austrian. The plan of these two diplomats was to provoke a war of Italy and Russia against Austria without drawing France or Germany into it. This turned out to be a vain hope and a dream. They failed in the very first stages of their conspiracy.

"Then the two diplomats changed their plans. Titoni suggested the Tripoli operations, with Isvolsky's sanction, in order to involve Austria, through the Balkan States and Turkey. Italy was eager to occupy Albania, but England and France blocked the scheme and prevented it.

"The war between Italy and Turkey was limited to Tripoli, and thus the two accomplices were defeated in their machinations once more.

"Then came the Agadir affair, the blow of Germany against France in Morocco. Isvolsky sought to influence the French Premier to go ahead and declare war, but England urged that the affair be settled peacefully. This was done, and Isvolsky's plot was upset again.

"In the beginning of 1912 Poincaré became Premier. He had already been interested in Isvolsky's pet schemes and was now ready to assist him.

"In August, 1912, Poincaré went to St. Petersburg and met the Tsar. When the Tsar asked him whether he would lend his aid to Russia in her efforts to secure control of Constantinople, Premier Poincaré replied:

" 'I am only the French Premier. You know that a Premier, who is only the temporary head of the Cabinet, cannot give you a definite answer to this question. Only the President of France could give you a definite and perhaps also a satisfactory answer.'

"Isvolsky and the Tsar understood the meaning of Poincaré's words.

"Soon large sums of Russian money made themselves felt in France. Isvolsky handed enormous sums to the French newspapers, and with the aid of about six million francs, Poincaré was elected President of the French Republic in 1913.

"Isvolsky, encouraged by Poincaré, influenced Russia to allow Bulgaria, Serbia and Greece to declare war on Turkey, in October, 1912. Poincaré sent to Austria the note in which he practically demanded that Austria remain neutral and keep out of the conflict. That note was quite offensive to Austria.

"Then Isvolsky, by his methods of provocation for the purpose of involving Austria in the war, expressed his opinion that Austria should intervene, but England succeeded in influencing the great powers to act calmly and wisely, and the intervention of Austria was prevented.

"Thus Isvolsky and Titoni lost their game once more.

"But if Austria acted wisely and kept out of the conflict, it was due not only to the pressure brought to bear upon her by the other great Powers who counselled peace, but also to the influence of the heir to the throne, the Archduke Ferdinand, who was a resolute and firm adherent of peace.

"Isvolsky knew this and commenced a new campaign. Before long the Pan-Slavists, led by Isvolsky, resolved to remove the Archduke who stood in the way of their plans and ambitions. This was accomplished. It is now an established fact that the leader of the plot against the archduke was the Russian Minister to Serbia, who died three days after the assassination of the Archduke. That man was Isvolsky's agent in Serbia.

"Then came the Austrian ultimatum to Serbia.

"On the day of the ultimatum Poincaré was in St. Petersburg. When the Tsar asked him this time about Constantinople, whether France would help him to secure it, Poincaré answered:

" 'Now that I am the President of France I can promise to help Russia to secure Constantinople.' "

"It was then that Russia, under the pretext of protecting little Serbia, commenced to mobilize upon a large scale, thus practically starting the war.

"Isvolsky accomplished what he wanted. And now Titoni also realized his hope—a war with Austria. But they had miscalculated. They had not counted on Germany coming to Austria's rescue.

"Isvolsky, the son of a Russian priest, had long been a fanatical adherent of the Pan-Slavic movement and has dreamed of a Europe dominated by the Slavs.

"The French Republic, through the President and certain members of the Cabinet, has become a pawn in the hands of this Russian intriguer.

"Under these conditions you will not be surprised that the French press has not published anything about the Jewish atrocities committed by the Russian government during the war.

"Of course, the people of France are beginning to realize the blunders that have been made. But it is too late. Russia's defeats, and the causes of these defeats, have opened the eyes of the French people, and there are many now who are quietly expressing their indignation. But the mass of the people do not know of the intrigues that led to this most dreadful of all wars."

Thus ended the French diplomatist's account of Isvolsky's part in the world catastrophe.

The military parties in all the countries now at war suddenly came into their own element. Some were prepared. Others only boasted of their preparedness. Some kept preparing quietly and efficiently. Others threatened, preparing in a haphazard manner.

About a month before the outbreak of the war certain newspapers in Russia boasted of the preparations Russia was making, of the reforms she introduced in her army, and of her readiness to measure her strength with Germany's in—1916.

The powder was dry. The air was electrified. The military parties everywhere commenced to assert themselves. And when the Russian intriguer, spurred on by the dream of Pan-Slavic domination and Russia's greed for Constantinople, dropped the match all of Europe was set aflame.

The dogs of war were suddenly unchained. Passions broke loose. The efforts of the statesmen to save the situation proved futile. It was too late to check the enormous wave of war-madness that had come upon Europe.

There was a man in France who worked for peace and for reason till his last breath.

On the eve of the war he addressed 100,000 persons in the city of Brussels. He spoke of peace—he brought them a ray of hope that there may be no war. On the following afternoon came the news that Germany was determined to enter the war. He rushed back to Paris—to the Foreign Office—where he was received by Under Secretary of State Abel Ferry. He said to the representative of the Minister of Foreign Affairs:

"The stronger you are bound by your treaties, the firmer must be your will to do everything possible to spare us this war. I fear you have not told our ally, Russia, that in the event she does not accept England's proposal for mediation she must not count on our aid against Austria.   We make this demand loudly in the hour of the gravest danger. We will do it even if we are threatened to be shot down. For in this way we clear Socialism of the responsibility and at the same time point out the only way in which peace may be saved."

The Foreign Office answered:

"We assure you that we have never stopped bringing pressure upon Russia in the manner you have indicated."

But another man, M. Ferry, of the Foreign Office, remarked a little later:

"It cannot be stopped!"

On July 31, 1914, the man who labored so passionately to save the peace of Europe declared that the Russian Ambassador, Isvolsky, was the chief instigator of the war.

On the same day he declared to the Under Secretary of State, M. Ferry, that he was determined to resume an energetic campaign against France entering the war.   He was warned against this in the following phrase:

"You may be shot down in the street."

On that same day the man who sought to save his country from war madness planned to commence his campaign by a powerful appeal in the form of "J'accuse!"   This became known in the reactionary spheres in the afternoon, and in the evening of July 31, 1914, this hero of peace, M. Jaurès, was murdered in a restaurant in Paris—shot through a window.

The famous and courageous champion of justice in the Dreyfus affair now paid with his life for his courageous fight to save the peace of Europe.   This time Isvolsky, Poincaré and Delcasse won.

Before I left France a witty Frenchman said to me:

"We have three invasions in France. First, the German invasion, then the Belgian invasion caused by the tragedy of Belgium and, last but not least, the British invasion. The British seem to be trying to run France, as if they were the masters here."

"But you have forgotten to mention another invasion," I remarked, "the Russian invasion of France. And this invasion was probably responsible for the other invasions."

ALEXANDER KERENSKY

Petrograd, 1917.

THE man of the hour was Alexander F. Kerensky. Simple and dominating, he was idolized everywhere. His sincerity and fiery eloquence won for him universal confidence among soldiers and civilians. The most picturesque popular figure brought out by the great revolution, he was hailed, as the "sweetheart" and the "hope" of the new Russia. He was its composite hypnotic force, concentrated in one soul.

Kerensky really participated in the preparatory work for the revolution, then rose to the very top of the revolutionary wave, above other Russian leaders, and became the inspiration of liberty-loving Russia.

A member of the socialist revolutionary party, he had grown more or less conservative under the burden of the great responsibility he had assumed. Because of this he incurred the animosity of certain members of his own party. The extremists despised him even as the counter-revolutionists among the reactionaries feared him more than any other Russian leader.

The German government, realizing Kerensky's tremendous influence and power, used every means of discrediting him. Vile stories were spread about him, accusing him of having accepted bribes of British and French gold, of having sold out to the bourgeoisie. For months the press of the world was fed on stories of Kerensky's critical physical condition. Vivid descriptions of his illness and his sufferings were published. As a final attempt, it was even sought to discredit his influence by circulating a story that he was a Jew, in order to arouse the reactionary elements against him.

Kerensky paid little attention to the gossip and wild rumors circulated about him. He went on with his work, strenuously trying to consolidate Russia, to reorganize the army in order to continue the war efficiently, to guide the ship of state safely to the Constituent Assembly.

His popularity meanwhile assumed legendary proportions.

Then came the July riots. Nicholas Lenine and Leo Trotzky challenged his strength in the first, futile attack on the Provisional Government.

July 13, 14 and 15 were days of horror in Petrograd. The bolsheviki organized riots, in which hundreds of men, women and children were killed or wounded in the streets of the Russian capital. Petrograd was in the grip of the bolsheviki for three days and all Russia felt the shock.

With cinematographic picturesqueness and rapidity Russia's political situation was changing. Sensation followed sensation, so that thousands stood in line, buying the evening newspapers. Long lines were fashionable then. There was a bread line, a shoe line and a tobacco line. Hundreds of thousands were waiting, waiting, waiting.

Only heroic men and measures could save Russia and her liberty. Mr. Kerensky, who rose on the top of the revolutionary wave, still remained on top. He was still the nation's idol, full of revolutionary fervor and courage. All looked to the special defense committee, composed of Kerensky, Savinkov and Nekrasov, co-operating with General Korniloff, to act energetically in reorganizing the army for a continuation of the war.

When the Premier was still in control of the situation, with the cabinet reorganized and the leaders of the Workmen's and Soldier's Council, as well as the constitutional democrats, supporting him and the new government, I sought his views. He received me on August 13, in the library of the former Tsar Nicholas, at the Winter Palace.

"The main problem before us now," he said, "is the national revolutionary defense of our country. Whenever those who fall into despair here or abroad think Russia has collapsed and is falling apart, I would remind them of the French Revolution, pointing to documents of history and comparing them with the present picture.

"In the army thus far we have no Lafayette or other generals who remained loyal to the fallen monarchy. Our officers and army are worthy of the highest praise. Despite misfortune, at the front, and disorders, they have shown great heroism.

"Our offensive attack opened a great wound, which is discharging the decay. The Russian organism is now undergoing a painful operation. We are applying energetic radical remedies to heal and strengthen it.

"Such is the inevitable course of revolution. All that was secretly falling apart under the old régime is now illumined under the bright but burning rays of truth and liberty.

"I am convinced that we shall have enough strength and power to come out of these extraordinary trials with honor. The birth of a free nation is always very painful.

"I value particularly American aid and support. America is thus far the best organized democracy. It is free from European prejudices, and we ourselves are inclined to become a nation without historical prejudices.

"I wish the great democracy would, especially at this moment, come to our assistance energetically; for only in the hour of need can we best test our friends. A deep, strong source of moral power is insufficient just now. It is necessary to add material support. If the old Russian régime was unable to crush the spirit and the soul of the Russian people, it did succeed in demoralizing the body and robbing the wealth of Russia.

"Among all modern statesmen I consider President Wilson the most worthy of emulation, deserving the world's attention and praise."

London, April, 1919.

In an exclusive interview with me to-day Mr. Alexander F. Kerensky made his frankest statement since he escaped from Russia. He had just returned from seclusion in the country, having reached London yesterday.

"How easily the people of the Entente countries have forgotten Russia's sacrifices and contribution in the war for the Allied cause," Mr. Kerensky lamented. "To-day Russia is considered a conquered country, like Germany."

"If the people do not know, surely the Allied statesmen must know what the Russian armies did until after the 1917 offensive, which upset Ludendorff's plans to strike with his full force against the western front," he continued.

"The Russian revolution of March, 1917, was an attempt to save Russia from a separate peace with Germany. In January, 1917, there were 1,800,000 deserters from the Russian army. Demoralization continued, enabling Germany to continually withdraw her armies from the eastern front. Within two months after the revolution the Russian army was almost regenerated. By the middle of May Germany stopped withdrawing her troops from our front. By June the normal condition of the Russian army was restored, and when I began the offensive against Germany her forces opposing us were larger by ten divisions than they had been ever before.

"The German General Staff had planned to attack the western front before the Americans could come in, but Russia blocked Ludendorff's designs.

"Allied statesmen know revolutionary Russia could have made an advantageous separate peace, but we knew no Russian front. To us it was the Allied front. We fought not only for Russia, but for the Allies. We made supreme sacrifices but we held the front for some time.

"Allied statesmen knew that Russia was more isolated than Germany was. They could not help us effectively. We were absolutely blocked during the first two years of the war. Indeed, French and Russian troops practically bore the burden of the war on land during this time. Of course, the British fleet did wonderful work on the seas, but the British army was adequately organized only after Russia had carried even a greater burden than Germany did.

"Many Russians now blame me because I would not make a separate peace with the Central Powers. Do you realize what a separate peace concluded by Russia with Germany at that time would have meant to France?

"Now all this is forgotten. Russia is ignored and treated as if she were non-existent."

Mr. Kerensky declared that no nation can forgive when its sacrifices are ignored and the blood of its sons betrayed.

"Statesmen at the peace conference are busy creating

barriers," he continued.   "They are giving Roumania territory almost down to Odessa and giving to Poland almost
up to Moscow.   They are dividing Russia into little states.
They are doing that which Napoleon tried to do more than
a century ago.

"They should understand that a combination of the
Powers with Poland against Russia means a combination
of Russia and Germany against France.   Then neither
America nor England could save the situation.

"Russia's catastrophe and chaos usually are attributed to
barbarism and the tinge of Asiatic blood, but almost the
same has happened in Germany.   When the limit of a
nation's exhaustion and destruction is reached state organism collapses.

"Compare what America contributed to France and what
was contributed to Russia.   You will then realize under
what hardships we fought and lost more men than any
other one of the belligerents.

"Now small states are created around Russia, artificially,
but there is nothing terrible in that.   Russia is experiencing
her gravest crisis now, but the Russian people, whose contribution to the world's literature and art and science is
considerable, will be regenerated.

"That which is taken from Russia now will come back.
The history of the beginning of the nineteenth century
will repeat itself."

Paris, May 1, 1920.

Paris is now the center of Russian leaders and "saviors."
Each of them has a remedy of his own, and each of them
considers his remedy as the only one that can save Russia.
There are Russian leaders here of every shade and color,

from radicalism to ultra-reaction and monarchism—beaten generals of the Tsarist régime, statesmen trained in the ways and intrigues of the autocracy, ambassadors "representing" non-existent governments, politicians and officers praying and working for a new Tsar, and Russian democrats who believe that only a constituent assembly could reconstruct Russia upon a democratic basis.

There are Russian nobles here who live on their pearls— a pearl a week—and they are rapidly coming to the end of their strings.

All these Russians are divided on almost every question affecting Russia, for each of them wants a different Russia —but on one point they are all united. They all believe that the Allies, instead of helping, have injured Russia.

Among all the Russian leaders here Alexander Kerensky is beyond doubt the most picturesque and dramatic figure. On the crest of the wave of the Russian revolution he rose to dizzy heights and became the favorite of the Russian people immediately after the collapse of the Romanoff dynasty.

I met him as Premier, when he was in his glory; I met him several times since then, and now I find him in his modest little room in Paris, where he lives in seclusion.

I asked him about Russia, about the Allied policy toward Russia, about the recognition of the Soviet Government.

There was a tinge of bitterness and a certain degree of cynicism in his comments on the Allied attitude, but it was clear that his love for Russia was as profound as his confidence in the eventual readjustment of Russia as a great and powerful country.

"America," he said, "had the greatest opportunity to save Russia, but she lost it. Immediately after the overthrow

of the Romanoff dynasty Germany supported the Bolsheviki, while England and France supported the monarch-
ists and reactionaries in Russia. Then America had the
greatest opportunity, and we Russians hoped that she would
help the democratic elements that sought to rebuild Russia.

"The Wilsonian peace policy was patterned after the
policy of the Provisional Government of which I was the
head. We outlined it first immediately after the revolution, but it was a policy distasteful to England and France.
So they did everything they could to undermine us. They
did not want us to participate in the liquidation of the war
along the lines of our peace program. And we would
not have been puppets at the Peace Conference.

"When President Wilson proclaimed his fourteen points
the Allies maintained silence. They were glad that President Wilson created such sentiments. They knew what
effect his speeches must have on the morale of the German
people, and upon certain elements of the people in the
Allied countries. But the Allied statesmen themselves did
not regard President Wilson's statements seriously. They
plotted to carry out their own program.

"Before President Wilson arrived in Europe the first
time, a prominent British official said to me: 'We are not
afraid of Wilson. He is not sufficiently familiar with
European affairs. Lloyd George will be able to accomplish
whatever he pleases.' And so it actually happened.
Lloyd George has done whatever he pleased.

"England is now pursuing with regard to Russia the
same policy that Germany pursued. England is now eager
to dismember Russia, almost along the lines of the Brest-
Litovsk treaty, and England will soon recognize and help
the Bolshevist government, as the Germans did in 1918.

"I am asked by Allied statesmen whether it would be wise to recognize the Bolsheviki and whether such a move would not lead to the spread of Bolshevism to other countries.

"My answer to them is this: 'Why did you not ask these questions two years ago, and why did you not take the advice given to you at that time?

" 'You have done nothing for Russia. On the contrary, you have caused us grave injuries. What difference does it make to us whether you recognize the Bolsheviki or not, whether Bolshevism will spread to France and England and Italy?

" 'Russia has had her Bolshevism, has suffered from it, has passed its worst stages; the terror is already a matter of the past—our concern is for Russia, not for other countries which have not only failed to help us, but have actually harmed us.'

"Russia needs locomotives, clothing and boots, and if she gets these things, so much the better for Russia. If governments based upon the system of private property discredit themselves through such deals, it is now of little concern to Russia.

"Either Russia is dead or she will come back stronger than ever. Among the Allies there are many who think that Russia is already dead, and they trample upon her grave. But we Russians believe that Russia is recovering. She is experiencing the pains of growth.

"And there is no nation that can help Russia except the Russian people themselves. The Allies have pursued only selfish interests in Russia, and have thus contributed to her ruin. Now the Russian people themselves must work out their salvation.

"I have long been opposed to military intervention and to the blockade. I pointed out long ago that these things, and the fronts of the reactionary generals, would galvanize the Bolshevist régime and make it stronger.

"Open Russia to the world, open the frontiers, and the world will then discover the myth that is so popular that Russia can feed Europe.

"Europe is demoralized and exhausted. France is quite helpless. Italy is on the brink of a volcano. England is now conducting the same policy that Germany would have conducted if she had won the war.

"England is now the supreme dictator of the world, outside of America. Of course, she does it skillfully and she has indeed a democratic system of government, in England.

"Italy needs Russian trade badly, and she is urging the recognition of the Soviets, not only to please her own radical elements, but also her reactionaries and her financiers. Italy has practically recognized Soviet Russia.

"Japan's recent occupation of Siberia is a new international outrage, and even America has not done anything to curb Japan's policy of aggression there.

"In Siberia Japan is fighting not a Bolshevist government, but a democratic representative government of the Zemstvos which has been recognized by the Bolsheviki. There Japan is crushing Russian democracy.

"People spoke of the great war as the last war. It was only the beginning of a series of wars. Instead of disarmament the nations will have to build ever more new big guns, aeroplanes and dreadnaughts.

"Russia can be revived only by her own powers, within Russia. She cannot be helped to come to herself by any other Power or group of Powers.

"The establishment of normal relations with Russia must lead to the failure of the Communist régime. Either they will quit of themselves or they will be overthrown. And I am sure that England will help the Communists as Germany helped them in the beginning."

PRINCE PETER KROPOTKIN

Moscow, 1918.

I TRAVELLED from Petrograd to Moscow to see Peter
Kropotkin and some of the other great champions of Russian emancipation. This journey, under the Bolshevist
rule, was connected not only with numerous hardships and
inconveniences, but also with risks and dangers. But if it
was difficult to reach Moscow from Petrograd it was much
more difficult to find the address of the famous Russian
leaders. Most of them were in hiding. No one knew the
whereabouts of Tchaikovsky, the "father" of the Russian
revolution, or of Catherine Breshkovsky, the "grandmother"
of the Russian revolution. No one could tell where Milukov, Boris Savinkov or Kerensky was.

After the brutal murder of Shingaryev and Kokoshkin,
two of the noblest liberal leaders, who had devoted all their
energies to the service of the Russian people, it became un-
safe for prominent Russian revolutionists to walk in the
streets or even remain in their homes.

After considerable difficulty I found Prince Peter
Kropotkin, the world-renowned scientist and revolutionist,
the author of "Memoirs of a Revolutionist." The genial
"Grand Old Man," who was one of the most feared personalities during the reigns of Alexander III and Nicholas II
was now classed among the counter-revolutionists.

Kropotkin, exiled by the Tsarist government, lived in
England about forty years.

When the revolution broke out last year he returned to his native land, where he was received with the greatest honors a free nation could bestow upon her favorite sons. Now, Prince Kropotkin lives with his wife in two rooms and but few intimate friends know their address. Twice the Kropotkin couple were forced from their rooms by the Bolsheviki and their little home was searched.

On my way to Kropotkin I saw the armored trucks crowded with Red Guards rushing toward the headquarters of the anarchists, who were supposed to have organized an uprising against the Soviets. They fired shots at random, killing and wounding many innocent people in the neighboring houses.

I asked Kropotkin for his views on the conflict between the Bolsheviki and the anarchists. He replied:

"The Bolsheviki are not Socialists, and the Anarchists are not Anarchists,—they are expropriators, ordinary criminals."

When I asked him for a statement on the present condition of Russia for publication in America, he said:

"Much as I should like to give such a statement to you, especially for America, I cannot do it now. I make no statements now. I deliver no speeches. I give no interviews to anybody. This is not the time for writing or speaking."

I told him that if the real leaders of Russia maintain silence, when their utterances might help Russia, their statements later would be of little significance or avail, as Russia was rapidly drifting into chaos. He agreed with me and said:—

"I will try to write a few words to-night in the form of a message to the American people. Just a few words."

Discussing the condition of Russia at that moment he said that as a result of the Brest-Litovsk treaty an enormous feudal capitalistic empire was created in the center of Europe, haughty because of its victory, full of hatred for its neighbors.

"We do not know what this empire will be in the near future," he went on, "but until now Germany and Austria, together with Russian autocracy, were the main strongholds of willful monarchical government in Europe and Asia. Their 'Holy Alliance' in 1815, and then the 'Alliance of the Three Emperors' in the sixties of the last century were the bitterest enemies not only of a republican but even of a constitutional form of government. They worked openly and secretly against any manifestation of the spirit of equality and freedom in Europe. They opposed in every way possible the democratization of any State, and especially worked energetically against socialism. And wherever the socialists in Switzerland, Italy and Spain, or even in France, showed an inclination to translate some of their ideals into life, the German government demanded immediately—and demanded rudely—that the governments of these countries make an end to this propaganda of the working people.

"The Russian autocracy naturally considered the German and Austrian emperors its chief supporters and allies, and a Russian democratic republic must be considered by Germany and Austria as their most dangerous enemy. Before the declaration of this war, Wilhelm wrote Nicholas that their own safety—and the safety of their thrones—demanded that they unite in an attack upon France and England.

"There is but one thing we can do just now—and this

is, while controlling ourselves in pain and agony, we must start an uninterrupted, daily, hourly struggle against the forces that have led Russia to the present condition of a vassal State of German imperialism and German capitalism.

"But first of all we must not reconcile ourselves to the thought of a possible monarchical restoration. Against this we must exert all our efforts. We do not want a repetition of the hangings and shootings by Nicholas and Stolypin.

"But it is still more urgent that we commence a powerful fight against all the forces that bring the victory of Germany into Russian life. And especially in the villages, through the co-operative organizations, the peasants may become the strongest fighters against Germany—her spirit, her culture, her commercial domination.

"First of all we must rid ourselves absolutely of our sense of worship of Germany in our schools, in our literature, in our political life, in the circles of our intellectuals, which have developed in Russia since the Napoleonic France was defeated by Germany.

"I know the Tsarist government, with its Ministers of Education, encouraged this worship, but we are also to blame for it to a great extent. Our intellectuals were carried away too much by German kultur and forgot that above kultur stands civilization—the striving toward equality, toward an ideal. Instead of familiarizing our people with the kultur of Germany, we must familiarize them with the Western World, its history, its life, its ideals of self-government."

On the following day Prince Kropotkin said to me:—
"I want to thank you for having made me work all night.

I have prepared a message to the people of America, which I ask you to transmit to them."

And he handed me the following message, written in his own hand:

"Russia is now living through one of those great commotions which have taken place in different countries of Europe at intervals of from one hundred and thirty to one hundred and forty years.   After England, which lived it through in 1639–1648, and France in 1789–1795, it fell now upon Russia to overthrow by means of a revolution her antiquated forms of life and to take a new departure in all her development.

"The social reconstruction, which is now to be accomplished in Russia, had been so long postponed and prevented by her rulers that it necessarily took on a violent character. Some historians have made the remark that once a social and political change, which has become necessary, is made to assert itself with violence in the streets, the change takes the form of a revolution, with all its consequences.   This remark is confirmed now in Russia—unfortunately under the most disastrous conditions.

"The Russians have to fight an enemy who was scheming for forty years the conquest of Russia—military, commercial and financial.   And that conquest was prepared not only in Germany herself, not only in her army, her trade, her banking system, her science, and so on.   It was also prepared in Russia by the intellectual demoralization of the Russian democratic thought.   And this was done with the aid of the autocratic government of Russia, which not only opposed the spreading of general education, but worked also to prevent a close intercourse of its subjects with the advanced thought of the Western democracies. What the Russians were permitted to learn they learned from Germany.

"The results of this double policy are now so awful—and I feel them so painfully—that I am quite unable to write about them. It is too hard to write about the sufferings of a beloved mother.

"I can say only one thing. After all, Russia *will* recover from her terrible illness—in the shape of a federal democratic republic, moving toward the higher ideals of equality and fraternity.

"But what is to be done now? What *can* Russia's friends do for her? In what way can they help her? Full of vigor and working capacities, animated with the best and friendliest intentions toward the Russian nation —as I *know* it is—what can the American nation do to help us? It can do very much, and already it does it in France, where every blow that the Allies will strike at the German invaders, both on land and on the sea, will help Russia and all the Slavonian nations to free themselves from the claws of the two imperial birds of prey.

"As to the help that the nation of the United States can give directly to Russia, it is immense.

"The pressing need of the moment is to save Northern Russia from imminent starvation. We still receive in Moscow our quarter of a pound of bread every day and one pound for the factory operatives; but even this insufficient allowance is supplied under the greatest difficulties, and in the provinces around Moscow whole populations cannot get even that regularly. *Conditions much worse than these are imminent.* And, with her population reduced to starvation, Russia risks to lose even the liberties she has conquered.

"Send us corn. Make it on a large scale. And be sure that the mass of the Russian people will fully appreciate this manifestation of friendship. Dissipate in this way the insinuations of the German agents who fluster in the ears of our people that the Allies use Russia as a catspaw for their imperialistic aims.

"Then send us at once as many tractors as you can spare. They are badly needed for plowing in the fall—already in August. Do it at once—there is no time to lose. . . . You see, I speak to you frankly, openly, as a brother must speak to a brother.

"And with the tractors, if you can spare men (I know they are needed there in the west of Europe, where the two different civilizations meet now in a mortal fight!)—if you can spare men and women, send us small brigades of energetic, active people to show our plowmen how the work is to be done. Send also seeds—your splendidly organized experimental stations know already what sorts of seeds are needed for the different regions of Russia.

"All over the northern half of Russia the conditions are such that the wheat and rye which were left for the spring sowing will be eaten during this month and the next, and the same is expected to happen by the end of next summer.

"Finally—and this is as important as the above mentioned, if not more so—help us to bring our dilapidated railways and rolling stock into a working order. The help you gave us by sending railway engines was invaluable. What we need now is fully equipped railway brigades of trained men for rapidly repairing our railways and engines. Of course, there will be grumblers and agents to spread and to repeat the German insinuations concerning the imperialist schemes of the United States. But, after what has happened in Russia on her western front, such insinuations will find less echo than they found a year ago.

"And then, the disinterestedness of the United States becomes every day more and more evident. And it will be still more so if all that you do to help the Russian nation takes the character of a popular work, coming from the depths of the American nation itself. *A direct gift and a friendly service from nation to nation.*

"And be sure that such a step—which will be soon followed by other steps of mutual intercourse—will do more to put an end to wars than anything else could do.

"I beg you to transmit my heartiest greetings to the American nation and my deep-felt respect for the attitude it took in the present struggle between two different worlds—the democracies of Western Europe and the two Central Empires, dominated by the military and financial astes of Germany.

"P. KROPOTKIN."

LEO TROTZKY

Petrograd, March, 1918.

I WENT to Russia to see what the Russian people thought of Bolshevism.

I interviewed a large number of representatives of factions, groups and parties of every political shade of thought in Russia.

I was particularly eager to meet Leo Trotzky, the cleverest among the Bolshevist leaders.

I sent a card to him by messenger, stating that I wanted to interview him for the American newspaper which I represented. The messenger returned to my hotel saying:—

"Comrade Trotzky asks you to meet him to-morrow at eleven o'clock in the morning at the Smolny Institute."

Next morning on my way to the Smolny Institute, the Headquarters of the Bolsheviki, I read in the newspapers a dispatch from Moscow stating that Trotzky had arrived in the new capital of the Bolsheviki, together with the other Commissaries, to be present at the conference of the Council for the ratification of the Brest-Litovsk peace treaty. I hesitated awhile, then decided to go to Smolny, notwithstanding the report that Trotzky had left the city.

The Smolny Institute, guarded by troops, with machine guns in front of the huge buildings, was almost deserted. The corridors were dirty. No one seemed to know anything about the departments that still remained in the Smolny.

Finally I found my way to the rooms occupied by Trotzky, who still was Commissary of Foreign Affairs, although he had resigned several days before. A young Red Guard in a fur cap, leaning on his gun, stood at the door reading a Russian version of a Conan Doyle detective story. I asked him whether Trotzky was in his office. He replied he didn't know.

"Can you find out whether the Commissary is here?" I asked.

"No," he said, turning to his novel again. Then I suggested that he send for Trotzky's secretary. He answered that he could not do that, because the bell was out of order, and he had no right to leave his post.

I waited awhile. Finally some one entered and I asked him to send out Trotzky's secretary. Within a few minutes a young woman came out. She had bobbed hair, a man's coat was thrown over her shoulders and she smoked a cigarette.

"Is Commissary Trotzky in?" I asked.

"Comrade Trotzky is not in," she answered, without removing the cigarette from her mouth.

"Are you sure he is not in?" I asked.

"He is not in," she replied, ready to go back.

I handed her my card and asked her to give it to Mr. Trotzky. Without saying another word she went away.

About two or three minutes later Leo Trotzky came out. He whispered something to the guard and opened the gate.

He extended his hand and said in English:—

"Do you speak English?"

"We may speak Russian if you like," I answered. Then he led me through the spacious bare rooms of the Smolny Institute and apologized for the appearance of the rooms.

"You know we moved to Moscow and things are in disorder here," he remarked.

He took me to his room. There was a bare writing table and three chairs. A man was cleaning the large window of his room at the time. Several times some one would enter without knocking and tell him that he was wanted on a very important matter.

"We want you there for only five minutes," the man persisted.

"I am busy now," Trotzky said.

Trotzky looked pale, exhausted.

I asked him how he was pleased with the Russian situation on the day the Brest-Litovsk peace was being ratified in Moscow. He stared at me awhile, then said:—

"Russia's position is more affected now by foreign than internal affairs. We have been called German agents, as you know——"

"Yes, I know, we published a number of articles dealing with this matter."

"But," he interrupted, "the Allied representatives in Russia did everything to spoil things for us and for themselves, and in that way they helped Germany more than we did."

"What are you referring to?" I asked.

"Certain members of the French and British missions blundered by supporting the Polish legions, the Ukranians, by stirring up the Roumanian armies against us, but the Polish legions, the Ukranians and Roumania all helped Germany," Trotzky answered quickly.

"The American representative took no initiative in any of these matters," he went on, "but he permitted foolish things to be done. We have been called German agents, but I can tell you that Germany has no greater enemy than our party. Nevertheless, the Allies helped General Kaledin. Of course, Ambassadors always deny that they are interfering with the internal affairs of the country to which they are accredited. So they also denied they interfered with the internal affairs of Russia. The American Ambassador acted honestly, but he didn't understand the situation in Russia."

"According to your opinion, then, the Allies are to blame for all the things that are happening in Russia to-day?" I asked.

"No, the Allies are not altogether to blame for it. There have been other mistakes, too. Revolution is necessarily accompanied by violence and disorganization, but we have creative forces which they overlooked. It was our intention to carry the revolution to Germany. The general strikes in Berlin and Vienna show that we have already accomplished much in that direction. But we lacked power of organization and Lenine favored a breathing spell for the revolution. So we accepted peace."

Trotzky paused awhile, then he added quickly:

"Now the Allies are preparing to make a new blunder. Japan is about to strike at Russia, but this will be a terrible blow to the Allies themselves."

"Just what do you mean?"

Trotzky looked at me fixedly as he answered:—

"I have information that Japan has an understanding with Germany regarding the division of Russia."

"When was such an agreement signed?"

"I don't know that," answered Trotzky.

"Do you know that such an agreement was signed?" I asked.

"I don't know that, either," he answered. "But I have reason to believe that there is an agreement which is based upon Germany's interests in the West and Japan's interests in the East. Germany wants a part of European Russia and Japan wants a part of Siberia. The Allies know of this understanding between Germany and Japan, but they close their eyes to it, fearing lest the secret agreement may become an open agreement. Other countries are prompted by the motive of crushing the social revolution."

Then the Bolshevist leader remarked:

"I must say that though Germany is employing methods of violence she deals after all with the realities of life, and that is why Germany is successful. The Allies, on the contrary, deal with appearances, with dreams rather than realities. Besides, they are six months too late. Any one who tells me that Japan is pursuing unselfish interests in Siberia is using a wretched diplomatic phrase. Japan is striking at Russia while we are organizing an army to resist German domination."

I looked at Trotzky in amazement. He was making this statement on the day the Bolsheviki were ratifying the Brest-Litovsk peace treaty.

"How long do you think your peace with Germany will last?" I asked.

"We are continuing the war against Germany in the Ukraine right now," answered Trotzky. "Neither we nor Germany consider our peace of long duration."

"May I know how you expect Bolshevism to work out in Russia side by side with German imperialism?" I asked.

"The Russia of soviets and militaristic Germany are absolutely incompatible," replied Trotzky. "We are not yet in the position of Persia or Armenia, but Russia is being torn to pieces and our party is now working for national defense. We will continue the war."

"Do you really think that the army you demobilized, that the peasants who have been sent to their homes, could be induced to fight for Russia again?" I asked.

Trotzky answered:—

"We are taking the military experts of the old régime. We are not afraid of them. We want their experience, their knowledge, but not their politics in the army. We will have a much smaller army than before. It will be composed of young peasants and workingmen."

He opened a telegram which lay on his table and said:—

"I have just received this telegram informing me that I was appointed head of the Military Committee. In fact, I consider the reorganization of the army so important that I resigned my post of Commissary for Foreign Affairs in order to take charge of this work."

I asked Trotzky what the Bolshevist government was planning to do in the near future.

"We will move from Moscow if necessary. We will make the Ural our base if we must. We will fight until the social revolution triumphs."

"How soon do you expect that to happen?"

"Before the end of the war," he snapped.

Several days after this interview I succeeded in securing the historic letter which Leo Trotzky sent from Brest-Litovsk to Lenine and Stalin, in which he suggested the famous formula, "We announce the termination of the war and demobilization, without signing any peace," and in which he predicted the revolution in Germany.

The following is a translation of this remarkable document:

"Dear Vladimir Ilyitch:

"It is impossible to sign their peace. They already have agreed with fictitious governments of Poland, Lithuania, Courland and others concerning territorial concessions and military and customs treaties. In view of 'self-determination' these provinces, according to German interpretation, are now independent States, and as independent States they have already concluded territorial and other agreements with Germany and Austria-Hungary.

"To-day, I put these questions squarely and received a reply leaving no room for misunderstandings. Everything is stenographed. To-morrow, we shall present the same questions in writing. We cannot sign their peace. My plan is this:—

"We announce the termination of the war and demobilization without signing any peace. We declare we cannot participate in the looting war of the Allies, nor can we sign a looting peace. The fate of Poland, Lithuania and Courland we place upon the responsibility of the German working people.

"The Germans will be unable to attack us after we declare the war ended. At any rate, it would be very difficult for Germany to attack us, because of her internal conditions. The Scheidemannists adopted a formal resolution to break with the government if it makes annexationist demands of the Russian revolution.

"*The Berliner Tageblatt* and the *Vossiche Zeitung* demand an understanding with Russia by all means. The centrists favor an agreement. The internal strife is demoralizing the government. Bitter controversy is raging in the press over the struggle on the western front.

"We declare we end the war but we do not sign a peace. They will be unable to make an offensive against us— *Verteidigungskrieg*. If they attack us our position will be no worse than now, when they have the opportunity to announce *kuendigung* and declare us agents of England and Wilson (after his speech) and to commence an attack.

"We must have your decision. We can still drag on negotiations for two, three or four days. Afterward they must be broken off. I see no other solution than that proposed. I clasp your hand.

"Your TROTZKY.

"Answer by direct wire:—'I agree to your plan' or 'I don't agree.' "

In Christiania the captain of the vessel on which Leo Trotzky left New York last year described to me how he was taken off by the British authorities at Halifax, who suspected that he was going to Russia to carry on a campaign for separate peace. Trotzky refused to leave the vessel when the officers asked him to follow them ashore. He was carried off by several men.

"Who knows?" said one of the British officers to me at Halifax. "If we had kept Trotzky here perhaps the war would have been over long ago and history might have taken a different course. We wanted to hold him, but Milukov and Kerensky insisted upon our releasing him."

GENERAL SUKHOMLINOFF

Petrograd, 1918.

I MET General Sukhomlinoff, former Minister of War, in the Prison of the Crosses in April. With him, in the same ward, were former Minister of Justice Scheglovitoff and former Minister of the Interior Khvostoff. These men were characteristic representatives of the autocracy that committed suicide.

General Sukhomlinoff, who was Minister of War for eight years under the Tsar, was made the scapegoat for the reverses of the Russian forces in 1915 and was thrown into prison by the government of the Tsar charged with high treason and graft. He was accused of making misleading statements to the effect that the Russian armies had all the necessary munitions at a time when Russian troops were forced to fight the Germans and Austrians with sticks and stones instead of guns and bayonets.

General Sukhomlinoff was placed on trial by the provisional government, headed by Alexander Kerensky, and was sentenced to imprisonment for life. Mme. Sukhomlinoff, his beautiful young wife, who was kept in solitary confinement in the fortress of Peter and Paul for about six months, charged with having aided her husband in affairs involving graft and treason, was acquitted.

Recalling the sensational trial and some of Sukhomlinoff's references to the causes of the reverses of the Russian armies, I was eager to hear his story and the details

concerning the outbreak of the war.   But the problem was
how to enter the Prison of the Crosses.

I had heard of the terrors that prevailed in the prisons
under the Bolshevist régime.   I had heard how prisoners
were taken out at night by the guards and shot in the yard
without any trial or hearing.   I had heard of prisoners
shot on the way by the soldiers who were to transfer them
to other prisons or hospitals.   And I felt that perhaps because of this chaos it might be easier to visit the Prison of
the Crosses, where members of the Tsar's régime were kept
together with the members of the Kerensky government.

I soon convinced myself that the affair was much simpler
than I had imagined.   I spoke to several friends about my
desire to interview Sukhomlinoff.   One of them told me
that he knew the commissary of the prison, as he had frequently visited his friend, who had been imprisoned by the
Bolsheviki.   I asked him to accompany me and introduce
me to the commissary.

We came to the Prison of the Crosses in the afternoon.
A large crowd was waiting outside the iron grating, with
cards in their hands.   It was visiting day and those who
had permits had to wait for their turn.   There were many
women in mourning, pale-faced and sad-eyed.

We walked to the head of the line and asked the soldier
at the gate for the commissary.   I mentioned that I represented the *New York Herald*, and he opened the gate.
My friend led me through the stifling corridors to the office
of the commissary.   The commissary and his assistant
were eating at the time.   My friend introduced me to the
commissary and asked whether I could see Sukhomlinoff.
The commissary exchanged glances with his assistant and
said:—

"I don't think I have the right to permit you to speak to him."

The assistant added: "No. We can't let you see him."

"I just want to see how you keep the symbols of the Tsar's régime in prison," I said.

Suddenly the commissary asked:—

"Didn't you have an interview with Trotzky?"

"Yes."

"What would you talk about with Sukhomlinoff?"

"I will talk to him only about the past—about the Tsar's régime and the war. Not a word about present conditions."

He hesitated, then said:—

"Well, you may go in, but do not discuss with him anything concerning present conditions."

My friend and I went into the ward where the former members of the Tsar's Cabinet were sitting. Sukhomlinoff was drinking tea near his cot. A little distance away Sheglovitoff and Khvostoff were talking quietly.

My friend introduced me to all the three. Sukhomlinoff invited me to have tea with him and we talked for more than two hours. General Sukhomlinoff, who is seventy years old, but looks older, commenced by saying:—

"From a Minister of War I have become a proletariat in the real sense of the word. My trial was slow in coming and the judges were neither just nor merciful."

"During your trial you mentioned that the Tsar telephoned you about a telegram from the Kaiser asking him to stop mobilizing the Russian army. Can you give me the details of that conversation?" I asked.

"It was on July 1, past midnight," replied General

Sukhomlinoff. "I was called to the telephone to speak with the Emperor at Peterhof. The Emperor said to me that he had received a telegram from Wilhelm informing him that he did not start the mobilization of the German army and asked him to stop mobilizing our army. I replied that according to the information of our General Staff the mobilization of the German army was going on in full swing and that it would be impossible to stop our mobilization just now, because for technical reasons it would delay our mobilization at least two months, and by that time the Germans could take Petrograd.

" 'Do you think the Kaiser is deceiving me when he writes that he has not commenced mobilizing the German army?' asked the Emperor.

" 'I think he is not telling you the truth,' I answered, advising him to communicate with the Chief of the General Staff concerning the information in his possession on this subject. This ended my conversation with the Emperor over the telephone that night.

"I immediately telephoned to Chief of General Staff Yanushkevitch and told him that the Emperor would call him on the telephone soon and asked him to give the Emperor all the information in his possession about the course of the German mobilization and the danger of stopping our mobilization.

"About twenty minutes later Yanushkevitch telephoned to me, informing me that the Emperor had spoken to him, that he told the whole truth to the Emperor, but the Emperor insisted that the mobilization of the Russian army be stopped.

" 'And I am telling you not to stop the mobilization of

our army!' I said to Yanushkevitch. Next morning we
received official information that the mobilization of the
German army was going on rapidly throughout the country. Then the Emperor thanked me for my firmness. It
was quite clear that the Kaiser tried to deceive the Tsar in
order to gain time."

"I understand that you met the Kaiser several times
and that you discussed with him the question of the secret
treaty between Germany and Russia. Is it true?" I
asked.

"I met the Kaiser three times. Twice I met him at
Russian manœuvres, and the third time I lunched with him
at Potsdam. We did not discuss the Russo-German treaty.
The only thing the Kaiser seemed interested in was the
question of Turkey. After lunch he invited me to his
study, and taking out a map of Turkey he asked me a number of questions regarding that country."

I noticed that General Sukhomlinoff did not want to talk
frankly about his interview with the Kaiser. I turned our
conversation to his own case. Then he spoke freely.

"Our reverses in Eastern Prussia were due entirely to
the blunders made at our headquarters," said the former
Minister of War. "They looked around for a scapegoat.
They wanted to find as big a scapegoat as possible, and
they selected me, the Minister of War. It was embarrassing to hold the commanders at the front responsible for
the reverses, because the Commander-in-Chief directed their
activities and interfered even with their instructions.
Since affairs took a sad turn at the front they looked around
for a scapegoat in the rear—and they held me responsible
for everything. They blamed me for all the reverses, al-

though Grand Duke Nicholas never confided any of his plans to me, and even arranged matters so that I could not be present while he was reporting to the Tsar when he came to the headquarters.

"When people familiar with military affairs were astonished at the absurd experiments of the Grand Duke which resulted in the defeat of our three armies, those responsible for the fiasco explained that everything was due to the lack of munitions and provisions in our armies. They contrived this intrigue and insisted upon my removal. But it was necessary for them to prove that I had neglected my duties. They appointed in my place an enemy of mine and organized a commission under the chairmanship of the senile General Petrov for the purpose of investigating the causes of the lack of munitions.

"General Polivanoff, with the aid of A. Gutchkoff, commenced to attack me in the press and in the Duma, circulating all sorts of gossip and slanders. The past master in shady affairs and espionage, Prince Andronikoff, manufactured an anonymous denunciation of myself and my wife and sent it to the investigating commission.

"Among other things, I was convicted on the ground that I had neglected my duties. I was appointed Minister of War in 1909. During the five years preceding this war I succeeded in accomplishing a great deal for the Russian army. In 1904 the Germans did not yet consider themselves ready for a war at two fronts, and they rejoiced that we were being beaten in the fields of Manchuria, even though their factories supplied us with munitions. But that war left our armed forces so disorganized that after the conclusion of peace our most important problem was the reorganization of the Russian army."

I asked General Sukhomlinoff, former Minister of War, in his prison cell, whether the Grand Dukes interfered with the War Department, and whether their work during the war was helpful. The old man, who but a short time ago was one of the most powerful figures in the Russian Empire, replied:—

"During my stay in prison I have worked upon my memoirs, in which I describe in detail the blunders made by the Russian government during the war. I have not the manuscript with me, but my wife knows where it is. If you like, I will be glad to give you a note to my wife, and she will let you examine the manuscript. You are at liberty to select for publication any passages you may be interested in."

He gave me a note to Mme. Sukhomlinoff. On the following day I familiarized myself with General Sukhomlinoff's memoirs and selected a number of extracts for reproduction.

Speaking of Grand Duke Sergius Mikhailovitch, General Sukhomlinoff said:—

"When he was appointed Inspector of the Artillery it was understood that he was to co-operate with me and follow my instructions. Instead of this he took charge of the entire artillery department, gave instructions without consulting me or General Polivanoff, who was really responsible for the work of the department, and reported to the Tsar personally without informing us of the contents of his report.

"I criticised such an abnormal state of affairs, and the Grand Duke never forgave me, mobilizing all his talents for intrigues against me. For instance, when I visited the Perm munition works and found that certain guns were not made in eighteen months because no reply was received from the Grand Duke regarding a misunderstanding in the design I criticised the 'red tape' in his department. Then the Grand Duke insinuated that I travelled to the Perm munition works and to other places merely for the purpose of getting travelling expenses from the government.

"He was personally so partial to the Schneider-Krezo munition works that the mention of other firms which could produce munitions more quickly and reasonably aroused his indignation and he again insinuated that I was materially interested in these firms. Thus a vicious circle was created and the strongest opposition to the establishment in Russia of any new great munition works, as in other European countries. The Schneider orders were filled also through the Putiloff works. The Grand Duke interfered directly with any orders placed by other departments without his knowledge. When I criticised him he tried to prove that I interfered in behalf of other munition works because I was personally interested in them.

"As to the accusations that I betrayed Russia, it is an absolute fabrication, and however hard the judges tried to convict me on this point they were unable to do it. My work was interfered with by the grand dukes, especially Nicholas and Sergius. On account of them we lost four years of most valuable time. Grand Duke Nicholas misled the Emperor and failed to do his work as chairman of the Council of Defense of the Empire. He hindered the work of the commanders in their preparations in the event of war. He kept me from being present when he reported to the Tsar, fearing that his prestige as commander might be affected. He wasted war supplies unnecessarily when he knew that we had to use them judiciously.

"He permitted the inexcusable operations in Eastern Prussia and the march to the Carpathians, thus destroying three of our splendid armies. He abused his authority with regard to military courts and stopped at nothing in order to rehabilitate himself. He could hardly boast of chivalrous conduct becoming a Commander-in-Chief.

"My trial was a travesty on justice. Instead of placing me upon the bench of the accused they should have tried a few grand dukes and other high dignitaries of that government.

"I am seventy years old now. Under the old laws of the Tsar's government any criminal reaching the age of seventy in prison is set free. But here I am in prison under a socialist régime."

Before leaving the Prison of the Crosses, I had a brief talk with former Minister of Justice Scheglovitoff, who was responsible for staging the Beilis affair. I also spoke with Khvostoff, Minister of the Interior of the Tsar's government.

"I understand that you, as Minister of the Interior, tried to organize the assassination of Rasputin. Is that true?" I asked.

"Rasputin was the evil genius of the Tsar," he replied. "He made and unmade members of the Cabinet and exerted the most terrible influence upon the Tsar, even in matters relating to the war. I did make an attempt to have him 'removed,' but I failed. I didn't do it cleverly enough. So they caught me."

This is the simple story Khvostoff related as to how he, as Minister of the Interior, tried to bring about the assassination of Rasputin. The reasons he gave for his attempt on the life of the lewd, illiterate Siberian peasant who dominated Russia for many years is an eloquent commentary on the last days of the Tsarist régime.

"Do you think the Germans are coming to Petrograd?" he suddenly asked me.

"Why do you ask this question now?" I asked.

"Because I am in a most peculiar position," he answered. "When I was a member of the Duma for several years, I fought in every way possible Germany's commercial domination of Russia. I prepared an exhaustive memorandum on the subject and outlined a plan of combatting this German invasion even before the war. And now I find myself in the peculiar position that I may be freed from this prison by the Germans if they enter Petrograd. Such is the irony of fate."

As I walked out of the prison I heard some of the returning visitors say that there had been disturbances in the prison the night before and that several prisoners had been shot by the guards. Outside the prison gates, here and there, the sidewalk was stained with blood.

"Every night they shoot prisoners here," said one of the women visitors dressed in mourning. "They always give an excuse that the prisoners attempted to escape."

Mme. Sukhomlinoff related to me how she was kept in solitary confinement in the fortress of Peter and Paul for six months.

"It was filthy and stifling there, and the food they gave us was unfit to eat," she said.

The young wife of the former Minister of War had a taste of what some of the noblest men and women who had dreamed of Russian freedom experienced for years. Then she told me of her efforts to obtain her husband's release from prison.

"I have visited most of the Bolshevist Commissaries," she said. "I have pointed out to them that under the Tsar's laws my husband, who is seventy years old now, would have been released, and I asked them to free him. I said to them General Sukhomlinoff is not only too old to be dangerous to any political party, but he is so discredited by the stories brought out before the trial and at the trial that you could not find three men who would support him or any movement in which he might be interested. Each one of the Commissaries I visited agreed with me, and said that he would have no objection to set him free. I asked each of them to give me these statements in writing, but they all declined. They said they were afraid that my husband would be killed by the soldiers if they released him."

General Sukhomlinoff, Minister of War under Tsar Nicholas, who spoke to me so frankly in his prison cell about the blunders of the Russian autocracy, continued his remarkable revelations which he made in his hitherto unpublished memoirs. Describing his removal from the post of Minister of War, he said:—

"During 1914 I reviewed at a special audience with the Tsar all that had been done in my department. He examined the report I submitted and expressed great surprise that so much had been accomplished during five years.

"But Grand Duke Nicholas, to rehabilitate himself both at home and abroad as Commander-in-Chief, considered it of the greatest importance to place upon me all the blame for all his unsuccessful experiments, and endeavored to stage the whole affair so that he could not be held in any way responsible for our defeats.

"He urged the Tsar to have me removed. Instead of an official order I received a personal letter from the Tsar, which shows clearly that he removed me not because he believed I had neglected my duties, but because of the pressure brought upon him by Grand Duke Nicholas.

"This is the letter the Tsar wrote me in his own hand:—

" 'Headquarters, June 11, 1915.

" 'Vladimir Alexandrovitch:

" 'After long consideration I have come to the conclusion that the interests of Russia and the army demand your leaving the post of Minister of War at this moment. Having had a conversation just now with Grand Duke Nicholas Nikolayevitch, I am convinced of this definitely.

" 'I am writing to you so that you may learn of this from me first. It is painful for me to express to you this decision, especially since I saw you only yesterday.

" 'We have worked so many years together and there have never been any misunderstandings between us. I thank you heartily for all your work and for all the energies you have spent for the welfare and upbuilding of our army. Unprejudiced history will give you a verdict more generous than that of your contemporaries.

" 'God be with you.

" 'Respectfully yours,

" 'NICHOLAS.' "

"When I became Minister of War in 1909 the Russian army was not fit to fight. In 1914 the army was in condition to mobilize rapidly and to fight," General Sukhomlinoff continued. "The reason why Russia was not prop-

erly equipped with war supplies was that none of the belligerents had expected so long a war.   All that could be done
in less than five years was done, but we had neither the
time nor the means for better preparations in a country so
backward in her industrial development as Russia.

"But Grand Duke Nicholas interfered with my department much more than that.   He was a Grand Duke, but
not at all a great commander.   But he exerted tremendous
influence upon the former Tsar and hated me because I had
predicted the failure of his project to reorganize the army.

"The tutor of Grand Duke Nicholas, General Skalon,
thus characterized his pupil:—'He is cruel by nature,
heartless, haughty, impulsive, base and cowardly.'   This
characterization is merciless, but true.   I may say that he
spoiled whatever he undertook to do.

"The late Premier Stolypin, speaking of the Grand
Duke's work as chairman of the Council of the Defense of
the Empire, said it was the work of an inmate of an insane
asylum.   He introduced a number of measures which
served as the beginning of the liquidation of the Russian
army and which culminated in the downfall of our military prestige.

"Grand Duke Nicholas was my enemy ever since my
appointment as Minister of War, and I could not depend
upon his co-operation.   Besides, he was accorded the privilege of making personal reports to the Tsar concerning the
military district of Petrograd without the knowledge of the
Minister of War.   As a result of this a number of serious
blunders were made.

"Thus, for instance, General Hazenkampf, the assistant
to Grand Duke Nicholas, lost the plans of the Fortress

Committee concerning the defense of the Gulf of Finland. All the efforts of the secret police department to find these most important documents proved futile.

"Not a word was said to me at the time the papers were lost. When I learned of this I mentioned it to the Tsar, but he remarked that the Grand Duke had already adopted measures to find the documents. It is quite possible that these documents fell into the hands of the German Embassy and proved very useful to the German government during the war.

"In reviewing the troops the Minister of War is regarded higher than the commander of the army. In my case the Grand Duke violated this rule. I considered it an insubordination and mentioned this to the Tsar. The Grand Duke, who was very ambitious and vain, never concealed his animosity to me and deliberately tried to offend me. When I reviewed the troops and greeted them he turned away demonstratively and continued to talk to the members of his staff.

"Taking advantage of the weak character of the Tsar, he acted as he pleased, and my assistant, General Polivanov, eager to ingratiate himself with the Grand Duke Nicholas, betrayed me.

"In 1911 I suggested to the Tsar that the commanders of our armies meet in Petrograd for a strategical conference in view of the possibility of war at our western front. The Tsar liked the idea very much and ordered half of the Winter Palace set aside for this purpose, as he desired to participate in the conference in the rôle of Commander-in-Chief. The General Staff prepared an elaborate program for the conference. The commanders of the armies arrived in

Petrograd. Then the Grand Duke Nicholas invited them all to dinner and told them that he was opposed to the conference. After the dinner he presented them to the Tsar, and an hour before the opening of the conference I received a note from Tsarskoye Selo informing me that the conference was postponed.

"I explained to the Tsar that the questions to be considered at the conference would be of great importance to him personally, that he would thus be able to familiarize himself with the commanders who might have to lead millions of men to fight, that in the event these commanders were not sufficiently equipped for their important tasks we would have time to replace them by abler men.

"But the Grand Duke did not like this plan. He said that the Minister of War wanted to examine the commanders and that such a thing should not be permitted. He urged Count Frederiks to tell the Tsar that the holding of such a conference at the Winter Palace was almost a sacrilege.

"The Grand Duke succceeded in convincing the Tsar that the conference should not be held. Thus I was placed in a position where I had to resign. Unfortunately, the Tsar refused to accept my resignation. Although the commanders had been ordered to return to their posts the Tsar despatched new orders to the commanders and the conference did take place under my chairmanship. The Tsar was not present, nor was Grand Duke Nicholas. He was afraid of the examination, and, unfortunately for Russia, he proved during this war that he failed to pass his examination.

"As chairman of the Imperial Defense Committee, he

wasted four years, interfering with my work, and afterward blamed me for all his blunders at the front, after he had practically ruined the three armies.

"The Grand Duke's animosity toward me was so widely known that even the German press frequently published accounts of my leaving the post of Minister of War on account of the differences existing between Grand Duke Nicholas and myself.

"In addition to his weaknesses as Commander-in-Chief, he was so influenced by his passion for spiritualism, in which his wife, Anastasya Nikolayevna, believed blindly, that he frequently sought in spiritualism solutions for some of the most serious military problems.

"My stand with regard to the mobilization of the Russian army averted a grave danger.

"At first the Tsar wanted to assume the chief command himself, but the Council of Ministers persuaded him to remain in Petrograd. Then the Tsar offered me the post of Commander in Chief of the Russian armies. I did not accept it because I knew that with Grand Duke Nicholas remaining in Petrograd near the Tsar, upon whom he exerted an enormous influence, my work would be constantly hindered.

"Then the Grand Duke was appointed Commander-in-Chief.

"The beginning of our campaign of 1914 was very favorable to us. Our army was so quickly concentrated that the Germans believed we had undertaken our mobilization secretly long before the war.

"The energetic operations of our northern armies in Eastern Prussia, our successful resistance of the German forces by our centre and the occupation of Galicia by our southern armies—all this indicated that the march of our armies to Berlin might be successful.

"The Austrians were driven to the Carpathians. Then, instead of the plan of action I elaborated, which would have assured our success, operations were undertaken by our northern armies in Eastern Prussia, which led to a catastrophe, and at the southern front we left Lemberg for some reason and undertook an offensive beyond the Carpathians, where we suffered another great defeat and thus definitely paralyzed our center.

"An old philosopher once said that in war many claim credit for a victory, while defeats are usually heaped upon one man, who is made the scapegoat. In this instance I was made the scapegoat. And yet Grand Duke Nicholas Mikhailovitch, in his memoirs published in 1917, describing his own impressions of the army, wrote:—'The Commander-in-Chief made many blunders not only from a strategical point of view, but because he failed to coordinate his operations with those of the Allies.'

"No great commander is insured at all times against a defeat, but the Grand Duke did not want to bear the responsibility for any of his failures and looked about for a convenient victim. Then the Grand Duke commenced to urge the Tsar that I be removed from the post of Minister of War.

"Grand Duke Nicholas offered his services to the Tsar and submitted a project for the reorganization of the War Department.

"In 1905, when I came from Kiev to Petrograd, the Tsar asked my opinion concerning the Grand Duke's plan of reorganizing the army. I considered it my duty to oppose the plan of the Grand Duke. The project concerning the

Chief of the General Staff was prepared by General Palitzin and was a poor translation of the German plan. Without hesitation I declared that such a plan was worthless for Russia, and that while it might be suitable for Wilhelm it was not for Nicholas.

"The Emperor agreed with me at the time, but after I had returned to Kiev the Grand Duke Nicholas insisted upon his plan and it was adopted. The Grand Duke never forgave me for my criticism. According to his project, the various departments in the War Office worked independently and there was no unity of action. In 1909 everybody recognized that the Russian Army was not fit to fight. The reports of the various commanders submitted to the Emperor left no room for doubt on this point.

"My prediction came true, and I had to undertake to repair that which was so thoroughly spoilt. We had no army and no fleet which could guard our country against an enemy's attacks, and we surely were not in a position to threaten any other Power with an attack.

"Just before I was appointed Minister of War, in March, 1909, there was a conference at Tsarskoye Selo under the chairmanship of the Emperor regarding the annexation of Bosnia and Herzegovina. General Rediger was asked whether our army was ready for active operations. He replied that our army was not ready. When Minister of Justice Scheglovitov, who is sitting right here, asked General Rediger whether our army was in a position to defend our country against attacks upon us the General answered categorically that the Russian army was not fit to fight. The Japanese war exhausted us, and the immediate demobilization completely disorganized our army."

After I had left Russia I learned that General Sukhomlinoff and a number of other prisoners of the old Tsarist régime had been released by the Bolsheviki.

The story of Sukhomlinoff is a characteristic page of the incompetence, intrigues and rottenness of the Tsar's régime, which collapsed so easily.

MARQUIS OKUMA

Tokio, September, 1918.

BEFORE entering Siberia I sought the views of Japanese statesmen concerning the Allied expedition in Russia. I interviewed Marquis Okuma, formerly Premier and the Chancellor of Wasada University, perhaps the foremost Japanese statesman best known as the "Sage of Wasada" or the "grand old man" of the land of the Rising Sun.

I asked Marquis Okuma what Japan was doing for Russia and what Japan's motives were in this expedition. Marquis Okuma said:—

"It is most important to restore Russia as a great state. It is most important for the world to adjust the balance of power by restoring Russia. Russia may readjust herself as a constitutional monarchy or as a republic of federated states like the United States, but I have not the slightest doubt that Russia will be once more a great state.

"Recently I outlined the way of saving Russia. I urged the Allies, and particularly the United States, which entered the war for motives of justice and humanity, to pay more serious attention to the present disordered state of Russia and to do their utmost to save Russia from complete ruin. In order to save Russia there is nothing that is more urgent than the reorganization of her army. Japan, as Russia's close neighbor, is geographically best situated to take the lead in relieving Russia. If Russia is saved and her disbanded troops are reorganized, how much would it conduce to the welfare of the hundred and eighty million people of Russia who would again prove themselves worthy supporters of the Allied cause!

"There is only one way to save Russia and that is to reorganize her troops and supply them with munitions and war materials. The territory of Russia is so vast that a victorious Allied expedition into Siberia could hardly expect to pass the Urals. The Allies themselves can hardly rehabilitate Russia completely, but they can act as advisers and guardians. In my opinion it is our task to help reorganize the Russian troops and then the Russian people themselves will take in hand the rebuilding of the national structure of Russia.

"If left alone Russia is sure to come into her own at some future day, but we cannot afford to lose time by waiting.

"When I compare Russia with China," went on Marquis Okuma, "I find that it will be much easier for Russia to adapt herself to the present conditions of the world. China has her own ancient civilization. She neglected to adopt the new civilization, therefore it is so difficult for China to adjust herself to the standards of other great nations. Her own old civilization has made things complicated for her. But it is quite different with Russia. Russia is comparatively young. Russia has no such ancient traditions to hinder her. The Slavic people have assimiliated Western culture and civilization. Therefore Russia's plight is, after all, not quite so complicated as that of China.

"Russia is so vast that it will be hard to restore a monarchical sovereignty. I believe that a democratic form of government would be far better for the restoration of Russia. I really feel that a form of government similar to that of the United States would be ideal for Russia. And it is most important for the entire world that the various forces within the Russian people should be united under a democratic government—indeed it is most important for the future of civilization that Russia shall be a great factor in the affairs of the world. The restoration of Russia as a great state will contribute much to the welfare of the world and maintain universal peace."

Marquis Okuma paused for a time. Then his face brightened with a broad smile, his eyes beaming good-naturedly, as he continued:—

"When I was a boy I had the impression that Russia was terrible. That was the general impression in those days in Japan. We looked upon Russia as upon a great Power full of terrors for us. We firmly believed that some day she would spring upon us and crush us. The people of Japan always feared Russia believing that she was bent on aggrandizement. Naturally we had to prepare ourselves for self-defense.

"But when we came into closer contact with Russia, when we commenced to understand her, we realized that she was not terrible at all. The Russian people are honest, simple, innocent; on the whole they are good people. The fear we entertained of Russia was due to a great extent to the machinations of several bureaucrats, who were ambitious and selfish and who were the power behind the Russian throne.

"I feel absolutely confident that Russia will become our friend, just as the United States and Japan have become good friends. Russia has experienced and is still experiencing an awful misfortune. We have a deep sense of sympathy for the Russian people. And, as I have said before, since Russia is not burdened with deeply rooted traditions, she will soon shape her new destiny under a democratic form of government."

I asked Marquis Okuma for his views on Bolshevism, and whether he thought that it would spread to other countries. He replied:—

"The disease of Bolshevism is a product of special environment and special circumstances. Bolshevism in Russia was caused by the excesses of the former Russian government. Bolshevism seems to contain a part of the doctrines of Karl Marx. Now consider how Marxism is operating even in Germany, the home of Marx. The social democrats there modified Marxism to a great extent. When we examine the program of the social democrats we find that it is nothing else than simple democracy, without extremism. Circumstances alter and modify theories, and actualities mitigate doctrines even in Germany. All these extreme theories in the United States and in England and France are greatly modified. But in Russia the former government was bad beyond belief. Thus extreme reaction gave birth to extreme Bolshevism. On the one hand Russia had Tolstoyism, with the doctrine of non-resistance, and on the other Russia has Leninism with the doctrine of terrorism. These sprang as a result of terrible oppression and the unfair distribution of wealth and land. It is most deplorable that men like Lenine, who had dreams and fancies of social reconstruction, should be working indirectly as the instruments of militaristic Kaiserism.

"It is possible that new forces may find a response among various nations, but these theories will be modified under healthy conditions—in England or the United States, for instance—for Bolshevism cannot thrive in these countries, for the very simple reason that there are no grounds to justify such extreme ideas. It is true that the distribution of wealth is not perfect anywhere and a period of reconstruction must come, but it will not be accompanied by extremism."

I asked whether Bolshevism was not spreading to Japan. Marquis Okuma answered:—

"We have no reason to fear the spread of this disease in Japan. Moderate socialism may meet with some success here, but there is no room for extremism in Japan. After the war there will be a tendency in every country for more democracy and for a more just distribution of wealth, but Japan has little to fear Bolshevism, for, though our country is a monarchy, the fundamental principle of our government is democracy. It has been so for many years. Our government is concerned with the general welfare of the people. Ours is indeed a government for the people. We have a real democracy without using the term democracy. It is the very keynote of our government. Therefore there is no place in Japan for such extremism as wrecked Russia."

Regarding the readjustment after the war Marquis Okuma said:—

"I have always admired America's spirit of justice, especially her participation in this war for humanitarian, unselfish motives in the struggle for the allied democracies of the world. If Germany is completely defeated and the militarism of Frederick the Great is swept away it will not be difficult to secure durable peace. There have been certain groups of bureaucratic statesmen, especially the militarists of Germany, who were prompted by the mistaken idea of aggression, and these people have frequently been the cause of trouble. Wars have almost always been the products of such mistaken ideas. Now the most important issue before the world is whether militarism can be completely crushed or not. If this war ends by crushing such dangerous militarism absolutely the peace conference will find smooth sailing in the new adjustment. As a rule international conferences have been burdened with difficulties and have proved unsatisfactory. The diplomatic tricks, intrigues and secret ambitions that prevailed at such conferences were caused by militarism and so long as international conferences are ruled by such tricks and mistaken ideas no real readjustment is possible. But when the fundamental cause is removed, when militarism is crushed, the international conference will find a proper solution for the world problems. There will be no room for the spirit of military aggression in such a conference. The conference will be ruled by a new spirit—by the spirit so often and so eloquently expounded by President Wilson. When the purpose of the Allies is achieved there will be real national freedom. The national map of Europe will be changed. Even then the readjustment will be easy, because the spirit of national freedom will prevail. New nations will come up, small nations will secure their independence and the peace of the world will not be disturbed.

"I am looking forward not only to a political but also to an economic improvement and readjustment after the war. When the world order will be readjusted at the close of this war commercial and economic relations will no longer be dictated for political purposes. Economic relations will become independent of political intrigues. Then free competition—in the best sense of the term—will prevail, and the welfare of masses will be promoted everywhere.

For the general welfare of the world I hope that peace will be concluded by the achievement of America's purposes and by the realization of President Wilson's plans for universal durable peace and world justice."

ROBERT CECIL

On the day of my arrival in London I interviewed one of Europe's foremost statesmen, Lord Robert Cecil.

My first question was about the League of Nations, but this he declined to discuss, saying:

"I am afraid I cannot speak on this subject as there is danger that whatever I say about it might be misconstrued in America particularly at this moment."

I then asked Lord Robert Cecil whether there would be a change of policy toward Russia in the near future and whether he was in favor of resuming trade relations with Soviet Russia. He replied:

"I have always been opposed to a policy of military intervention in Russia after the armistice. Since we are not going to fight the Soviet Government of Russia, why not trade with Russia? Even if we disagree with that government, why should we starve the Russian people? Such a policy is both unfair and unwise. It seems to me that trade relations with Russia will be resumed before long. In fact, I understand that considerable commercial relations have already been established with Russia through Esthonia which concluded peace with the Soviet Government. England has not yet been trading there, as far as I know, but I am told that other countries, including America, are dealing with Russia right now—that is, they are dealing with Esthonia which is dealing with Russia. I can of course understand the difficulty and embarrassment on the part of some governments in treating officially with the Soviets, in giving them official recognition just now, but I cannot see why the Russian people should be made to suffer because of this. We have no quarrel with the Russian people."

I asked Lord Robert for his views concerning the terms of the peace treaty of Versailles. He said:

"The territorial arrangements affecting Germany as stipulated in the treaty are not so bad. The territorial arrangements with Austria are of course much worse. But the economic arrangements with both are utterly indefensible. It is only right to say that the device adopted—the undefined indemnity—was not an American invention."

"Could not the United States, then, exert sufficient influence at the peace conference to prevent this device from being embodied in the treaty?" I asked.

Lord Robert Cecil answered:

"Of course strong efforts were exerted, but in the end a compromise was made."

"Would you say, on the whole, that you are pleased with the outcome of the war?" I asked.

To which he answered:

"Of course it was better to win the war than to have been defeated by Germany."

"That goes without saying," I remarked. "What I meant was whether you are pleased with the outcome of the peace as worked out in Paris."

"I certainly am not," he replied. "The economic arrangements of the German peace treaty are an insane policy. In effect the Allies have said to the Germans: 'However hard you work, you cannot count on reaping any benefit from your exertion. The more money you make the more will we take from you by way of indemnity.' This has contributed to the demoralization of the will and energy of the German people which so many observers report. It has helped to render a section of them desperate and hopeless, ready for any adventure which may change their lot. It has been I am convinced one of the greatest incentives to German Bolshevism. It has also made it difficult if not impossible for Germany to obtain outside credit. Who would lend to a debtor the whole of whose assets are already pledged to others? Finally, by keeping alive in the minds of some of the belligerent nations a hope of receiving very large indemnity it has prevented them from making the efforts and sacrifices required by their financial position."

"Do you think there will be any changes in the terms of the treaty with Germany?" I asked.

"Yes, I believe there will be changes," he answered. "Our Prime Minister has recently asked Germany to submit new economic proposals and has promised to consider them favorably if at all reasonable. Strangely enough, the most important questions were not those that attracted most attention at the Peace Conference. The questions that were most widely discussed—for instance, as to what shall be done with Danzig and the Saare Valley—were comparatively unimportant. The really vital matters were economic. The result was deplorable and some way out will unquestionably have to be found. It may be that the Reparation Commission will make a drastic use of its powers in modifying the terms of the indemnity. It may be the Treaty itself will have to be amended. But whatever is done, no time should be lost. The economic position in Europe is steadily getting worse and may become past remedy. What a pity we have not the full influence of the United States to prevent the threatened disaster."

The following letter from Lord Robert Cecil is characteristic:

"Foreign Office,
"*October 7th, 1915.*

"*Dear Mr. Bernstein:*

"I am much obliged to you for your letter from Rotterdam, as well as that from Berne. I am sorry that I did not reply to the Berne letter; I quite thought that I had done so, but I suppose I must have overlooked it.

"I am most grateful to you for sending me the further information about the position of the Jews in Russia. Everyone must sympathize with them in the sufferings which they have endured. Indeed, quite apart from any other cause, the mere evacuation of the conquered territories both by Jews and Russians has entailed, I am afraid, terrible hardships. Great efforts are, I understand, being made to assist these poor people, both by sympathizers outside Russia, and by the Russians themselves. It is incidents of this kind which make one realise what really lies underneath the glories and glamour of war, and the man who is responsible, whoever he may be, for having loosed upon the world this terrible series of calamities, is surely one of the greatest criminals in the world's history.

"Your sincerely,
"ROBERT CECIL."

In response to a letter of mine, accompanied by my

article entitled "In Sackcloth and Ashes," depicting the tragedies of Belgium, Poland and the Jewish people in the World War, Sir Edward Grey sent me the following remarkable note:

> "Foreign Office,
> "*June 5th, 1916.*

"*Dear Mr. Bernstein:*

"I am much obliged for your letter enclosing a pamphlet which you have written and which has safely reached me.

"As regards the questions which you asked in the last two paragraphs of your letter, since the latter was written I made a speech in the House of Commons with regard to terms and prospects of peace. There is really nothing I can add to this when it is taken in conjunction with the other pronouncements made both by the Prime Minister and myself on the subject. In case what I said has not been reported fully in the United States press, I enclose a copy taken from the official records of the House of Commons in case you care to have it.

"I believe the best work neutrals can do for the moment is to work up opinion for such an agreement between nations as will prevent a war like this from happening again.

"If nations had been united in such an agreement and prompt and resolute to insist in July, 1914, that the dispute must be referred to Conference or to the Hague and that the Belgian Treaty must be observed there would have been no war.

> "Yours very truly,
> "E. GREY."

LEONID KRASSIN

London, 1920.

SEVERAL days after Leonid Krassin's arrival in London in 1920 I met him and discussed with him the problems which stirred the whole world at the time. He was in the midst of conferences with the British Foreign Office and was besieged by interviewers representing the leading newspapers of the world. He refused to give any interviews for publication. Finally I succeeded in meeting him at midnight and secured the following important statements from the ablest and most reasonable representative of the Soviet Government abroad:

You ask me to describe contemporary Russia. Soviet Russia is the State of the working people and the peasants who have taken away the land from the estate-owners and made it the property of the laboring people, who have expropriated the factories and the shops and given over their management into the hands of the workers themselves and to the organs of the Government which they have established.

The war, which was started in 1914 by the Tsar's Government and which hastened the wrecking of the Tsarist throne, has exhausted the entire country, has cost millions of lives and undermined the very foundations upon which the economic life of the people rested. It was the war that called forth the revolutionary eruption, which did not stop at the overthrow of the autocracy, but ended, toward the

close of 1917, in the victory of the peasants and workers
who removed from the Government the weak bourgeoisie
which was incapable of guiding the ship of state, and have
taken the Government into their own strong hands. The
storm of the revolution, accompanied by the quaking of
social foundations, naturally brought about disorganization
of the economic and industrial life, and of the transport
system of Soviet Russia. Thus the economic condition of
the country at the moment the Soviet Government came
into power was extremely critical indeed. In this respect,
however, Russia is not an exception among the other countries of Europe which participated in the world war.
Neither in Austria nor in Germany, at least until 1919, did
communism play any significant rôle in the direct conduct of
their governments, nevertheless the economic and industrial
conditions of those countries are desperate. The absence
of Bolsheviki in the Governments of these countries has not
made their condition any better than ours, and even some
of the victorious countries, such as France or Belgium, for
instance, are struggling against a desperate crisis in every
domain of their economic life.

But Soviet Russia, aside from the miseries caused by the
war of 1914–1917, had to drink a still more bitter cup.
During the very first months of the existence of the Soviet
power in Russia, it was subjected to a series of attacks and
attempts to overthrow the Soviet Government, first on the
part of Germany, and afterward, on the part of the Allies
who mobilized against Soviet Russia some of their own
troops, as well as those of other Governments, aided by
those elements of the old landowners of capitalistic Russia
who could not be reconciled to the overthrow of Tsarism
and were interested in the restoration of their lands and

their property. These separate attempts shaped themselves in 1918 into a series of desperate military campaigns organized against Soviet Russia, requiring enormous financial and material expenditures, munitions, all their perfected arts of warfare, aiding the armies that attacked Soviet Russia with technical and military experts and advisers sent by the Allies who had already won their war. Soviet Russia had to resist a number of attacks in the West, East and South. The front in this war of Soviet Russia against her enemies was about ten thousand kilometers long. Toward the end of 1918 Soviet Russia was cut off from the provinces where bread, coal, metal and naphtha were in abundance, and yet more than eighty-five per cent. of locomotives of the Russian transport system depended on coal and naphtha for their operation. Not contenting themselves with attacks from without, the Governments of the Allies endeavored to organize within Russia itself a number of conspiracies for the overthrow of the workers' and peasants' Government. Until the end of 1919 Soviet Russia was indeed a besieged fortress, and the only materials which Soviet Russia received during that time consisted of the bullets which the enemies directed against it from the other side of the fronts. It seemed that there was nothing that could save Soviet Russia, and yet owing to the indirect support of the proletariat of Western Europe, who expressed their will unmistakably on a number of occasions, refusing to ship materials and supplies needed for the war against Soviet Russia, stopping trains and ships, interfering with the sending of troops destined for the fronts against Russia, Soviet Russia succeeded in defeating and crushing the greater part of the armies that fought against it. The war would have been completely over and the workers and peasants of Russia would have had the opportunity to concentrate the work of the entire government apparatus and all the local organizations for the purpose of improving the economic welfare of the country, if in April, 1920, Poland did not start her attempt at overthrowing Soviet Russia.

All the efforts of the Russian people had to be directed again in defense of their country against the aggression of their enemies. Again all the industries and the transports had to work chiefly for the needs of the war. But our position is already infinitely more favorable than before. Siberia, Turkestan, the Baku region and Kuban are again united with Soviet Russia, and the crisis caused by the lack of necessities, that ring with which it was intended to strangle Russia in 1918 is already broken and can never be set up again. Soviet Russia will not end the war before the Polish Government of landowners and capitalists is overthrown—the Government that incited the Polish people into fratricidal war against the Russian people who did not and do not want to violate the independence of the Polish State.

The internal condition of Russia is, of course, very difficult, particularly as far as the industrial centers of Central and Northern Russia are concerned. A considerable portion of the employees of the factories and shops are continually serving in the army at the fronts, defending the socialist state with their breasts, organizing and leading detachments of the Red Army, regulating the transport of troops and war supplies. The delivery of foodstuffs to the cities is difficult because the greater part of the transport must be used for purely military materials. The position of the city population was particularly hard during the past winter owing to the lack of fuel. But when we consider the majority of the Russian population, the peasantry, it must be said that their condition had never before been so favorable as during the past few years. The peasant not only secured his land, but the greatest portion of his products which used to be sent to the cities before, remains in the villages now. The Soviet régime absolutely protects the vital interests of the farmer. Having experienced the régimes of Kolchak, Yudenitch, Denikin and other Tsarist generals, who had tried to wage war against Russia, the Russian peasant who en masse is of course not a communist, has nevertheless become the most enthusiastic adherent of the Soviet régime and the Soviet State, because the Soviet régime protects to the fullest extent the vital interests of the peasantry. In the fact that the Russian peasants have become adherents of the Soviet régime, you will find one of the main causes of the invincibility of Soviet Russia. An even more important rôle in the success of the great struggle was played by the splendid organization of the Russian working class, whose endurance, heroism and superior discipline manifested themselves both in the military struggle and in the organization of labor and industry.

The further slow or rapid development of Russia now depends upon the foreign relations with Russia. Without machines, tools of production and materials for the reorganization of our transport, the reconstruction of our economic and industrial life will progress but slowly. For years to come the Russian workman and the Russian peasant are doomed to a comparatively wretched existence, but Russia has nothing to fear for its future, even under such circumstances. Russia is great and vast. Her resources of all sorts of raw materials, bread, lumber, fuel are enormous. The population of Russia, notwithstanding the privations caused by the war, is increasing more rapidly than the population of any other country. The Russian people has within it great forces which will manifest themselves in various spheres of human endeavor. And as now all the fruits of the work of the Russian workmen and peasants belong to themselves, the lack of necessary supplies, in the absence of support from abroad, will to a certain degree be replaced by a greater perfection of its own social organization. If, however, the Western European Governments, and particularly the Government of the United States, will realize that any further efforts to destroy by force the established Soviet régime of Russia will lead only to useless and hopeless waste of money and supplies, to the loss of hundreds of thousands of human lives, and the interruption of the economic development of Russia at the cost of the further impoverishment also of Western Europe, then there is hope of a more rapid economic and consequently also cultural development of Russia with the support of the more industrially advanced countries.

The aims and ideals of contemporary Russia consist of the rapid and complete development and utilization of all our economic possibilities in order to raise the cultural and spiritual level of the entire working people.

As for the demands made of the Soviet Government in various countries, especially in France, concerning the payment of the debts contracted by the defunct Tsarist Government, the Soviet Government of Russia is ready to discuss and examine them only at the beginning of official negotiations regarding the restoration of peaceful relations between Russia and other countries. There is no sense in considering this question before the opening of such negotiations.

The progressive elements of the Russian people warned the bourgeoisie of the whole world as far back as 1905 that the Russian people will not pay the debts which the Tsarist Government contracted in Western Europe for the purpose of securing the necessary means to enslave and oppress the Russian people or to prepare for such wars as the Russo-Japanese war which the Russian Government started in order to divert the storm of national wrath from problems of international reconstruction to the alleged danger which threatened Russia from other nations. The Petrograd Soviet of Workmen's Deputies in 1905 made public an appeal addressed to all the powers of Western Europe in which it was specifically pointed out that the loans then made to the Tsarist Government would not be recognized by the Russian people, and that when the Russian people will take the reins of government into their own hands, the Russian people will not honor these debts. That appeal was signed not only by all the socialistic parties, but also by the group of "Liberation" and the Constitutional Democratic party organized at the time, and by such representatives of that party as Struve and Milukov.

The Soviet Government does not decline to discuss these and other demands which may be made, but such discussions cannot be conducted in newspaper interviews or in private negotiations, not even during the negotiations for the resumption of commercial relations. These questions we will discuss only at an official peace conference of all the Powers where we are willing to examine all demands and where we will present also our own demands for the damage and losses caused us by the two years of war which we did not want and for the termination of which we appealed to the Governments of all the countries from the very first day of its start.

The importance of America for the economic regeneration of Russia and for the liquidation of the consequences which Russia, like other countries of Europe, received as an inheritance of years of war, is very great. America has enormous resources, highly developed industries and technique, the most scientific modern methods of production, and, above all, great initiative, daring and quickness of decision, which the cultured countries of Western Europe lack. The importance of the American market to Russia is very great even at the present time, as a large number of the most vital industrial enterprises in Russia, particularly our transport, could quickly be readjusted with the aid of American materials and machines. America is perhaps the only country which, notwithstanding her participation in the war, has materials and machines in quantities which admit of exportation abroad. Leather, coal, cotton, various sorts of steel could be exported to Russia in considerable quantities. America is perhaps the only country which could furnish to Russia quickly a considerable number of ready locomotives and thus within a few months radically improve the condition of our railroad transportation, and consequently render tremendous help to our industrial development. The delivery of cars, of railway materials of every kind, as well as machines and supplies necessary for the repair of boats and railways, various factories and shops, could also be easily accomplished by American industries.

But the importance of America's aid to the industrial regeneration of Russia is not exhausted by furnishing these materials during the coming months, for some of these materials may be secured also in other countries. American industry could play even a more important rôle through its supply of capital, of technical powers in the exploitation of the natural resources of Russia and in organizing upon a large scale the factories working on the production or securing of raw materials. The industrial utilization of the most promising naphtha region on the Ukhta could be brought about in the near future only with the aid of American enterprise. Another great project is the building of a railroad from the port of Soroki on the White Sea to Kotlas and from Kotlas along the parallel to Obi, thus crossing many millions of acres of the richest forests as yet untouched by human feet. In those regions various ores and metals could be exploited, large factories and mills established for the production of paper, celluloid, etc. There is an enormous opportunity for American enterprise in the world's richest coal fields, in the Kuznetsk basin and the Southern part of the Government of Tomsk. That region bordering on one side of the province of Altay, abundant in all sorts of ore and mineral wealth, and on the other of Minusinsk, the granary of Siberia, which is connected with all Siberia by navigation.

The proper exploitation of naphtha in Baku, Grozny, Maikop and also in the region of Emba and the Urals may be brought about upon a large scale only with the participation of American capital.

The Soviet Government has often considered the possibilities and conditions upon which American industries and enterprises could be attracted for the purpose of elaborating the natural wealth of Russia and in this connection certain conditions have been worked out which enable me to state definitely that this task can be realized absolutely, and that the Soviet Government is in position to present to American representatives of industry such conditions for the exploitation of the natural wealth of Russia under which the establishment of the above-named factories will prove absolutely practical, commercially sound and sufficiently profitable.

CHAIM WEIZMANN

April, 1921.

DR. CHAIM WEIZMANN, the president of the World Zionist Organization, Professor of the University of Manchester, is a famous chemist, who rendered invaluable services to the cause of the Allies by most important discoveries at a very critical period of the war.

Dr. Weizmann has been conspicuously identified with the Zionist movement for many years. During the World War the Zionist Organization was crippled because of the peculiar position of the Jews, who found themselves in the armies of all the nations at war, in the ranks of both the Allies and of the Central Powers.

The mantle of Dr. Theodor Herzl, the brilliant founder of the modern Zionist movement, fell on the shoulders of Dr. Chaim Weizmann, whose achievements for Zionism have gained for him the recognition of the Zionists throughout the world as the leader who actually succeeded in transforming the dreams and hopes of the Jews into a reality.

It was he who secured the Balfour declaration in 1917 in favor of making Palestine the National Homeland of the Jews. It was he who was most instrumental in the San Remo decision of the Supreme Council which ratified the Balfour declaration on April 24, 1920.

On that historic day for the Jewish people Premier Lloyd George and other Allied statesmen said to Dr. Weizmann at San Remo:

"We have given you the start. Now it is your task to bring about the rebuilding of Palestine. If you fail, the fault will not be ours."

To this Dr. Weizmann replied:

"The Jewish people will not fail."

I was with Dr. Weizmann at San Remo at the time. Humble and modest despite his great achievements, he fully realized the enormity of the task before him and the Jewish people. On that occasion he outlined to me some of the work that must be done by the Jews without delay in order that Palestine be made rich and great again, that it be developed economically, industrially, culturally and agriculturally.

On the day of the San Remo decision Dr. Weizmann wrote the following lines in my notebook:

"To-day Israel entered once more as an active factor on the world's stage. No more a passive sufferer, but with a great opportunity to apply his energies and the accumulated experiences of ages for the upbuilding of his ancient home, which he ought to make into a shining beacon. Judea capta is no more."

After the San Remo conference I travelled with Dr. Weitzmann in Switzerland. The Jews everywhere were hailing the San Remo decision as the redemption of Israel, and Dr. Weitzmann as the redeemer. He sought the quiet of Switzerland to escape the first demonstrations and the praise that was showered upon him from various parts of the world. During the days that we were alone, I had occasion to discuss with him Palestinian problems from practically every angle. In the course of these interviews Dr. Weitzmann said:

"The restoration of Palestine to Israel now is nothing

short of a miracle. It is up to the Jewish people to make good the golden opportunity that is offered to them by the world. We can rebuild Palestine by hard work only, and I know that the Jews are ready to make enormous sacrifices for the regeneration of their ancient home.

"As for the Arabs, the differences between them and ourselves will be more easily removed now that they know our status. They used to look upon the Balfour Declaration as a war promise that would not be kept when peace came. I hope they will no longer be misled by irresponsible agitators. We need the Arabs and they need us, and with good will on both sides we can adjust our differences. As some one has wisely said, once we get out of the talking stage and start on the working stage, all these misunderstandings will disappear."

I asked Dr. Weitzmann to describe the beginning of the work on the Balfour Declaration. He answered:

"When the war broke out, the Zionist organization was concentrated on plans of work in Palestine, with no political horizon, with indifference on the part of the Powers, and opposition on the part of Turkey. The war divided our forces, as we were separated by gulfs and trenches. Russian Jewry was practically broken up. The pale of settlement became the theatre of war, and in the wake of the contending armies came ruin and misery.

"There was a small band of our workers in England who thought it their duty to utilize their position to save what could still be saved. We were a small, unofficial, unrecognized band of workers, but we knew that we voiced the sentiments of the great masses of the Jewish people, and we set out to create a political position for the Zionist movement.

"We reasoned thus:—'It is possible that as a result of this war Turkey will disappear. It is therefore possible that the territories constituting the Turkish empire may be considerably readjusted and recast. The whole political structure of the Old World will go by the board. Therefore, the Jewish claims must be clearly formulated, and we must secure the recognition of these claims by the Allies. We further thought that the war was really a duel between Germany and England.

"We felt that if we could get England to understand the achievements of the Jews in Palestine and thus secure England's support for Zionism, half the battle would be won. That was our theory. I agree it was a gamble, but a gamble worth taking. We had strong opposition. We were a small band of foreign Jews and against us were the might and prestige and bank accounts of the established leaders of the British Jewish community.

"But we were inspired by the righteousness of our cause, and we said to the British statement:—'The Jews will get Palestine, whether you want it or not. There is no power on earth that can stop the Jews from getting to Palestine. You gentlemen can make it easy for them, or you can make it hard for them, but you cannot stop them.'

"They asked us how many Jews there were in Palestine, and what they had accomplished there. We opened our books to them. It is true, we had very little to show as yet. We said, 'All that you see has been achieved under most trying circumstances, always in the teeth of opposition on the part of the Turkish government, and also of your rich Jews who tell you that the Zionist movement is merely the fancy or hope of a few enthusiasts.

" 'We tell you we have behind us the millions of Jews

who are inarticulate now and we speak on their behalf.'

"It took at least two thousand interviews with British statesmen to get them to understand Zionism. I myself made more than a thousand visits to British statesmen in order to familiarize them with the true meaning of Zionism. Of course, we had the great support of American Zionists, which was most helpful. People have criticised me because I asked only for a national home for the Jews and not for a Jewish state. They said the Balfour plan did not mean a Jewish state. It certainly did not mean a Jewish state.

"The Jewish colonists who went to Palestine years ago and who have done there such wonderful work really prepared our political claim for Palestine. They were the real political leaders of the Zionist organization. We only supplemented their work."

In answer to my question whether it was true that the British military authorities in Palestine were at that time more sympathetic to the Arabs than the Jews, Dr. Weitzmann said:

"It may seem strange, but it is true that almost all Englishmen, after visiting Jerusalem, were at first unsympathetically inclined to the Jews. But I can easily understand the reasons for that. The first reason is due to the appearance of the Jews in Jerusalem. The Englishmen saw long-coated, long-bearded, old Jews, with carlocks — the so-called Chalukah Jews. They had expected to find there the Jews of the Bible. So the officers and soldiers asked themselves, 'Is it for these Jews that we were called upon to make so many sacrifices, and shed our blood that they shall have Palestine?'

"The Arabs, on the contrary, seemed to them to fit much better into the scenery of the Orient by their picturesque garb.

"The second reason is that the British officials found the Jews more difficult to deal with than the Arabs, who obeyed their orders. They found the Jews intellectually their equal, and they resented it.

"The third reason is a personal one. Among the British troops there were clerks and businessmen who naturally looked for future opportunities, and some of them regarded Palestine as a good field for their activities after demobilization. Some of them had their eyes on certain concessions, but when the Zionists stopped these concessions, the British soldiers did not realize that it was done for the purpose of preventing speculation and exploitation. They simply attributed that to the eagerness of the Jews to grab everything in Palestine.

"I can understand the reasons why they liked the Arabs better than the Jews. But, then, I am not pleased with Jerusalem as it is, either. Jerusalem must be cleaned up. The Chalukah Jews, the Jews depending upon alms from abroad, must be changed. I know it is difficult to change the old generation. But the young generation can still be changed. We shall build Yeshivahs, houses of Jewish learning, for the younger element, for we must not destroy before we build.

"There are so many fine intellectual qualities in these Jews that we cannot afford to lose, now that so many of the important institutions of Jewish learning have been destroyed in Russia and Poland. We must build them anew in Palestine. We must introduce the most modern

methods in our schools there, but we must make every
effort to preserve some of the finer traditions of Israel in
the educational institutions."

I interviewed Dr. Weizmann in Washington in April,
1921, after he had been received by President Harding to
whom he explained his mission to the United States and
described his recent impressions of Palestine.

Answering my questions, Dr. Weizmann said:

"Since the decision of San Remo, we have had the appointment of Sir Herbert Samuels as High Commissioner
of Palestine, and the beginning of immigration to Palestine.

"Since the doors of Palestine were opened for immigration, Jews have come there at the rate of from 1,000 to
1,200 a month. They are mostly young men and women,
sturdy, educated, open-air people, from Poland, Bessarabia
and Southwestern Russia. Some of them have come from
no man's land.

"Most of these immigrants have been through the war,
have seen and lived through all the hardships and tribulations of present-day Eastern Europe. No work is too hard
for them, and the very rigorous medical examinations have
yielded about 86 per cent. of people fit for the hardest work
possible, in which they are actually engaged.

"They are breaking stones and building the roads of
Palestine. They are organized in camps, in various parts
of the country, and one can hear on the roads of Palestine
their merry Hebrew songs mingled with the sounds of the
hammers and shovels.

"That these people took their immigration to Palestine
seriously, and that they have not come there merely as
refugees, may be gathered from the fact that though the

majority of them are intellectuals, they are prepared for agricultural pursuits, and about 70 per cent. of them have learned the Hebrew language before coming to Palestine.

"This immigration is at present limited, but we know that there are about 30,000 young men and women of this same type living in the hell called the Ukraine. Some of these are managing to escape at great peril. And thus we get a stream filtering through Bessarabia and Poland.

"About 50,000 are waiting in Bessarabia to be admitted to Palestine. To our great sorrow we are not in a position to bring them all to Palestine at present, as we must reckon with the present limited resources and undeveloped state of the country. And also with our limited means.

"But we feel certain, and we have the authority not only of our own experts, but also of the Administration of Palestine, that if we had but the means, room can be made in Palestine for a very considerable immigration to that country within a comparatively short time.

"The Executive Committee of the World Zionist Organization is in possession of elaborate plans for colonization, the establishment of hydro-electrical power, house building, education and so forth.

"Palestine seems to be at present the only place in the Near East which is beginning to settle down to constructive work, and although it is surrounded by countries disturbed by unrest, the new settlers in Palestine are permeated by the spirit of building up a commonwealth socially just, economically healthy, and intellectually high.

"This would serve as a great stabilizing factor in a part of the world which is destined once more to play an important rôle in the development of mankind. This is symbolized already in the effort to erect a university on Mount

Scopus.   Great Jewish intellectual forces like Albert Einstein are endeavoring to make it a success.

"The Jews of America can give not only financial aid, but also some men and experience in the task of reconstruction.   We see the beginning of this in the work of the American Zionist Medical Unit.

"I am sure that the Jews of this great country will make a glorious contribution to the ancient Jewish Homeland.

"Almost a year has passed since the Supreme Council at San Remo made its decision with regard to Palestine. The Jewish people is on trial.   We are scrutinized by all the nations of the world, and we must make good, for we have both the forces and the resources necessary for the upbuilding of Palestine.

"While opportunities in Palestine are numerous and most enheartening, two-thirds of the Jewish race in Eastern Europe are living at this moment under intolerable conditions.

"On the eve of its renaissance Jewry stands wounded and mutilated.   It has only one hand free for constructive labor, and with the other it is desperately struggling to ward off blows that threaten it with destruction.   The Jews of America are providentially the remnant that may now liberate the larger part of Israel."

In 1923 Dr. Weizmann discussed the situation of Palestine and the Arab-Jewish problems in the Holy Land as follows:

"The mandate has been ratified.   It has met with the approval of the civilized world.   The resolution of the American Congress will rank with the Balfour Declaration, and to us Jews this is one of the most important documents in the annals of our history.

"We are attempting to build a home in Palestine and we are conscious that this building can only be successful if it will be done in co-operation with the peoples and population of Palestine. We are coming into Palestine not as conquerors. We are coming into Palestine not to dominate anybody. We are coming to build up Palestine together with the people there, taking our place according to our merits and our achievements. The other people in Palestine, the Arabs and Christians, have to recognize that we have a right to do what we intend to do. Just as we recognize that Palestine is going to be the common homeland for Jews and Arabs, we want the Arabs to recognize that we have a right to come into Palestine to establish ourselves there, not on the back of anybody, but with them, to work and create new values of which Palestine is capable.

"Palestine has a population of about 700,000 non-Jews, an overwhelming majority of Moslems, a small minority of Christians and another small minority of Jews. Roughly speaking there are 500,000 Moslems, 100,000 Christians and 100,000 Jews. Since the war and even before the war there has been a striving on the part of the Arab people for a revival, and being anxious for the revival of the scattered Jewish people, we treat with respect and reverence any attempt of revival amongst other people.

"We recognize to-day, that between us and the Arabs in the Near East, and particularly in Palestine, stand many forces—perhaps destructive forces—which try to emphasize this estrangement that has taken place between these two races which are akin to each other. But we also see as present in Palestine that the tendency which was so marked three or four years ago—the tendency of two entrenched camps watching each other with suspicion, is grad-

ually declining. We are trying to co-operate with them.
We work with them. We are looked upon with a certain
amount of suspicion. We are looked upon with suspicion
particularly because we represent to the Eastern races the
West, and the West is looked upon with suspicion at present
in the Near East. The various tribulations through which
Europe and the East is passing to-day, Bolshevism, Kemal-
ism, the unsettlement of European affairs, all these reflect
on the fancy of an Oriental people. Every rumor in the
East is exaggerated. Every vibration in the political
world is reflected and exaggerated in Palestine. Palestine is a peculiar country. There is no country in the world
where the distance between the sublime and the ridiculous
is so small as in Palestine. One stands constantly with
one leg on the sublime. Eighty generations look down
upon you. Palestine is like a sounding-board. Every
noise goes forth over all the world. If a Jew is killed in
Piccadilly, the Ukraine, or run over by a motor car on
Broadway, it is an ordinary affair. If something of that
kind happens in the Holy Land, it becomes an act of state,
an act of violence,—two races clashing. All these factors,
the tribulations of Europe, mental and moral strife, contribute to make life in Palestine much more difficult than it is
elsewhere, but making allowances for all that there is a
growing tendency to co-operate, to meet, to work together,
and I think the Arabs are beginning to accept us, as we have
made it quite clear that we have got to live with them, work
with them, not to establish our home on their back, but to
co-operate with them. Every unbiased observer would confirm and bear out this particular point of view. It is a
difficult task. We must work slowly, and we must overcome a great deal of friction and prejudice, but I think

we are a sufficiently tenacious and stiff-necked people and we shall carry through.

"As for the Jewish side of the problem, we knew the Jews were capable of coming into a civilized country, of adapting themselves very rapidly to this civilization and performing a very useful rôle in this civilization, but whether the Jews would be capable of laying the foundations of a civilization and doing all that is necessary in the fight with nature, overcoming all these difficulties in order to build up a country from its very elements, that we did not know.

"We have now convinced ourselves that we can do it. We have to-day in Palestine a generation of Jews that come from everywhere, by the most complicated roads. I can almost hear the tramp of these people over the various roads of Europe and Asia, finding their way and knocking at the gates of Palestine. They come from the Ukraine, from Morocco, from Mesopotamia, from Canada, from India and Russia. They are divergent in their culture and education, language and habits. They are different in types. The one thing that unites them is the upbuilding of this Home. You see these people coming from 'No Man's Land,' politically and morally, you see them on the swamps of Palestine, on the hills and valleys, working as common laborers on the roads—people with high standards of education, sometimes with university degrees, and here they are draining swamps, breaking stones, building roads, afforestating the country, doing all that which is known to American or European civilization as pioneering. Here you have all these scattered people, suspended morally, politically and physically, finding not only a mere refuge— for refuge is a tent—but finding a center for their spiritual life, application for their energies—their constructive energies become more constructive. The swamps are being drained, the hillsides are blossoming, the roads are being built by the idealistic onslaught of these people. They come in thousands and thousands will follow. Behind these thousands stand other thousands and behind these, others.

"I was in Jerusalem three years ago at the time of the so-called 'pogrom.' I have seen pogroms in many parts of Europe, but there was one distinctive feature in the Jerusalem pogrom. We counted our dead. There were 20, and the Jews of Jerusalem said to me, 'For the 20 who have been killed there will be 20,000 coming in to take their place and take the same risk and face it all.' That is a real force—and more than that—it is a force which makes for civilization, which makes for stability. For a long time to come the Near East will be a troublesome region. In Egypt, Mesopotamia, Transjordania and Central Arabia there are many forces which defy European civilization and culture. Coming not as conquerors but with peace in our hearts and minds, we who still have a great deal of the East and who have gone through Western schools, could interpret the West to the East and the East to the West and we could perform an act of civilization which no other people could perform—to serve as a bridge between two cultures that watch each other to-day with suspicion but might be united to-morrow. And—perhaps the day will come when there will be another seat of the League of Nations, a real seat of peace, harmony and justice, a seat for all these humanitarian ideals which have formed the bedrock of our civilization—in Jerusalem. The prophets are not dead yet. They are silent to-day but they may speak to-morrow."

ALBERT EINSTEIN

New York, 1921.

PROFESSOR ALBERT EINSTEIN, who introduced a new scientific conception of space and time and of their relation to the physical world, has come to America not to expound his theory of relativity, but to interest the Jews of America in the building of a Hebrew University in Palestine.

The foremost Jewish genius of our age is a modest, unassuming, kindly gentleman, almost childlike in his simplicity, with a keen sense of humor.

Professor Einstein, who is a Swiss citizen and a professor of the University of Berlin, suffered from attacks directed against him by German anti-Semites when their agitation was intense. Writing to the London *Times* he thus characterized wittily the present tendency to discriminate between men of science on nationalist grounds:

"The description of me and my circumstances in the *Times* shows an amusing feat of imagination on the part of the writer. By an application of the theory of relativity to the taste of the readers, to-day in Germany I am called a German man of science, and in England I am represented as a Swiss Jew. If I come to be regarded as a bête noire, the description will be reversed and I shall become a Swiss Jew for the Germans and a German man of science for the English."

I interviewed Professor Einstein regarding the purpose of his mission in America and the needs of the University of

Jerusalem. Answering my questions, Professor Einstein said:

"The purpose of my visit to America at this time is to enlist both the moral and material support of the Jews of America for the building of a Hebrew university in Palestine.

"Such a university would assist enormously in the up-building of Palestine, for it would become a spiritual center of Jewish education and culture for the Jews in the Holy Land. Later this university would also attract Jewish students of other lands, who would come to study in Palestine.

"But, above all, I consider it most important that there exists this great common Jewish cultural enterprise, which is of the utmost significance for all Jews.

"Through my contact with Jewish students in various parts of Europe I have arrived at the decision that such an institution of learning in Palestine is essential.

"I have met the Jewish students of Austria, Hungary and of Russia, who are clamoring to complete their education in European universities. I have seen the difficulties and hardships which these young men and women are experiencing. I have observed the discriminations, which have become intensified since the war.

"Poverty, the economic collapse in Central European countries, has fanned the flames of national hatreds, and the Jewish students have suffered in Germany, in Poland and especially in Hungary. A large number of Jewish students are barred from the universities on religious grounds.

"The situation has been aggravated also by the fact that a number of universities in Eastern Europe have been closed altogether.

"Many of the students have come to me for aid. I have

seen their helplessness, their hardships and their needs.
And in this way I came to the realization that a Hebrew
University in Palestine is an absolute necessity for the Jew-
ish people.

"The traditional respect for knowledge which we Jews
have maintained intact for many centuries of severe persecution makes us feel all the more keenly the present discrimination against so many talented sons and daughters
of the Jewish people who are knocking in vain at the doors
of the universities of Eastern and Central Europe.

"And those who have gained access to the spheres of
free research had to do so by undergoing a process of assimilation which has crippled the free and natural development of the spiritual character of our people and deprived
them of their cultural leaders.

"It seems to me, it is also the duty of the Jewish people
to preserve, through the university we are planning to establish in Palestine, the neglected branches of Hebrew literature, language, archæology and history.

"Distinguished Jewish scholars in all branches of learning are waiting to go to Jerusalem where they will lay the
new foundation of a flourishing spiritual life and will promote the intellectual and economic development of Palestine.

"The Hebrew University in Palestine would become a
new 'Holy Place' to our people.

"Despite the crude realism and materialism of our times,
there is a glimmer of a nobler conception of human aspirations. The American people exemplified this by the part
they played in recent years in the affairs of the world.

"The Jews of America are at this time the most fortunate portion of the Jewish people. Europe is sick and suf-

fering, and the Jews of Europe are experiencing greater
sufferings, discriminations and persecutions than ever before.

"So I have come here with feelings of hope that my
spiritual aims with regard to the university in Jerusalem
will find a sympathetic response in America, and will be
realized through the support of American Jewry.

"A group of physicians has been formed for the purpose
of raising funds for the medical faculty of the university.

"A general committee is also being organized, including
a number of prominent academicians and financiers.   With
the help of these people I hope to secure the required moral
and material support to enable us to build the university
without delay.

"Not only Zionists are realizing the importance of this
university, but a number of distinguished American Jews
not identified with the Zionist movement have expressed
their interest and sympathy for this cultural enterprise and
have promised to assist me in making it a success.

"I am not an organizer myself.   The university will be
organized by specialists.   I shall be glad to work with
them, and help them in every way possible.   I am at the
disposal of the university, and am prepared to participate
in the scientific department.

"Not being a prophet, I cannot foretell whether my mission in this country will be successful.   All I can do is to
do what I can.   But the sympathy and interest for this
work I have found in this country both among the Jews
and the Gentiles is most encouraging.

"Various considerations have led to the selection of the
following University Institutes for the initial scheme:

"1—A department of Jewish and Oriental studies—

philology, literature, history, law, archæology, religion and philosophy, mainly Jewish but including also Arabic and Semitics in general. This department is to be a university school for scientific studies, able to offer training to both graduates and post-graduates and empowered to confer degrees.

"2—A research institute for the Hebrew language, the object of which will be to guide and assist its modern development by the study of its vast treasure-house of literature.

"On the scientific side it was decided to begin with Research Institutes, as suggested in 1913 by Dr. Weizmann and the University Committee, in which the chief scientific adviser was the late Prof. Paul Ehrlich, and not with teaching faculties. The initial plan comprises the institutes for physics, chemistry and microbiology.

"In the advancement of science Jews have always taken a noble part, but the fruits of their labors have not been reaped by Jewry.

"Is it conceivable that, in addition to the tragedy of Jewish science without a home, there could exist a Jewish National Home without science? The traditional pride of the Jewish people in their learned men would never suffer such humiliation.

"And there is no doubt that to those non-Jewish idealists and believers in spiritual values who have supported Zionism a Jewish Palestine means, perhaps mainly, a real renaissance of that Jewish genius of which they have seen so many examples scattered in many lands."

MAX NORDAU

London, 1921.

I HAVE met Dr. Max Nordau many times. I visited him practically every time I came to Europe before the World War, and since the war. I corresponded with him while he was in exile in Spain during the war.

Dr. Nordau, one of the intellectual giants of our time, the brilliant philosopher, publicist and critic, and one of Israel's most courageous leaders, discussed in the course of our numerous meetings literature and art, war and peace, and particularly the Jewish question in its various aspects. A modern Jewish prophet, fiery and eloquent, fearless and far-sighted, he was nevertheless almost childlike in his simplicity, which is the outstanding characteristic of all true greatness.

Our last meetings took place in London, in 1921. I visited him in his little room in the Zionist offices there, and he called on me at my hotel. He talked about his latest works and complained of the indifference with which some of his more serious productions were treated.

"I do not read the reviews of my books," he remarked on one occasion, with a smile. "What can the critics tell me about my work that I do not know myself? If they praise me, I could praise my own work better than others could, and if they damn me, I could damn myself more effectively than others could, for I know my own faults and my qualities better than the critics do."

During the last interview I had with him he analyzed
the Jewish problems after the war, the tragedy of the Jewish people and the hope that lay in the realization of the
Zionist ideal of rebuilding Palestine as a National Jewish
Homeland. He said:

"The World War was a war of the Jewish people. There
have been proportionately more Jews in the firing-line than
even Frenchmen, although these have furnished the highest
percentage of mobilized soldiers. They have fought at
least as heroically as the English and the Americans who
have covered themselves with the greatest glory, to judge
by the number of distinctions and honors they have won.
They have suffered more than the Serbians and the Bel-
gians who were considered to be the most lamentable victims
of the conflagration, and the conclusion of the peace treaty
leaves them in a worse condition than the Austrians, the
Germans and the Russians who are justly, if cruelly, punished for having been the cause of the scourge which has
tortured and martyred mankind for five years.

"It is easy to substantiate these affirmations with figures
and facts. The number of Jewish soldiers in the ranks of
all the contending armies is estimated as being between
850,000 and 900,000. Assuming that there are thirteen
millions of Jews in the world, including those of the neutral
countries, this means that approximately seven per cent. of
the whole Jewish population has worn uniforms, which is
more than can be said of the English and the Italians, and
far more than the Americans. Eighty thousand Jews have
fallen in battle or died from wounds, while the casualties
amount to a little under two hundred thousand. These are
the direct losses which do not include the numberless victims

of that infamous scoundrel, the chief commander of the
Tsarist Russian army, the mass-murderer Grand Duke
Nicholas who, at the beginning of the campaign, ordered
the whole Jewish population of the war area in Poland to
be driven out of their homes and to be hunted in the interior of Russia where half of these unfortunate women,
children and old men perished along the roadside, like
beasts of the wilderness, from cold, hunger, exhaustion and
ill treatment.

"So much as to our active and passive share in the war.
But now the tragic difference between Jews and the other
nations that participated in the horrifying adventure.
These people all fought for an interest which they understood, which was clear to them, which they felt to be worth
every, even the supreme, sacrifice. The aggressors broke
the peace in greed for domination, for profit, for conquest,
for glory, for gratification of vanity. The assaulted nations knew that they were bound to risk everything, all that
they possessed and their life as well, in order to defend
their national existence and honor. But we Jews, what did
we fight for? For one thing only—for the accomplish-
ment of our duty toward the state of which we were citizens
or subjects. Far be it from me to minimize this reason
of our heroic effort. We had always protested of our
patriotism, we had boasted of it, we had gloried in it, it was
only fit and just that in the hour of supreme danger, when
feelings are tested as to their sincerity and vigor, we should
prove by acts the value of our words.

"But if this holds good of the Jews of such countries as
the United States, England, France, Italy, where the laws
make no difference between natives of different creeds and
races and where all citizens enjoy the same rights, it is

heartrending to think that our brothers had also to brave death for states like Germany and especially Russia where they were despised, hated and persecuted, where the Governments treated them worse than criminals. Yet even in the German and Russian armies the Jewish soldiers did more than their share, as is proved by the number of casualties as well as distinctions bestowed on them, surely not out of favor, but because even the most hardened, unjust and anti-Semitically biased superiors could not help acknowledge, most reluctantly, with a bit of ribbon or a cross of inferior rank, conspicuous deeds of valor accomplished under the eyes of their comrades in arms.

"And now that the war is over, at least theoretically, the nations draw up their accounts and establish the balance sheet of profits and losses. The vanquished, of course, have no reason to rejoice. They are inexorably punished for their sins, they have to atone for the abominable crimes of their rulers, whom they have enthusiastically cheered when they were led on to murder, arson and pillage, whom they have followed, not only without revolt or even mere reluctance, but with overbrimming joy. They are ruined, humiliated, dishonored, and it will take a century of honest work and decent behavior before they will be pardoned for their misdeeds.

"The victors in the struggle, although badly damaged, also have good reason to be dissatisfied. The United States has the proud consciousness of having fought with sublime disinterestedness for justice, right and freedom, of having been the glorious champion of the noblest causes, and of having saved civilization. England has crushed the most dangerous rival she had ever encountered in her way, and destroyed the naval power which disputed with her flag the rule of the seas. France has gained back her lost provinces, immensely augmented her colonial empire and vindicated her ancient world position. Italy has completed her national unity and stretched her frontiers beyond Triest, to the long coveted Trentino, and probably Fiume. Poland has been re-established to an extent she never would have dared dream of in these last 150 years. A swarm of small nations has been called into existence and begins, full of glee and expectations, a new political and cultural life. They have obviously paid a big price for this achievement, but they have obtained it and cannot fairly complain of the bargain.

"But how are we Jews rewarded for our sacrifice? What have we gained with our superhuman efforts? What are our assets against our dead, our maimed, against the destruction of the health and property of an appalling number of our brothers in all the warring countries?

"Even in the victorious states of Western Europe with the express exception of Italy, which forms an admirable contrast to her neighbors and allies, a deep ground wave of anti-Semitism is welling up furiously and threatens to drown us.

"In France there is perhaps no open discrimination against the native Jew; but the foreign Jew is ever surrounded by an atmosphere of suspicion and contempt; he is the permanent object of police vexations, and in some parts of the country and the protectorates, even the native Jew has to suffer ignominious treatment. In Algiers Jewish students who served in the war as officers and won distinction for their gallantry have been rudely denied admission into the university associations, and in Tunis the Jews suffered from street riots and violent attacks of French and

Arab mobs without the local authorities lifting a finger to protect them against brutal assaults.

"In Germany they are made the scapegoat of all national crimes and follies. It is charged they have undermined the army, they have caused the cowardly flight of the former Emperor, the downfall of the empire, the domination of the Socialists, the Communist troubles, the famine, the depreciation of the German currency. They must be expelled from the Fatherland, or better still, exterminated on the spot.

"In Austria bitter hatred of the Jew vents itself on every occasion. He is hunted in the streets of Vienna, he is assaulted in the lecture rooms of the university, he is heinously libelled in the press.

"In Hungary pogroms of the most frightful character have occurred in dozens of places. Thousands of innocent Jews have been slaughtered with bestial fury. Those that remain are frightened out of their senses, so much so that they rush in panic-stricken throngs to the baptismal fonts and seek salvation in conversion, a collective cowardice and degradation without precedent in the annals of our history.

"The horrors of Poland, Russia and foremost, the Ukraine, are too well known, alas! A hundred thousand mutilated corpses of Jews—men and women, old people and children—are strewn over the cursed soil of those countries which have drunk streams of Jewish blood shed by fiendish mobs. Unutterable terror is maddening those that have not yet been actually killed, tortured, sullied or robbed of all they possess, but are day and night trembling under the present menace of death in its ghastliest shape. Millions of Jews are condemned to perish most miserably. Their only chance is rapid flight. But where to? Even America, the land of refuge, the haven of salute, the Mother that has ever opened her arms to human beings, even America takes on a sternly hostile mien and extinguishes the torch of the gigantic statue at the entrance of New York Harbor—Liberty enlightening the world!

"There would be no redeeming point in this desolate picture of the present unparalleled distress of our race, but for one event which I would unhesitatingly call a miracle if I were inclined to use mystic language.   England, with the consent of her allies and associates, has promised the Jewish people Palestine, to establish there their national home. Interpret this term as you like—at all events it means that as soon as England receives from the League of Nations the mandate for assuming the administration of the country of our fathers, she will throw it open to us, so that our threatened, ill-treated, ruined, famished despairing masses may find a spot on the face of God's earth where they may know rest, peace, security and comfort, perhaps joy of life again.   The blessed land where the shade of Rachel will welcome with maternal tenderness her returning children and where the hallowed memories of our great ancestors will inspire and guide them, will hold out before them bright hopes and magnificent ideals.

"The most tragic, the most burning problem is that of East European Jewry.   You know the fearful plight of the millions of our people living in the former Russian and Austro-Hungarian empires and in the Roumanian kingdom. Did I say that they lived there?   The word life is too fine for the miserable existence to which they are condemned. They are unprotected and rightless.   Even if they are theoretically recognized as citizens of their birthland, they are practically outlaws.   They are treated as pariahs.   Gov-

ernments and administrations cruelly discriminate against
them. They bear all the burdens of the state, but enjoy none of its benefits. Their Christian countrymen
look at them with eyes of contempt and hatred, constantly
threaten their personal security and often actually attack
their life and property. They are practically excluded
from the public schools, and compelled to go abroad in
search of higher instruction. The respect of the human
personality, the dignity of free men are brutally denied
them and they have ever to tremble before the whimsical
hostility of the ruling class and the sanguinary instincts
of the mob.

"The problem of the Western Jew is of a different character. It is a moral problem. They are not materially
endangered. If they are callous, they may be content and
happy. If they methodically shut their eyes, they may
dream themselves in a fool's paradise. But those among
them that have reached a higher degree of mental development, that are sensitive and delicate, that strive after unity
and harmony of feeling, have their heart rent and their
soul torn. They persuade themselves that they are legitimate sons of their country, they are proud of their political
nationality, they are the most loyal, the most enthusiastic
patriots, often to the point of vicious chauvinism, but they
experience permanently the mortification to be faced by the
undeniable fact that their Christian fellow citizens consider them as a distinct element, as half strangers, if not
as total aliens. They distrust the sincerity of their attach-
ment to their homeland, do not think one moment of iden-
tifying them with their own breed and nationality, and do
not credit them with the same color of emotions, the same
trend of thought, the same views of the world and life, the

same motives of action, the same ideals which they know or imagine themselves to possess.

"The notion of this abnormality, of this strange aloofness of their Christian environment, inflicts on the cultivated Jews an uneasiness which, in too many cases, reaches the stage of despondency and even despair and destroys the equilibrium of their being. Some are prompted to become contemptible renegades, others degrade themselves to rabid anti-Semites, many make desperate efforts to overcome their innermost nature and to change the deepest foundations of their sentimental and intellectual structure, with the result that they become enigmatic, suspicious and antipathetic to Christians and loathsome, or at best an object of pity, to Jews.

"The problem of East European Jewry seems the more urgent of the two. There it is a question of life and honor. For generations the Jews of the East have clamored for emancipation, convinced that this would be their salvation. In Russia they were slaves. They were pent up in certain territories where there was no room for development, for profitable exercise of their natural gifts, for wholesome manifold activities. They were excluded from all official careers. The percentage norm of all higher schools debarred them from the possibility of quenching their burning thirst for knowledge or forced them to seek in foreign countries, at the price of humiliation, of unbearable discomfort, of ruinous outlay, the opportunities which Russia roughly denied them. Infamous police practices, the Damocles sword of *Oblavas*, of arbitrary expulsion and incarceration, incessantly suspended over their heads, deplorably educated them to habits of bribery, of dodging, of all kinds of doubtful contrivances which in the long run could not fail to exercise a corrupting influence on their character.

"Now Russia has broken down. But the revolution and the destruction of the Tsarist state have not brought the Jews the liberty they have so long sighed for. In Great Russia the Bolshevist terror has indeed created the full equality between them and the Christian population, but it is an equality in misery and utmost distress. In Ukraine the most abominable pogroms have taken place and the Jews have been victims by the tens of thousands of the unspeakable horrors of torture, slaughter, shame and robbery. In Poland they have been hunted, vexed, ill-treated, and are now subjected to a disastrous economical boycott which must end in utter ruin, if continued for any length of time. Finland dishonored itself by an hostility which takes all sorts of forms, also the most cowardly and contemptible—that of mass expulsion.

"Hungary, which was, for so long, considered a sort of paradise, at least for lukewarm Jews, which was a stronghold of extreme assimilation, even more so than the countries of the Occident where Judaism had drifted the farthest away from its national traditions, Hungary, whose capital, Budapest, was sneeringly nicknamed 'Judapest' by the anti-Semitic idiots of Austria, has rushed with the lust of a preying hyena into the ranks of the pogrom-lands and does its best, or its worst, to make up for lost time, with particularly enraged carnage.

"Roumania, and what is left of Austria and Germany, do not go to the length of murder and open pillage, but there is no kind of moral ill-treatment which they do not inflict on their Jewish inhabitants. They surround them with a suffocating atmosphere of hatred and contempt; they hin-

der them by all sorts of cunning devices in the peaceable
pursuits of their callings; they put officially or officiously no
end of insurmountable obstacles in the way of their careers;
they expel war refugees by the thousands and hermetically
shut their frontiers with locks and bars against all Jewish
immigrants, even those that in Austria come from the provinces which were formerly parts of the empire and have now
become Roumanian, Czecho-Slovakian or Polish territories.

"What hope is there for these eight millions of stricken
Jews in Central and Eastern Europe to see their unbearable
situation ameliorated?   What remedy is available for the
healing, or be it only for some relief, of their moral ills?
The civilized powers have made attempts, which, however, give an impression of being make-believe rather than
prompted by a really serious purpose, to intercede in their
favor with their tormentors.   Great Russia must remain
outside of these considerations.   For the time being, it is
inaccessible to Western influence or intervention, and in order to excuse in their own eyes and in those of the world
their pitiable inactivity in the face of the heart-breaking
sufferings of so many millions of innocent human beings,
the Occidental powers favor the spreading of the infamous
lie that Bolshevism is a Jewish movement, that the Russian
Jews have invented it, and propagate it, so if they suffer
and perish in Russia, they have only what they deserve,
and the conscience of the idle onlookers remains at rest.

"Denikin has been mildly advised to curb somewhat the
gangs of cowardly murderers and thieves under his command; but there is no indication that either he or his bestial
officers and men have paid the slightest attention to these
soft whispers from the West.

"With the new states that owe their existence or aggrandizement to the good will of the Allied Powers, the latter have dealt somewhat more authoritatively. They have inserted in the peace treaties, which constitute the fundamental charters of the states, clauses prescribing respect for the rights of national minorities. These articles should in reality bring about the full emancipation of the Jews and their equality before the law with all other citizens of the several countries. But the governments of the new independent states established by the grace of the peace conference, demurred as long and as obstinately as was possible against this obligation, and when finally they could not help signing the treaties, they manipulated matters so that the solemn document remains a scrap of paper as far as the Jews are concerned. Roumania is an old adept at the sport of poking fun at accepted stringent obligations, and Poland, Finland, Austria, as well as Hungary, bid fair to compete successfully with her in this rôle. As to the Allied Powers, they connive benevolently at this shameful breach of faith and contempt of given pledges.

"This is the Eastern Jewish problem. And its solution? I see only one—emigration! It is difficult to move millions? Undoubtedly; it is much easier to let them perish on the spot without lifting a finger to save them. But where shall they go? There is the rub. Australia and America, where there is still room for some two or three hundred millions of human beings, will not consent at present to receive our unhappy wandering brothers in search of a home. So they must stay and submit to the awful conditions of their present existence? This would be terrible. I am still an optimist, in spite of the actual ghastly aspect of the world; I still believe in progress and do not abandon the hope that even the sub-human Slav peoples will rise some day to the human level. But this will take a long time, and in the meantime our unhappy brothers will perish if they are not led out from their hell.

"At the root of this attitude of the non-Jews lies the new-fangled preposterous theory of the superiority of the so-called Aryan races, which condemns the Jew, on the ground of inferiority, to the rôle of a Pariah. For this problem there is also a solution, and only one: the existence of a Jewish nation, recognized formally as such, received on terms of equality in the League of Nations, qualified by this status to claim the treatment of peers by all the other nations of the world.

"Zionism is the only solution of the Jewish problem.

"Zionism opens to the millions of the East, the land of refuge—Palestine. Zionism gives the Jews a legitimate place in the League of Nations and guarantees their real equality."

WALTER RATHENAU

Berlin, July, 1922.

When the Rapallo Treaty was signed between Germany and Russia, the Allied statesmen were thrown into consternation. Germany was sharply rebuked for having upset the plans of the economic conference. In France protests and threats were hurled against both Germany and Russia. The Rapallo Treaty was denounced as a new evidence of Prussian treachery. It was branded as the first step to a Russo-German military alliance replete with the gravest consequences.

In the course of my recent travels through Europe I discussed the Rapallo Treaty with the men who signed it for Germany and for Russia, and with others who are familiar with the inner workings of the various political and economic conferences that have vainly endeavored to readjust Europe.

One of America's best informed statesmen, who played a most important rôle during the war and the peace conference, and who had the greatest opportunities to observe European diplomacy at close range, discussing the Russian situation and the Rapallo Treaty, said to me:

"It is as sure as fate that Russia and Germany will get together, that the Rapallo Treaty is but a prelude to a military alliance between these two nations in the future. All that the Allies have done with regard to Russia and Germany necessarily forced these two nations to combine.

"Such an alliance holds within it the seeds of the gravest consequences, for the Atlantic powers some day will be confronted by a new and formidable combination of powers. The Allies by their action have practically forced such an alliance among all the nations on the other side of the Rhine—Germany, Russia across Siberia, as far as the Pacific, with perhaps Japan and even China, and the Islamic world, against the Atlantic powers. What a regenerated Russia, a readjusted Germany, an aroused and irritated Islam, with Japan and China as their allies, could do in a conflict against the Atlantic powers within twenty-five or thirty years is a situation too terrible to contemplate."

Several days before the assassination of Walter Rathenau, Germany's Minister of Foreign Affairs, and one of Europe's foremost constructive statesmen, I had a long interview with him at the Foreign Office in Berlin. At first he was willing to give me a frank expression of his views, but not for publication. Afterward, however, he consented to my publishing an interview, provided I submitted to him a copy of the manuscript. He revised this interview on the eve of his tragic death. I received the manuscript, with his revisions, at eleven o'clock on Saturday morning at the Foreign Office. About ten minutes before, Rathenau had been murdered by agents of the monarchist organization near his home in Grunewald, on his way to the Foreign Office. His secretary had not received the news of his chief's assassination when he handed me the interview which Rathenau had revised during the previous day.

As Rathenau was practically the father of the Rapallo Treaty between Germany and Soviet Russia, I was particularly interested in his views on Russo-German relations. He denied that the Treaty was a step to a military alliance

between these two nations. He was particularly emphatic
in denying that the Treaty contained any secret provisions.
Then he asked me, with a smile:

"Do you think we would sign a secret treaty with the
Soviet government of Russia? The secret would be out
in twenty-four hours."

In revising the manuscript, Rathenau changed these
words to read as follows:

"We have made no secret treaty with Russia, and we
will not make any."

He explained to me his reasons for concluding the treaty
with Russia at Rapallo while the Genoa conference was in
session, as follows:

"The treaty we signed is a peace treaty between Germany
and Russia. It is neither a military, political, nor even a
trade treaty. We negotiated it some time before the
Genoa conference and could have signed it before. But
we did not desire to prejudice the work of the Conference.
We signed it during the Conference because we learned that,
according to a memorandum prepared in London before the
Genoa Conference, it was planned to make Russia also a
creditor of Germany. Russia was to be asked to insist also
on reparations—perhaps not for herself, but for the other
powers—she was to be asked that Germany's debts to Russia should be paid to the other powers. Practically all the
great nations were our creditors, and Russia was to be added
among our creditors. Before the Genoa Conference this
was decided upon by the powers. Germany was the only
power that was kept out of a series of secret preliminary
conferences held at the Villa d'Alberti. It was then that
we resolved to sign the Rapallo Treaty. We were blamed
and sharply criticized for having done what we were actu-

ally forced to do.   Two other powers did the same thing—
they also negotiated treaties with Russia at the same time,
only they signed them later, but they were neither criticized
nor censured in any way.

"After the Rapallo Treaty we acted as mediators between Russia and other powers, and some of the statesmen
of the other powers thanked us for our efforts in that direction.   We helped to bring Russia closer to the Western
powers.   We encouraged the more conservative elements
of the Russian government, as is evidenced by the fact that
the only criticism in Russia against the treaty came from
the ranks of the extreme Left."

In answer to my question whether there was any ground
for the opinions that the Rapallo Treaty was but a prelude
to a Russo-German military alliance in the future, Dr.
Rathenau replied:

"The Rapallo Treaty is nothing else than a peace treaty,
by which we recognized the Soviet Government.   We have
no secret treaties of any kind with Russia, and we will not
make any.

"Russia's reconstruction can come about only through the
united efforts of the powers, and the sooner that is started
the better for all.   Every day of delay now will cause much
more than a day of delay afterward in bringing about such
a reconstruction.   Germany, knowing Russia well, and having come into closer contact with Russia in the past, will
naturally be in a position to do most for Russia's readjustment, through our organization ability, our technical experience and our familiarity with the required methods."

"What is most essential for the purpose of the readjustment of Europe and its reconstruction?"   I asked.

Dr. Rathenau replied:

"First of all it is essential to demobilize the public opinion created during the past seven years. Thus far the demobilization of this public opinion has not yet begun. For seven years the Allied countries and the United States heard only one side of the case. It was not a fair trial. The other side has really not been heard to this day. Whatever was said by us or in our favor was immediately branded as propaganda. As soon as any statement presenting our case appeared in any newspaper outside of Germany, hundreds of other newspapers declared such a statement to be a falsehood inspired by German propagandists.

"We are now going to publish twenty-two volumes of documents relating to the World War. We are throwing open the archives of our Foreign Office to the whole world. It is to be a scientific work, prepared under the supervision of unprejudiced historians. What other government is going to do the same? For seven years our side of the case was not heard. Now the 'criminal' is telling everything, while the innocent lambs will be taciturn on this subject. They are not going to open the archives of their Foreign Offices which could reveal some very interesting facts. The demobilization of prejudiced public opinion should begin at once, if the world is to be readjusted.

"The United States will have to help in the reconstruction of the world. The United States will eventually discover that it cannot disregard the plight of Europe. I can understand why the United States dislikes Europe now, or why it is disgusted with it, or tired of it, but it will find out that it cannot continue to maintain this attitude of of indifference. The United States decided the outcome of the war and the United States decided the peace. The

United States is thus really responsible for the consequences of the peace. It is true that it did not ratify the Treaty of Versailles, but the Treaty between the United States and Germany contains the stipulation that the advantages secured by the Treaty of Versailles shall not be forfeited by the United States, and in this way the United States recognized that peace treaty.

"The condition of Europe is now worse than it was before the war. Before the war Alsace-Lorraine was perhaps the sorest spot. How many sore spots are there now after the end of the world war?

"The only sign of returning reason was to be seen in the recent conference of the bankers in Paris. They have practically made it clear that the reparation clauses in the treaty would have to be revised to meet facts instead of theories. The money-lenders understand this question better than anybody else. Without them the world can hardly be readjusted now. At present there is so much unemployment, idleness and laziness. Instead of working, people seem to be holding one another by the throat. Under such circumstances nothing can be accomplished. The beginning must be made by the demobilization of prejudiced public opinion created during the war. For seven years the world was fed on falsehoods, and the atmosphere must now be cleared in order that reason may prevail."

GEORGE CHICHERIN

Berlin, July, 1922.

I INTERVIEWED George Chicherin, the Commissary for Foreign Affairs of the Soviet Republic of Russia, who signed the Rapallo Treaty for the Russian government. He received me at the Esplanade Hotel in Berlin and discussed the Russian situation at considerable length. Answering my question about the impression that the signing of the Rapallo Treaty produced in Russia, Chicherin said:

"The Russian people regard this as the model of all treaties to be concluded with other states by Russia. The principle of wiping out all claims, as fully laid down in the Russo-German Treaty, is considered by us as the only basis for future relations between Russia and other states.

"The ruling idea is that we must now build our new future. The needs and interests of foreigners are guaranteed by our new legislation and by the agreements with other governments and concessionaires—all these, of course, within the limits of our system of nationalized property, transport and soil.

"But the past must remain the past. We cannot take upon ourselves the old burdens. We also have our counter claims, resulting from the invasion of Russia and from intervention. The mass of our people is extremely sensitive with regard to these counter claims. Our people felt the calamity of intervention. It is therefore impossible for them to consent that the claims of Russia's creditors shall be recognized, while our counter claims are not recognized. It is the reciprocal wiping out of all claims— as in the Russo-German treaty—that the Russian people consider the only possible solution."

When I remarked that the fear has been expressed that the Rapallo Treaty was the beginning of a military alliance which may become a serious danger in the future, Chicherin answered slowly:

"The Russian government desires peace—with everybody. Its wishes regarding Germany are directed to economic collaboration, and we are equally desirous of securing economic collaboration with other countries. If other countries are afraid that we will unite ourselves too closely with Germany, the best way of preventing this is for them to enter into friendly relations with Russia. If everybody is hostile to us and only Germany is friendly to us, such hostility is imposed upon us by the other powers."

Discussing America's attitude toward Russia, Chicherin said:

"The American government is very poorly informed about Russia. It still seems to think that a change of government is imminent there. Every careful observer will absolutely refute this idea. The enormous majority of the Russian people is completely behind the government. It is impossible to maintain indefinitely a wall between the United States and Russia. It is inevitable that the American government will realize that it will have to deal with our government. It would be much better for both if that were done sooner. American trade can only profit from such an arrangement. At present, business between America and Russia is impossible, because American businessmen feel that since there are not even de facto relations, there can be no protection—and every business man wants trade relations resumed.

"If the American government were fully informed of the present state of things in Russia, it would not continue to wait for a change of government there. In some utterances made by the American government it is stated that there will be no relations with Russia until the Soviet government is replaced by another. In other utterances it is only a change of system that is demanded. So far as this change of system refers to security for foreigners and the guarantee of personal rights, it is already provided for in our new legislation. But so far as the American government demands a complete change in our system of property and the full reëstablishment in Russia of private property instead of our national ownership—which means that the American government demands a fundamental change of our whole economic system—in other words, the abandonment of our present régime—that is obviously impossible. The mass of workers will not reëstablish private property in the factories, and the mass of peasants will not permit the restoration of big land properties. The national control of foreign trade and big production in Russia is absolutely essential for the protection of our people against their enslavement by the predominant capitalist states. Our system is one of self-defense and of the protection of the political and economic freedom and independence of Russia."

Of intervention, Chicherin said:

"We are not at all sure that the French government has abandoned the idea of a new intervention. The French government is persistently hostile to us. The idea naturally arises that either the French government still hopes to overthrow our government, or it must try to come to terms with our government. Since the French government is rejecting all our offers for an agreement, our natural assumption is that it still entertains hopes to overthrow the Soviet government of Russia. Of course, I do not know the plans of the French government but *experience has shown that all attempts to overthrow us by force were doomed to complete failure, and on the contrary helped to cement more strongly the solidarity of the Russian people.*"

Those who regard the Rapallo Treaty as the beginning of a Russo-German military alliance found their opinioin confirmed by Leo Trotzky's recent threat. When it was reported that France was on the point of exerting military pressure on Germany by invading the Ruhr, Leo Trotzky, in a statement to the foreign press representatives, declared as follows:

"Suppose France brings military pressure on Germany. In that event Poland can hardly remain passive. If Poland acts against Germany, I question whether we can remain passive ourselves."

Karl Radek, the Soviet government's leading propagandist, discussing the Russo-German treaty, recently wrote:

"Many silly things have been said about a military agreement between Soviet Russia and Germany. We are alleged to have obligated ourselves to maintain an enormous army. If Poland and its more or less sincere friends decline to reply to the question concerning the limitation of armaments, it must begin to dawn even on the simplest mind that it is not because of a secret agreement with Germany, but because of a secret agreement between France and our neighbors that we must keep our army intact."

That Russia and Germany would some day be drawn together after the world war, was a foregone conclusion to those who knew the temper of the Russian and the German peoples after the Peace Conference. The Rapallo Treaty was but a gesture on the part of the two exhausted nations.

After the Russian revolution many solutions of the Russian problem were attempted by friends and enemies of Russia. Numerous blunders were committed in these attempts at saving Russia—in fact, few blunders were left uncommitted. The Russians knew the new Russia just as little as the non-Russians did. The blunders that were made forced Russia into the arms of Germany, and helped to keep the Soviet government in power.

An American friend, intimately familiar with the attitude of Col. Edward M. House toward the Russian problem, after the Revolution, during the war and at the peace Conference, said to me:

"Colonel House is one of the very few statesmen who understood the Russian problem immediately after the Revolution, who advocated a sane course in the treatment of Russia, and who in 1917 and 1918 cautioned the Allied statesmen against the dangerous consequences of the mistaken Russian policy pursued at that time.

"Colonel House was asked by French and British statesmen to agree to their policy of intervention, when he was in Paris. He told them at that time that the planned intervention would only help to keep the Soviet government in power. He was opposed to the French and British policy adopted toward Russia, and when he returned to the United States and presented his views on this subject, he was sustained by the President.

"Some time afterward, while Colonel House was away in Europe again, various French and British commissions came to the United States and kept impressing President Wilson with the urgent need of intervention in Russia. It was then that the President finally agreed to the sending of troops to Archangel and to Siberia, with the sad result that everybody knows.

"The policy of intervention by which the Allies sought to crush the bolshevist government of Russia, produced exactly the opposite effect. Various Russian emigrés and Allied statesmen tried to convince Colonel House—in order that he might influence the President—that all that was necessary was to raise the Allied flags in Russia, and the Russian people would rally to the anti-bolshevist forces and overthrow the Soviet government. Colonel House pointed out to them that their theories would only lead to greater confusion.

"Some time later, after several attempts at intervention had failed, Allied statesmen endeavored to convince Colonel House again that intervention on a huge scale was essential, and that this time their plan was bound to prove successful. They were anxious to have him exert his influence with the President in that direction. In answer to his question where they intended to get an army for such purpose, they assured him that they could raise an army of about two million men in Poland, Czecho-Slovakia and Yugo-Slavia, under the leadership of French officers, in order to invade Russia. His next question was, 'But where will you get funds to finance this enterprise?' Naturally they looked to the United States to supply the necessary money. Colonel House shattered their hopes by informing them that they could not get a nickel in the United States.

"Colonel House's plan to help Russia at that time was that the United States should do for Russia what it had

done for Belgium, that Herbert Hoover should organize in
Russia a system of relief upon a large scale, to aid the Russian people, helping province after province, without the
slightest interference with the internal affairs of Russia.
The Russian people needed relief even then, and he believed that first of all the Russian people who had just
liberated themselves from the worst autocracy that had oppressed them should be aided in their distress, and sec-
ondly, he regarded it of the utmost importance that the
world should know exactly what was going on in Russia.

"All of the information which came from Russia, with
but few exceptions, was based on propagandist materials
sent broadcast by the Bolsheviki, painting rosy pictures of
the blessings of the dictatorship of the proletariat, while
the inspired Allied and Russian anti-bolshevist propaganda
outside of Russia distorted the truth quite as much on the
other side.

"All that served to confuse the Russian situation in the
minds of the people everywhere, and the solution grew ever
more complicated and difficult. But the effect of it all
was that Russia and Germany were forced into each other's
arms."

EDUARD BENES

Prague, July, 1922.

"It is a mistake to think that the reconstruction of Europe can come through the reconstruction of Russia.

"The Genoa conference has shown it. The Hague conference now confirms it.

"The trouble is that there has not yet been advanced any definite constructive program for the rebuilding of Europe. Genoa has proved it. The Hague confirms it.

"Thirty-four nations came to the Genoa Conference with good intentions, but without any program. Even Lloyd George's program—the only more or less definite plan—was inadequate.

"My plan of the Little Entente was conceived for the purpose of establishing peace and friendship with our neighbors. After we have signed our treaties, nothing can happen in Central Europe without us or against us. We are as strong as the ancient Austro-Hungarian empire ever was.

"The main problem in Europe is not Russia but Germany.

"There must be a complete political and economic agreement between Great Britain and France. Only that would bring peace and stability to Europe."

These striking statements were made to me in Prague by Dr. Eduard Benes, the Premier of Czecho-Slovakia, the foremost of Europe's younger statesmen.

Though Dr. Benes represented a new state—one of the smaller states of Europe—he was nevertheless one of the most conspicuous and influential factors at the conference in which he participated. He is daring, picturesque, constructive, practical. Even his enemies admit his courage and his genius.

Benes, the father of the Little Entente—a sort of United States of Europe—believes in force—in the force of friendship united for peace. He realized that the strength of his country lay first in work and then in the good will and friendship of its neighbors. Czecho-Slovakia was surrounded by enemy states that had suffered economically and territorially because of the creation of this new state. It was surrounded by peoples that hated and envied the new state which started to work so industriously and which is making better progress than any of the new states and many of the older states in Europe.

A patriot, a philosopher, a publicist of note, a worthy pupil of Professor Masaryk, Benes suddenly rose to the task and responsibility of true statesmanship, so sadly lacking in Europe just now—and his fame and influence are rapidly growing throughout Europe.

Masaryk in Washington and Benes in Paris really created Czecho-Slovakia during the war and at the peace conference. Their eloquent pleas and their forceful arguments won to their cause the Allied statesmen, and particularly the deep sympathies of President Wilson and Colonel House. Czecho-Slovakia was created and set up as an important new state.

The story of the 40,000 Czecho-Slovak "prisoners of war" in Russia, whom the Russian Red Armies sought to disarm after the Brest-Litovsk treaty had been signed between Germany and Russia, and who were going through Siberia to the Western Front to aid the Allies, was one of the great dramatic events of the world war. The Czecho-Slovaks resisted the superior force of the Red Army, seized practically the whole of Siberia and became the masters of the situation along a line of about five thousand miles—from the Urals to Vladivostock. Their popularity with the Russian population of Siberia testified to the fact that they were not only courageous but also tactful and considerate as victors. They displayed extraordinary energy and genius for organization.

Shortly after the creation of the new state the people of Czecho-Slovakia employed the same energy, perseverance and organization ability to put their country in order. Amidst the chaos, confusion and idleness in Europe, they started to work and build; they created new centers of learning and culture, and also gave shelter to thousands of students and hundreds of professors, who had been deprived of the means of continuing their educational work in Soviet Russia.

Czecho-Slovakia worked, prospered and has grown strong. And this was accomplished so quickly mainly through the efforts of Masaryk, that practical idealist and savant, the President of Czecho-Slovakia, beloved by the people of Czecho-Slovakia, known as their "dear little father," and of Benes, the courageous young master builder of an empire of peace—of a united states of Europe.

This young man of 38, Dr. Eduard Benes, has become the most interesting and dominating figure in the affairs of Central Europe.

I sought his views regarding the questions that stir the minds of all who know the seriousness of Europe's ailment and who strive to find a solution of the puzzling and perplexing problems of the reconstruction of Europe. In the course of a long interview, Dr. Benes said:

"As you are travelling through Europe, you see that Europe is in bad shape. Europe is going through a period of political, economic and intellectual decadence.

"The World War was the worst in all history. More human lives, more property, more values were destroyed than in any other war in the past. It is quite natural that a period of terrible decadence, unrest, confusion, and chaos should follow in the wake of this destruction.

"But I am not pessimistic as to the outcome. It could hardly be expected that after such an enormous catastrophe, the reconstruction of Europe could come about in four years. Confidence and credits have been destroyed—the most vital things so essential for the restoration of normal international relations have been completely upset.

"Four great empires were destroyed—Germany, Russia, Austro-Hungary and Turkey. Austro-Hungary was partly destroyed. Russia is practically destroyed and ruined, and Germany is also destroyed economically.

"Out of the Austro-Hungarian empire new states have been formed. Ours is an entirely new state. We had to build everything, and we have built, and we are building. How far we have already succeeded may be judged from the fact that in 1920 we had an active export balance exceeding our imports by three billions of crowns, and in 1921 our exports exceeded our imports by five billions. No other country in Europe, with the exception of England, can point to such a record after the war. And our currency is stabilized. Our people are working hard, and as soon as there is a restoration to more normal conditions in our neighboring states, our own situation will naturally be still better.

"Europe cannot be reconstructed through Russia. If other powers give money to Russia, that may help Russia to a certain extent, but it cannot help Europe for many years to come. Russia is unable to give anything to Europe for a long time. It simply means that we would re-enforce the Bolsheviki. The Bolshevist theories and experiments have failed. Everybody knows it now. But the Soviet representatives cannot admit that much. They didn't admit it at Genoa, nor do they admit it at The Hague. They went as far as they could go, at Genoa. But the facts make their admissions unnecessary.

"The Russian communists went forward too fast, and they must retreat rapidly in order to save themselves. So they had to resort to all sorts of compromises and methods of evolution for the purpose of going back.

"It was a grotesque picture to see the Soviet representatives, after having criticized old Europe most sharply and having declared that it was doomed to utter destruction, asking that same old Europe for money in order that they may save themselves. In this way the Soviet régime admitted its failure. The Bolsheviki had sentenced Europe and its capitalism to political and social death. They declared war on capitalism, they prophesied its immediate collapse, and now these fundamental enemies of capitalism ask the capitalists for help, for money. What a wonderful theme for satirical caricaturists!

"The Rapallo Treaty between Russia and Germany is of no importance either to Russia or to Germany. Russia cannot give anything to Germany, and Germany in her present condition cannot do anything to aid Russia.

"The trouble is that no definite, constructive program and no plan of method for the rehabilitation of Europe have as yet been advanced by any of the statesmen.

"Thirty-four nations came to Genoa. They came with the best of intentions, with enthusiasm, with the desire for peace and for reconstruction, but without any program—without any plan or method of rebuilding Europe and restoring normal conditions.

"The only man who had some plan was Lloyd George. His plan was first to reconstruct Russia and through Russia the rest of Europe, and second, to have a pact for non-aggression signed by the nations.

"That plan was not adequate. Europe may be able to help Russia, but Russia does nothing now to help Europe. And as for the non-aggression pact, it is really of no importance, for no nation wants any new wars now.

"The intellectual life of Europe is in a state of almost complete collapse, too. In Vienna, for instance, there are 22 chairs vacant at the universities because economic conditions and the inadequate remuneration make it impossible for professors to exist there. Intellectual intercourse is practically at a standstill in Europe. In Germany, for instance, very few scientific books can be published because it is too expensive to produce them, and only very few scientists can afford to buy books and periodicals in Europe nowadays. The governments are unable to give any subsidies for these things now. They must help first of all the unemployed in order to avert disturbances and check unrest, and they must help the crippled veterans of the war.

"As for our own state, we first of all commenced by

eradicating the war psychology in our country. That is really the first requisite of peace.

"As a new state we were surrounded by enemies. Germany, Austria, Hungary, and Poland were our enemies when Czecho-Slovakia was set up as a state.

"In the chaos, in the anarchy in Central Europe, unchained by the war, we decided to build the spine—the backbone of a new organization, first on a basis of force, so that our neighbors should see that we were strong, that we were healthy, that we were working and building, that we settled down for peace; and then I knew they would realize that they could collaborate with us. We set out to establish a policy of friendship, first with Yugo-Slavia and Roumania. After our treaties with these countries were concluded, nothing could happen in Central Europe without us or against us. We became the center with which all other states in Central Europe were obliged to come into contact. It was easy then to negotiate with Austria. We were in position thus to prevent war with Hungary when Charles made two attempts to return as King. We were also able then to show Poland the insecurity and danger of her own position between Germany and Russia, and her advantages in joining the Little Entente.

"We made economic treaties with Austria, Poland, Roumania, Yugo-Slavia, Italy, Spain, France, and even Russia. The results of our Russian treaty are of no particular significance or value as yet.

"The rebuilding of Europe from the bottom up is necessarily a slow process, but after the destruction of four great empires, after the destruction of the achievements of many centuries, it is foolish to think that we can rebuild Europe in the short space of a few years.

"We must be patient. We must be strong. We must be industrious and energetic. We must oppose all demagogy, all unreasonable nationalism and chauvinism. We must be practical.

"In Austria, for instance, the question of reparations has so overwhelmed the people that they have lost all their courage, all desire to work, to grow rich. They have lost their energy, their nerve. They say, 'What is the use of working, if we are actually working for others?' With such ideas and in such a state of mind, Europe cannot be reconstructed. There is too much demagogy, too much of war psychology still prevailing in many countries of Europe.

"I prefer to work hard and grow rich, and give part of my wealth to my neighbors rather than lie down in idleness and drift to utter ruination.

"The main problem in Europe is not Russia but Germany. If Germany were helped toward readjustment, Europe would really be helping itself. If you give money to Russia, you cannot get anything in return for many years, and Europe cannot be helped that way. But if we find a plan for helping Germany, the effect on Europe would be immediate and helpful all around.

"I repeat, I believe in starting with the simple in order to have enough strength to cope with the more complex problems afterward.

"The Russian problem will require many years to be solved. There will be chaos and anarchy there, but Russia's salvation will come from within, from the Russians in Russia. So many blunders have already been made by various statesmen that the wisest thing is to let the Russian experiment prove its failure completely and unmistakably. In the meantime democratic sentiment among the Russian people is gathering strength, and I foresee a strong republican Russia emerging out of the ruins. But that, it is obvious, cannot come suddenly.

"If Russia were now recognized politically, she would become a political factor in the world, without being an economic factor in the reconstruction, on the contrary, the disorder and uncertainty would be intensified. The Bolsheviki would gain in prestige and power, and the labor organizations everywhere may again be misled, and thus the unrest might grow everywhere. It would mean that we would give Russia a voice in political affairs, without any economic advantages to be gained from such a measure for any other country.

"As for America's attitude to Europe and to Russia in particular, I can easily understand her reserve and caution in European affairs now. But my opinion is that the United States have thus far refused to participate in the conference for the reconstruction of Europe mainly because no concrete, practical program has yet been submitted to them.

"What can be done for the reconstruction of Europe? What are the preliminary steps which must be taken?

"First of all, there must be a complete agreement between Great Britain and France. Italy would fall in line with such an agreement. These powers must have a definite and reasonable economic and political understanding and agreement. That would immediately serve to restore peace and stability in Europe. Without such an agreement there can be no reconstruction.

"When these powers agree among themselves, they will finally have to take the first step in the direction of a definite understanding with regard to reparations. When that question is definitely and reasonably settled, there would be a real basis for Germany to start along new economic lines. That would also form a basis for an international loan, and the stabilization of the German currency, which would surely have an immediate and most beneficent effect everywhere and would hasten the re-establishment of peace and order in Europe."

STEPAN RADICZ

Zagreb, Croatia, July, 1922.

I WENT to Yugo-Slavia to familiarize myself with the blunder that was made there by the Peace Conference. It is a very serious blunder, for the population is in a state of intense unrest, and an explosion may occur there at any moment if precautionary measures are not taken in time to avert the new catastrophe where the World War was started.

The trouble in Yugo-Slavia is due to the fact that one portion of the population is for a militarist state and the other for a republic. The Serbians are trying to establish a strong military Serbia under the name of Yugo-Slavia, while the Croatians and the Slovenians want a peaceful national existence as a republic. Though they speak the same language, their ideals and aspirations differ widely. They are divided by differences of religion and their history. The Serbians belong to the Greek Orthodox Church, while the Croatians are Catholics. The Serbians lived for centuries under the rule of the Turk; they had hardly any opportunity for cultural development, and they see their glory in a powerful military state; while the Croatians, though only oppressed, by Hungary, enjoyed a certain degree of autonomy and assimilated Western culture.

After the lessons of the World War, the Croatians see their salvation and their opportunity for development under a republican form of government. Besides, there are about three quarters of a million Croatians in the United States, and through them the influence of their Americanization is felt practically in every village of Croatia. The Croatian peasantry dream of a United States of Slavs—under a republican form of government. But if that is impossible, if the Serbians must have their king, the Croatians want a republic in Croatia, with Zagreb as its Capital, and they are willing to be associated with the Serbian kingdom upon terms of friendship and equality.

The Serbians, flushed with victory and eager for a greater Serbia, are imposing their will upon the rest of the population by force of arms. Hence the grave danger of a new explosion, of a new war.

I discussed the Yugo-Slav blunder with various leaders and I talked with the peasants in the Croatian villages. There is no doubt that their movement for liberty is strong and genuine. Fortunately, the leaders of the peasants are level-headed men, with a profound sense of responsibility. They are courageous, they are conscious of their power, but they are not firebrands.

The most picturesque, influential and popular leader in Croatia is Stepan Radicz. A publicist of note, a philosopher, he is the idol of the Croatian peasants who constitute the vast majority of the population. The Serbians regard him as their most dangerous enemy—they call him a rebel —and they kept him in prison for almost two years. The Croatian peasants regard him as a martyr. They call him their President. They love him as their friend and their teacher. Seventeen times he was thrown into prison by the Austro-Hungarian authorities for championing the cause of the people's independence, and after the World War he was imprisoned for 21 months by the Siberian Government for a speech he made, advocating a republic for Croatia.

Stepan Radicz is not a revolutionist, as the Serbians call him. He is religious, though not a fanatic. He believes in progress, but he is not an advocate of violence. He is a real responsible leader of the people and he is inspired by a real sense of justice. He is a brilliant orator and a vigorous writer. He knows how to talk to the peasants in terms they best understand. His appearance in any village in Croatia is hailed with enthusiasm and joy. The peasants' homes are ornamented with his pictures. I travelled with Radicz through a number of villages in order to speak to the peasants themselves. Before going to the villages, Radicz wanted me to see the cemetery at Zagreb. He showed me the monuments erected years ago to Croatian poets, scientists, philosophers, martyrs—champions of justtice and liberty. He said: "Before you see our people in the villages, you must see that our nation always honored our intellectual leaders rather than our military heroes."

Then we went from village to village and talked with the people. Wherever we came the peasants dropped their work and greeted their "president." The children and the women in the villages greeted him with exclamations, "Long live the Republic!" The men complained of the high taxes imposed on them by the Serbian Government to maintain a huge army. They all said they wanted a republic, in order to be able to work in peace.

Stepan Radicz spoke to them. His speeches were brief and eloquent. He advocated liberty, but he always begged them to be patient and not to launch on any rash adventures.

During our trip through the villages Stepan Radicz outlined to me the aspirations of his people, the cause of unrest, and his fears of an explosion which may lead to a new catastrophe.

He said: "Those who have learned something from the war are the victors. Those who have learned nothing from the war are the losers, whether they are among the Allies or the Central Powers. Our people saw that the Tsar of Russia, the Kaiser of Germany and the Kaiser of Austro-Hungary had been overthrown. They saw that republicanism was the order of the day. Our simple people reasoned simply. They said that since the big monarchies were ended, it would be unwise to start smaller monarchies now. My own teacher, Professor Masaryk, made a grave mistake when he told the Allied statesmen that the Serbians were the most important factor in Yugo-Slavia, and that the Croatians were slaves, and that a union of these peoples under the leadership of Serbia was the best way of solving the problem. Thus a monarchy was forced upon us. Our people were not consulted. There was no plebiscite of any kind.

"A week before the armistice, on October 29, 1918, we Croatians proclaimed our independence. A month later the Constituent Assembly for Yugo-Slavia met. It was dominated by Serbia. One thing had been decided in advance —that all must recognize the monarchy—the dynasty. That was an insult to our intelligence and also to our spirit of democracy.

"Our people, the Croatians, the most cultured of the entire Yugo-Slav group, see and feel how the Serbians are forcing the monarchy and terrorist rule upon us by violence —by force of bayonets. The Serbians say that Serbia is surrounded by enemies, that seven nations are their enemies, and therefore a large standing army is absolutely essential.

Our people say, 'If all your neighbors are your enemies, you must be at fault.' Our people say that pigs do not grow on bayonets, that armies do not build a country, that peace and work are the only roads to prosperity. They are perplexed, because the Serbians who have learned nothing from the war have been made the masters in Yugo-Slavia.

"We Croatians received the majority of votes in our territory, but our views were not consulted and our wishes were not honored. The King is Serbian, the entire government is Serbian. We have a higher culture than the Serbians, who were for centuries oppressed by the Turk. They acquired some of the savage methods of their oppressors, and are now imposing a tyranny upon us even as it was imposed upon them by the Turk. Our peasants are persecuted for expressing opinions favoring a republic. We, the intellectuals, holding these views, were also thrown into prison, but we were liberated, while the peasants are still being persecuted, and herein lies the real tragedy. Our peasants see that the common people are handled unceremoniously, while the leaders are treated with consideration. Leaders, even revolutionary leaders, are ready to compromise when they find themselves in an awkward predicament. They sometimes even stoop to corruption. Not so the people. They want no compromises. They say, 'We are working hard, we are prosperous because of our work. The Serbians are concentrating all their energies on the army, on violence. We want democracy, freedom, while they want a monarchy, oppression. We cannot and will not bear their burdens!'

"We, the leaders, know that we have both the force and the ability to impose our will—the will of the people—on the government. But we have a higher sense of duty. We know where we would start, but we do not know where we would end. We cannot tell what temptations other governments may develop when they see civil war in our country.

"Politics, like business, must have a certain measure of idealism—otherwise it cannot succeed. We must think not only of the present but also of the future. A business man who thinks of the future must necessarily possess a certain degree of idealism, honesty and morality. These qualities are entirely lacking in the Yugo-Slav administration.

"I was kept 21 months in prison by the Serbian government. For eleven months not a soul was permitted to see me. My family was not sure that I was alive. I was imprisoned for a speech in which I said, 'Long live the King —in Serbia—not in Croatia. Our people want freedom— a republic!'

"At the end of 21 months, on election day, when it became apparent that I would get an enormous majority of the votes, I was pardoned by the King. I was asked whether there was anything I wanted. I said 'I want nothing for myself. I am fifty years old now—I need much less now than when I was twenty. I want nothing for myself. But I want freedom for my people. If you want my views on this subject I shall gladly give them to you. You are spending millions on an army. You have a bigger army than Great Britain has. You have an army three times as large as that of the United States. You have more than three times as many gendarmes as the empire of Austro-Hungary had. You are spending the greater part of the budget to maintain an organization of force and violence, and there is hardly anything left for schools and other constructive measures. This strength of yours is your greatest weakness. As for the King, I have nothing against him as a man, nor have I anything against him as a King, if the Serbians want him.   But my people want a republic.   We are willing to recognize and honor him in every way—we are even willing to be associated with the Serbian state, but equally as a federated state.'

"The state as constituted in Yugo-Slavia to-day not only fails to solve the oriental problem, but it aggravates it, and there will be no real peace here until this situation is adjusted through the moral pressure of the Great Powers who desire peace in Europe."

The vice-president of the Croatian Peasants' Party said:

"Serbia has an army of 200,000 men.   She has a huge number of gendarmes, and then she has the Wrangel army of more than a hundred thousand reactionary Russians. The Serbian government has started out with a wrong formula—raw centralization of violence.   They want to erect a great Serbian state by destroying the Croatian people—a historic, cultural and economic unit which had its own independent state thirteen centuries ago.   Therefore, since the Serbians constitute only four millions of the population of Yugo-Slavia, and the other nations together constitute more than eight millions, the Serbians had to create a wild military state.   In Dalmatia and Bosnia the Wrangel gendarmes are flogging the people and plundering them. Serbian troops are doing that, too.

"Besides, the government is organizing so-called patriotic bands, maintained on government funds, instructed by Serbian officers.   They are supplied with firearms, and are used for the purpose of intimidating the people by methods of terrorism.   Serbian chauvinism is rabid now.   Experienced and capable Croatian officials are dismissed from government posts, and replaced by incompetent and dishonest Serbs. The worst forms of corruption and graft are practiced openly. The security of the rights of person and property is destroyed by the militarist régime of Belgrade. Even religion is employed for political purposes. Many Greek Catholics are forced to join the Greek Orthodox Church. They think they can build a greater Serbia in that way.

"Corporal punishment has been introduced. Thousands of people have been beaten with sticks for no other reason that they said they were in favor of a republic. Many villages have been destroyed and thousands of people killed in Bosnia and Sandjak, as so-called enemies of the State."

Professor Shurmin, editor of the *Zagreb Obzor*, for 16 years a representative of the Croatian people, and a former member of the Cabinet, said:

"Croatia, as the most cultured of the nations in Yugo-Slavia, was always Western in culture and education. During the World War Croatia was heart and soul against Prussianism, because Prussianism always helped to oppress the Slavs.

"We are not opposed to the Serbs. They have the same language we have, though not the same culture. But we are opposed to the government that resorts to violence to destroy us as a nation. We are in favor of finding a way for co-operation. We are willing to remain together with them, but as equals. Our people are republican in spirit. Let the people, through the plebiscite, decide the form of government, and form of union to be established. Then peace will prevail in our country. We cannot submit to an oriental, Asiatic rule now. We always gravitated to Western ideals, and we cannot start on the dangerous road of militarism now that we see so clearly what has happened to the great military autocracies of Russia, Germany and Austro-Hungary."

The opening paragraph of the Constitution of the Neutral Peasant Republic of Croatia, adopted in March, 1921, reads in part as follows:

"We Croatians, as a nation of a very old peasant culture, have by the inevitable course of events of the World War been delivered from the oppressive aristocratic feudal Magyar centralism, and from the German militarist sovereignty of the Hapsburg monarchy.

" . . . Aware of all these factors in the emancipation of the country and in unison with the conservative West, we are preserving the foundations of civilization and of the production of wealth, and with the revolutionary East, we are simultaneously creating a State in which all cultural as well as wealth-producing elements, but particularly the peasant and working classes, shall have their fullest share in all branches of government and administration. . . ."

As we travelled through the villages, I met many Croatians who had been in America and who returned to their native land after the war. They had worked in American shops and factories, and brought the spirit of America to their native villages. Most of them were disillusioned. They had hurried back in the hope of finding liberty in their old home. I saw several homes decorated with American flags.

One of these peasants who had only recently returned from the United States said:

"I was in America about fifteen years. I have come back to my native country thinking that it was free now. I learned to work in America, and this makes me rich here.

But we are not free, and that makes me unhappy. I can't get used to this life."

A woman who came from America to her native village said:

"I love America because it is a republic. And I love a republic because I love my children. I don't want to lose them in the next war, and I don't think republics will have any more wars after this dreadful war we had."

As we rode through the villages we saw the fertile soil of Croatia. We saw the peasants at work. We saw their hospitality. We heard their folk songs and watched the national dances of the girls and young men after the day's work was done.

Late in the evening, on the way back to Zagreb, our automobile broke down. We waited all night in the fields. It was cold and dark, and a distance from a village.

The sun rose at about three o'clock. Shortly afterward we saw here and there young men and women coming out to the fields, beginning their new day's work. At first they were silent, and then we heard them singing as they worked.

At about five o'clock in the morning we found a pair of horses and a hay wagon and rode back to Zagreb, the capital of Croatia, fatigued but profoundly impressed with the industrious and picturesque little peasant nation that wants liberty and peace.

ARTHUR SCHNITZLER

Vienna, July, 1922.

I MET Arthur Schnitzler in his study in Vienna. A fine copy of Mona Lisa was conspicuous among the numerous portraits on the walls, and on his desk stood a statuette of Goethe. The brilliant Viennese dramatist and novelist, whose sixtieth birthday was recently celebrated by his friends and admirers, is youthful despite the gray in his hair and beard, and his kindly smile is as full of charm as ever. During the past few months many eulogies by the foremost dramatists, novelists and critics appeared in various European periodicals and newspapers.

Schnitzler is beloved by all who know him. All agree that his artistic works are marked with a peculiar charm and are of lasting value. He has portrayed men and women as they really are—with their dreams and their passions, their foibles and their follies.

Gerhardt Hauptmann, summing up the achievements of Schnitzler thus far, writes that to have an appreciation of Schnitzler is to have an appreciation of art and culture. Hermann Bahr predicts that Schnitzler will fare better than other writers a hundred years hence, for when future generations will want to study the traits, the modes of life and thought during the years of Austria's sunset, they will have to go back to Schnitzler who mirrored that sunset most clearly, who reproduced as no one else the last charm of

Vienna in the shadows, who was the doctor at her death bed, who loved her more deeply than anyone else, who was the last poet of her agony.

Schnitzler spoke with deep emotion of Austria's pathetic plight, of the beauty and grandeur of her landscapes and of her still undeveloped opportunities, of the curse of too much politics in Austria, and for that matter in the whole of Europe, and then he pointed to the growth of prejudice and hate after the war.

"What is becoming of Europe?" he said. "The hate which has been intensified by the war is growing and spreading, and the most dreadful feature of it all is that people are talking of new wars in the near future.

"On August 1, 1914,—on the day of the declaration of war—I wrote a letter to my brother of which I should have been ashamed a little later. I gave him my reasons why it was impossible that such a world war could take place. It was a foolish letter in view of the events that followed so rapidly, and that involved practically the whole world in the war. But only now—after several years of so-called peace, we see clearly that the war was really impossible. It was the most brutal of all wars. It destroyed more values than any previous war, and it has left the world in a much worse condition than it was before the war. We see chaos, poverty, ruination everywhere in Europe. And we see more hate than before the war.

"To check this spread of hate in various countries, it seems to me that it is urgent for intellectual leaders everywhere to create good will and a better understanding among the nations. A great campaign of education is essential in that direction. We have seen that Socialism has failed to meet the problems of war and peace effectively and has not exerted such an influence either in the war or in the making of peace.

"We must realize, first of all, that man is the worst of all animals—the most cruel of them all.   The difference between the human being and other animals is that the human being possesses such traits as joy at another's misfortune, and false indignation.   Animals have no such terrible traits.   We must also realize that while the human mind may be improved by education, the human soul cannot be improved—for it cannot be changed.   We may therefore hope that human beings will some day become wiser, but they cannot become better.   The mind may be improved, but not the soul.   Human beings are born egotists.   They do not love one another unselfishly—they hate one another.   All we may hope is that the intellectual leaders may succeed in showing the people that they must stop wars because it would be best for them to have no wars —because they would benefit more from peace than from war.

"Pacifism should not be sentimental.   That is useless. Pacifists should not say that it is wrong to kill, that it is unethical to destroy human life—that it is immoral to commit such a crime—that other people suffer from such destruction—and that war is terrible on that account. Everybody knows that war is terrible, that it leaves dead and maimed in its wake—that it destroys property, and retards what is known as civilization.   But such methods of reasoning, such arguments are of no avail.   Human beings are not impressed by them.   Human beings do not change their nature on that account.   Instead of sentimental pacifism, it is essential to convince them by education that peace would benefit them and save them—that in a roundabout way they themselves or their children may be the victims of war—the wounded, the mutilated, the dead.

"It is of very little value to preach love and the brotherhood of man, for it does not help. There are some people who believe that it is enough for them to preach or to listen to sermons on loving one's neighbor as themselves—and that by this they have already discharged all their duties to their fellow men. The quality of unselfish love is not inherent in human beings—and it is useless to demand of human beings to change that which cannot be changed. Besides, it is not necessary at all. I do not want people to love me. I do not want their kisses. I don't think it necessary that there should be too much love among the nations. The important thing is that people should realize that they must not wrong one another—that they must not hurt or injure one another. The important thing is that people should have the opportunity to work, undisturbed, in peace, that they should not interfere with others, that they should not destroy others, that they should not rob others. They must learn to realize that war will affect them directly in some way or other just as they believe war would affect their enemy—their neighbor.

"Yesterday, while my daughter was packing to go to the country, we found a batch of old newspapers published during the war. I looked at the headlines. 'The battle of ——. We captured 50,000 men. Tens of thousands slain.' And the jubilation over each victory! I remember how our people rejoiced when they heard that thousands of Russians were drowned in swamps. I was filled with terror as I recalled all this. Of course, the other side did exactly the same. They rejoiced when hundreds of thousands of our people were slaughtered. And I recalled with horror the indifference with which people afterward read about those battles.   When, for instance, they read that fifty thousand men had been slain, and on the following morning the revised figures showed that instead of fifty thousand there really were sixty thousand casualties, did that difference disturb the people's sleep, or did it affect their appetites?   Not in the least.   They went on eating, drinking and smoking their cigars.   In fact, the men at the front hated the 'enemy' less than the people in the rear—we know that at the front the men often fraternized with the 'enemy,' while the people in the rear hated the 'enemy' intensely— and this hate is continuing.   And in certain places it is even encouraged deliberately—fanned and spread artificially.

"If we read about some distant island sinking into the ocean with a population of a half a million human beings we would actually be affected by such news much less than by the natural death of someone on our block.   If a fire breaks out in our neighbor's house, we are upset and worried to the extent that we fear lest the fire should spread to our own house.   If a fire breaks out somewhere in our city, we are worried because it may destroy the house of one of our relatives or friends.   If we hear of a fire in a distant part of our city where we have no relatives or friends, we go on smoking our cigars undisturbed.

"I recall a simple, quite unimportant incident, but it is so characteristic that I will tell it to you.   Some years ago my wife had scarlet fever.   We had a nurse who attended her.   The nurse was very correct, devoted, efficient and intelligent.   When my wife recovered and the nurse was to leave, she had to wait about a quarter of an hour for an ambulance which was to fumigate her clothes in order that she may not infect other people.

"When I went out of the house a few minutes later, I noticed to my great amazement that the nurse entered a crowded street car, without having waited for the ambulance. She had no patience to wait fifteen minutes, and she went home by car without having taken the necessary precaution. She probably infected a number of people in that car with scarlet fever. Here was a nurse who knew well the dangers of such contagion. She was intelligent and it was her profession to look after patients, and to be careful. But that did not matter to her. She went into the crowded street car because the passengers were just ordinary people whom she did not know. They were strangers to her, and she did not care. But if, for instance, she were to learn that someone was infected in that car by her, and that such person carried the disease to a child who happened to be a schoolmate of her own child, and in that way infected her own child—and her own child died as a result of her recklessness and neglect then she would think and act differently in the future. Of course, if such a thing happened, people would say that it was an unusual case, a rare coincidence. But if people were to figure things out logically they would find that the wrong they do others in some way or other necessarily reacts on themselves—they would understand that, and would stop wronging others. As I have said before, human beings may become wiser, but they will never grow better. It is therefore the important task of intellectual leaders everywhere to organize themselves and start a campaign to enlighten the people that peace is in their own interests—that war will ruin them, while peace will benefit them."

"Why don't you develop this idea more elaborately in an article?" I suggested.

"I can't write articles," replied Dr. Schnitzler. "I have often been asked to write articles for the *Neue Freie Presse*. I have often discussed certain subjects with the publisher and editor of that newspaper, and he often said to me: 'Let me have an article on this subject. This is just what I need.' I have always declined to write articles. I often wonder why journalists and publicists underestimate their own ability to write articles and believe that novelists or dramatists must necessarily know how to write articles."

"But in this instance you have advanced the best reasons why you should write something on this theme, particularly when you pointed out that the intellectual leaders should at this juncture do the utmost to make people realize the effects of war and peace on themselves," I said.

"I am afraid you would be disappointed if I wrote an article on this subject. I really could not do it," he replied.

Our conversation turned to Schnitzler's dramatic works. Suddenly he asked:

"How would you account for the fact that some of my plays which were written 20 or 25 years ago are being produced only now? They seem to attract more attention now than when I wrote them."

"Your works were at least a quarter of a century ahead of their time," I answered. "Only now people are beginning to understand and appreciate them fully."

When I mentioned "Reigen," his sex play which created a sensation last year in Berlin and Vienna and which was at first suppressed by the German censor, Schnitzler remarked modestly: "'Reigen' is an ordinary play. The dialogues were written more than twenty five years ago. When this play of mine will long have been forgotten, the record of the Berlin trial connected with 'Reigen' will live. The stenographic report of the testimony at that trial is the most amazing satire of our time. The four or five figures that revealed themselves in that extraordinary document are types of hypocrisy that the greatest of satirists could hardly have invented or improved upon."

ROOSEVELT LETTERS

In the course of one of my interviews with Count Witte in 1908 in Petrograd I asked him to permit me to examine the more important documents relating to the Portsmouth Peace Treaty, in which Theodore Roosevelt played so conspicuous a rôle. Count Witte took out a large portfolio from his desk and said:

"There are only two sets of these documents in existence. This is the original, and the Tsar has the copy. The time has not yet arrived to publish these documents."

He hesitated a while, then added:

"I have another appointment now which will take about an hour. If you like, you may go into my library with these documents and examine them. You are at liberty to use any of the documents you can copy during this hour. But do not mention that you received them from me."

I examined the documents for half an hour, and then copied for half an hour. Among the various reports I found unpublished cablegrams which President Roosevelt had sent during the Portsmouth Peace Conference direct to the Tsar, through American Ambassador Meyer. I knew that these cablegrams, which threw a most interesting light on Roosevelt as peacemaker, had not been made public in America, and later I learned that Roosevelt had sent them to the Tsar without the knowledge of Count Witte, Russia's chief plenipotentiary at the Portsmouth Conference. So I selected these documents for reproduction. Exactly at the end of the hour, the huge figure of Count Witte appeared in the doorway of the library.

"Now I am interested to see what you have chosen," he said, smiling.

I pointed to the Roosevelt cablegrams.

"I must compliment you. You have selected the most interesting of all these documents," he remarked. "Roosevelt did not know that the Tsar transmitted the cablegrams to me."

I brought these documents back with me to America and published them in *The New York Times*.

Some time afterward, when Roosevelt became the contributing editor of *The Outlook*, he asked me how I had secured his cablegrams. I told him that while I was not at liberty to divulge the name of the man from whom I had secured the copies, I was absolutely certain that they were authentic, and therefore I published them.

He smiled broadly and said:

"They are authentic, but I am curious to know who gave them to you. The only reason I am sorry you published them is that I intended to publish them first in my autobiography."

The following is President Roosevelt's First Cablegram to Ambassador Meyer, August 9, 1905:

"Please see his Majesty personally immediately and deliver the following message from me:

"I earnestly ask your Majesty to believe that in what I am about to say and to advise I speak as the earnest friend of Russia and give you the advice I should give if I were a Russian patriot and statesman. The Japanese have, as I understand it, abandoned their demands for the interned ships and the limitation of the Russian naval power in the Pacific, which conditions I felt were improper for Russia to yield to.   Moreover, I find out to my surprise and pleasure that the Japanese are willing to restore the north half of Saghalien to Russia, Russia, of course, in such case to pay a substantial sum for this surrender of territory by the Japanese and for the return of Russian prisoners.

"It seems to me that if peace can be obtained substantially on these terms, it will be both just and honorable, and that it would be a dreadful calamity to have the war continued when peace can thus be obtained.

"Of the twelve points which the plenipotentiaries have been discussing, on eight they have come to a substantial agreement.   Two, which were offensive to Russia, the Japanese will, as I understand it, withdraw.   The remaining two can be met by agreement in principle that the Japanese shall restore or retrocede to Russia the north half of Sakhaline, while Russia of course, pays an adequate sum for this retrocession and for Russian prisoners.   If this agreement can be made the question as to the exact amount can be a subject of negotiation.

"Let me repeat how earnestly I feel that it is for Russia's interests to conclude peace on substantially these terms. No one can foretell the continuance of war, and I have no doubt that it is to Japan's advantage to conclude peace. But in my judgment it is infinitely more to the advantage of Russia.   If peace is not made now, and war is continued, it may well be that, though the financial strain upon Japan would be severe, yet in the end Russia would be shorn of those East Siberian provinces which have been won for her by the heroism of her sons during the last three centuries. The proposed peace leaves the ancient boundaries absolutely intact. The only change in territory will be that Japan will recover that part of Saghalien which was hers up to thirty years ago. As Saghalien is an island, it is, humanly speaking, impossible that the Russians should reconquer it, in view of the disaster to their navy, and to keep the north half of it as a guarantee for the security of Vladivostok and Eastern Siberia for Russia.

"It seems to me that every consideration of national self-interest, of military expediency, and of broad humanity, makes it eminently wise and just for Russia to conclude peace substantially along these lines, and it is my hope and prayer that your Majesty may take this.

"THEODORE ROOSEVELT."

President Roosevelt's Second Cablegram to Ambassador Meyer, August 13, 1905:

"My second cable was forwarded after the arrival of your first. Japan has now on deposit in the United States about 50,000 of the last war loan. Please tell His Majesty that I dislike intruding my advice on him again, but for fear of misapprehension I venture again to have these statements made to him.

"I, of course, would not have him act against his conscience, but I earnestly hope his conscience will guide him so as to prevent the continuance of war, when this continuance may involve Russia in a greater calamity than has ever befallen it since it first rose to power in both Europe and Asia.

"I see it publicly anounced to-day by the Minister for Foreign Affairs that Russia will neither pay money nor surrender territory. I beg His Majesty to consider that such an announcement means absolutely nothing when Sakhaline is already in the hands of Japanese. If on such theory the war is persevered in, no one can foretell the result, but the merged representatives of the Powers most friendly to Russia assure me that the continuance of the war will probably mean the loss not merely of Sakhaline, but of Eastern Siberia, and if after a year of struggle this proves true, then any peace which came could only come on terms which would indicate a real calamity.

"Most certainly I think it will be a bad thing for Japan to go on with the war, but I think it will be a far worse thing for Russia. There is now a fair chance of getting peace on honorable terms, and it seems to me that it will be a dreadful thing for Russia and the civilized world if the chance is thrown away. My advices are that the plenipotentiaries at Portsmouth have come to a substantial agreement on every point except the money question and the question of Sakhaline.

"Let it now be announced that as regards these two points peace shall be made on the basis of the retrocession of the north half of Sakhaline to Russia on payment of a sum of redemption of money by Russia, the amount of this redemption of money and the amount to be paid for the Russian prisoners to be settled by further negotiations. This does not commit the Russian Government as to what sum shall be paid, leaving it open to further negotiation.

"If it is impossible for Russia and Japan to come to an agreement on this sum, they might possibly call in the advice of, say, some high French or German official appointed by or with the consent of Russia and some English official appointed by or with the consent of Japan, and have these later then report to the negotiators. This, it seems to me, would be an entirely honorable way of settling the difficulty. I cannot, of course, guarantee that Japan will agree to this proposal, but if His Majesty agrees to it I will endeavor to get the Japanese Government to do likewise.

"I earnestly hope that this cable of mine can receive His Majesty's attention before the envoys meet to-morrow, and I cannot too strongly say that I feel that peace now may prevent untold calamities in the future. Let me repeat that in this proposal I suggest that neither Russia nor Japan do anything but face accomplished facts, and that I do not specify or attempt to specify the amount to be paid as redemption money for the north half of Sakhaline to be settled by further negotiation. I fear that if these terms are rejected it may not be possible that Japan will give up the idea of making peace or of ever getting money, and she will decide to take and to keep Sakhaline and Harbin and the whole Siberian Manchurian Railway, and this, of course, would mean that she would take Eastern Siberia.

"Such a loss to Russia would, in my judgment, be a disaster of portentous size, and I earnestly desire to save Russia from such a risk. If peace is made on the terms I have mentioned, Russia is left at the end of this war substantially unharmed, the national honor and interest saved, and the result of what Russians have done in Asia since the days of Ivan the Terrible unimpaired.

"But if peace is now rejected, and if Japan decides that it is better she will give up the idea of obtaining any redemption money or any other sum, no matter how small, the military situation is such that there is at least a good chance, and on estimate of most outside observers a strong probability, that though Japan will have to make heavy sacrifices she will yet take Harbin, Vladivostok, and Eastern Siberia, and if this is once done the probabilities are overwhelming that she could never be dislodged.

"I cannot too strongly state my conviction that while peace in accordance with the suggestions above outlined is earnestly to be desired, from the standpoint of the whole world and from the standpoint of both combatants, yet that, far above all, it is chiefly to Russia's interest and perhaps to her vital interest that it should come in this way and at this time.

"THEODORE ROOSEVELT."

After interviewing Roosevelt at the request of Witte, in 1913, in regard to a report that was circulated abroad to the effect that Japan was really tottering at the time of the Portsmouth Peace Conference and that she had induced Roosevelt to assume the rôle of peacemaker, Roosevelt wrote me the following characteristic letter:

February 10, 1913.

"Dear Mr. Bernstein:
" . . . You could have added to the statement you made to Count Witte, that it was also a preposterous falsehood to assert that any representative of the Japanese Government had directly or indirectly asked me to forward the negotiations on the ground that Japan was getting exhausted and could not continue the war.

"Faithfully yours,

"THEODORE ROOSEVELT."

In 1917 Theodore Roosevelt wrote the following introduction to my volume containing the "Willy Nicky Telegrams," the secret correspondence between the Kaiser and the Tsar, which I had secured in Russia and which I made public throughout the world:

Sagamore Hill, November 6th, 1917.

"*My dear Mr. Bernstein,*

"I congratulate you on the noteworthy service you have rendered by the discovery and publication of these letters. They illuminate, with a glare like a flashlight, the dark places of diplomacy of despots; they show what diplomacy in autocratic nations really is, and what it has done and sought to do, right up to the present time. The whole world ought now to understand that the despotism of Germany was one of plot and intrigue no less than of ruthless brutality and barbarism, and that with a cynically complete absence of all sense of international morality and good faith it sought to bend to its purpose of evil the poor feeble puppet who at the moment embodied the despotism of Russia. These letters should be made familiar to all civilized peoples.

"They show the folly of the men who would have us believe that any permanent escape from anarchy in Russia can come from the re-establishment of the autocracy, which was itself the prime cause of that anarchy—for the governmental condition was so intolerable that they put a premium on the production of lawless violence in the ranks of the lovers of liberty and justice and fair play to all.

"They show, furthermore, the wicked folly of all who would now treat with the German despotism for a negotiated peace, a peace without victory, a peace into which the wrong-doer and the wronged would enter on equal terms. This war was made by the militaristic and capitalistic autocracy of Germany, and it was acquiesced in and even promoted by the German socialistic party, which thereby proved itself traitorous to the workingmen and farmers of the world. With these documents before them, no Americans who hereafter directly or indirectly support the Prussianized Germany of the Hohenzollerns can claim to stand in good faith for human rights, for equal justice, and for the liberty of small well-behaved nations.

"Let me repeat, my dear sir, that in publishing these letters you have rendered a signal service to this nation and to all mankind.

"Very sincerely yours

"THEODORE ROOSEVELT."

WOODROW WILSON

Woodrow Wilson was a great idealist, and as a great idealist he was disillusioned. His tragedy lay in the fact that he was so far ahead of his time. The future generations of America will learn how to value the fine heritage of idealism he has bequeathed to the world.

"Fifty years from now there will be more plays written about Woodrow Wilson than there have been about Napoleon or any other distinguished personage in history. There is in his life a greater drama than Shakespeare ever pictured."

This statement, made several years ago by Alexander Moissi, the famous European actor, displayed a deep understanding of the dramatic in the life of the greatest American of our day, the supreme idealist who died this year, and who is destined to rank with Lincoln in the history of America.

The dramatic rise of Woodrow Wilson to heights rarely before reached by a human being, and his disillusionment will be better estimated in the years to come, for the events are too close at present to be seen in their proper perspective.

When Woodrow Wilson entered American political life, a new force made itself felt immediately, a great moral force with a passion for righteousness, for social justice, for a new freedom, for universal peace. Woodrow Wilson was a new type of American politician-statesman, strong and keen, determined to translate into life his lofty theories and humanitarian doctrines. But he was not a mere dreamer. His idealism and his dreams had a practical basis. He looked farther into the future than most of his contemporaries, and his tragedy lay in the fact that he was far ahead of his time—and therefore he was so often misunderstood.

During the World War, Wilson grew into the most important world figure, not only as the President of the greatest, richest and most powerful republic, but as the voice of mankind. His utterances carried a new hope to the world. It was as though in the madhouse of slaughter in Europe there suddenly appeared the conscience of a great young people—the aroused conscience of America—and President Wilson's simplest words, his finely-woven phrases embodying lofty ideals, sounded like a new gospel preached from Sinai. His formula of "self-determination of nations," though borrowed from the Russian radicals, thrilled the oppressed peoples everywhere with new hopes and filled them with yearnings for national self-expression. His advocacy of the League of Nations throbbed with sincerity, with almost naïve simplicity and with deep faith.

Out of the turmoil of combat, amid bloodshed and tears, above the din of cannon, came his ringing words that sounded like a new Sermon on the Mount, a new Ten Commandments. And the people, clamoring for a ray of hope, trusted Wilson's ideals implicitly.

I do not know whether the following anecdote is true or not. It is said that Clemenceau once asked President Wilson lightly: "Why do you insist upon your Fourteen Points when Moses gave only Ten Commandments to the world?" To this Mr. Wilson is said to have replied: "If you will guarantee that we can carry out the Ten Commandments at the Peace Conference I would be only too willing to give up my Fourteen Points." This story may be a legend, but it is characteristic that such legends have grown up around the personality of Woodrow Wilson.

He came to Europe as the great peacemaker. The people, particularly the oppressed nations, saw in him one of the world's greatest prophets—the embodiment of their hope and their salvation. The people worshipped him in Italy, in Belgium, in Czecho-Slovakia; they lighted ikons for him even in distant Siberia, and the defeated peoples saw in him their redeemer. His tour through Europe called forth a spontaneous ovation such as no king or religious leader ever received.

The statesmen and politicians of the victorious nations feared and respected him. They knew the energy, enterprise and determination of America—the great young giant across the seas, and they feared Wilson as the head of that giant. They dared not oppose him, even when they shrugged their shoulders at his excessive idealism. During the war they realized the effect of his sermons to humanity, they knew that those sermons were breaking down the morale of the Central Powers because the people everywhere believed him, and the Allied statesmen tried to convey the impression that they agreed with him by maintaining silence.

There is one definite, concrete service which Woodrow Wilson rendered to the world and which will be remembered after most of the statesmen of to-day have passed away and are forgotten. It will be recorded by future historians among the greatest achievements of our age. It was Wilson who actually broke down the Hohenzollern dynasty and crushed Kaiserism. It was he who first dared raise his voice against the militarist autocracy of Germany when the other statesmen were silent. They never wanted the downfall of Kaiserism, they could not conceive that it was possible to overthrow it. Wilson directed the moral and physical forces of America against Kaiserism and crushed it. It was a monumental achievement.

When it became known that Mr. Wilson would personally conduct the peace negotiations in Paris, the European statesmen became alarmed at first. They feared America as a new dictator in international affairs.

But Wilson was not familiar with the petty intrigues of European diplomacy, with its age-old rivalries and jealousies, and the great peacemaker, caught in the labyrinth of European diplomatic entanglements, found himself forced to yield and yield for the sake of maintaining peace in the Peace Conference. He believed in himself, in his ideals, he felt absolutely convinced that he was but voicing the desires and hopes of the American people, and for the sake of attaining his great ideal, the instrument through which a durable and righteous peace could be secured, he forced himself to make concession after concession. But when he raised his voice in protest against secret treaties in the matter of Fiume it was too late. His utterances seemed to have lost their charm. The miracle seemed at an end. And the concessions which Wilson was forced to make led to compromises that prevented the peace treaties from becoming real instruments of righteousness and durable peace. Europe, with millions of bodies strewn over her fields during the war, was now strewn with dead hopes.

I saw President Wilson in the Hotel Crillon, in Paris, on the day before he returned to America. I heard him speak to a group of American correspondents about the peace treaty. He was still inspired. He defended his acts and his concessions on that occasion much more effectively than at any time after his return to America. He realized that the peace treaty was not a perfect document, but that it was the best that could have been secured under the circumstances. He had fought for his ideal, and while he was compelled to yield on numerous points, the others at the Peace Conference were compelled by him to yield still more.

I shall never forget his brief answer to one of the correspondents who asked him whether he believed that America should concern herself with all the troubles of the world.

"Wherever injustice is done, whether it be done to a large group or to a small group, the moral force of America must be there to defend those who are wronged or oppressed."

When the Russian passport question began to stir the sense of justice of the American people, when Russia discriminated against a certain portion of the people because of their religious belief, and the spirit of the best American people was aroused against such discriminations, Wilson delivered an address that was the most inspiring and most important contribution to the cause of equal rights for all American citizens. In that famous speech he said:

"There lies a principle back of our life. America is not a mere body of traders; it is a body of free men. Our greatness is built upon our freedom—is moral, not material. We have a great ardor for gain; but we have a deep passion for the rights of man. Principles lie back of our action. America would be inconceivable without them. These principles are not incompatible with great material prosperity. On the contrary, unless we are deeply

mistaken, they are indispensable to it.   We are not willing
to have prosperity, however, if our fellow citizens must suffer contempt for it, or lose the rights that belong to every
American in order that we may enjoy it.   The price is too
great.

"Here is a great body of our Jewish fellow citizens,
from whom have sprung men of genius in every walk of
our very life; men who have become part of the very stuff
of America, who have conceived its ideals with singular
clearness and led its enterprise with spirit and sagacity.
They are playing a particularly conspicuous part in building up the very prosperity of which our Government has so
great a stake in its dealings with the Russian Government
with regard to the rights of men.   They are not Jews in
America; they are American citizens.   In this great matter
with which we deal, we speak for them as for representatives and champions of principles which underlie the
very structure of our Government.   They have suddenly become representatives of us all.   By our actions for them
shall be tested our sincerity, our genuineness, the reality
of principle among us."

In a letter, dated July 5, 1911, Governor Wilson wrote
me about the Russian passport question as follows:

. . . "I do not see how there can be any divergence of
feeling among patriotic Americans regarding the situation
in Russia with regard to the religious discriminations made
by the Russian Government.   The principle involved ad-
mits of no argument."

On January 23, 1912, Mr. Wilson wrote to me on the
same matter as follows:

"We have certainly abundant reason for thinking that

Russia has failed to keep her obligations under the treaty. . . ."

In September, 1911, when Woodrow Wilson was a candidate for the Presidency, I had the privilege to introduce him at the National Arts Club to a delegation of about one hundred journalists and editors of foreign language newspapers who gathered there for the discussion of the problem of immigration. Addressing the editors, I said: "You who have come to this country from various parts of Europe in quest of a home and of liberty, you are all American or striving to be American. You have brought with you your best traditions; your lofty ideals; your energy and earnestness; your love for your great literatures and your great cultures; the great past of your nations, and here in the land of tolerance and equal opportunity you are working out your future together with the great future of the American people. We are all deeply interested in a better America, and the better America will be, the better will be the rest of the world."

And Woodrow Wilson said on that occasion:

"I have always pleased myself with the idea that America in some degree exists in spirit all over the world, and that there are men coming to these shores who have displayed their force in our affairs, who bring to America a more vivid conception of what it means than those of us who were born and bred here ourselves entertain. . . . If I go to the country reputed to be a country of equality and liberty, I must expect to find constant visible and open signs of liberty and equality; and therefore, I carry to that country a demand which that country must satisfy. I carry it because I was really, without knowing it, born an American.

I wanted that thing that I thought I could get in America, and therefore broke the tender connections of old associations, the intimate connections of a birthplace and went to a far country looking for an ideal.

"I close as I began, by a very respectful protest against calling yourself foreign editors or anything with the word foreign in it. Your newspapers and magazines are published in languages which are not the general language of America, which is modified English, but at this stage of the melting-pot process every language in which you print a paper is largely used in the United States, and is used for the conveyance of American ideas. Now, I would just as well Americanize a language as Americanize an individual, and I welcome the process by which you are Americanizing other foreign languages as the rest of us have Americanized English, or speaking as someone wittily said, the 'English Slanguage.' All my interest is that you shouldn't regard the language in which you print your periodicals as a foreign language when printed in America for the conveyance of American thinking. Then we will have taken another step toward that combination of elements which is in the long run going to make America more varied, I dare say, in its natural gifts, more variegated in its genius than any other country in the world."

In July, 1914, President Wilson was reported to have made the following statement in the course of an address at the dedication of the American University:

"That is the reason why scholarship has usually been most fruitful when associated with religion, and scholarship has never, so far as I can at this moment recall, been associated with any religion except the religion of Jesus Christ."

I wrote him a note inquiring whether he was quoted correctly in the press, adding:

"I feel quite certain that you know that true scholarship has ever been and is now the very essence and foundation of Judaism, the religion which gave birth to Christianity. It seems to me that it would, therefore, be unfair to exclude Judaism from the religions with which scholarship has been intimately associated."

On July 9, President Wilson made public the following letter addressed to me:

"I am sorry that there should have been any unfair implication in what I said at the opening of the American University last week. You may be sure that there was nothing of the kind in my mind, for there certainly is nothing in my thought that would discriminate in the important matter you speak of, against Judaism.

"I find that one of the risks and penalties of extemporaneous speaking is that you do not stop to consider the whole field but address yourself merely to the matter directly in hand."

Woodrow Wilson has often been described as a cold, unfeeling, thinking machine. The people who characterized him thus did not know him. They knew neither his wonderful sense of humor, nor his deep sympathies for the suffering and the oppressed.

I remember how deeply he was moved when I related to him the sufferings of the people in Palestine during the early stages of the war, when they needed food and medicines and there was no way of sending these to them at the time. The Jewish relief committee had made vain efforts to secure a boat to send food supplies and medicines. At the request of Dr. Magnes, of the Relief Committee,

I took the matter up with the big-hearted, fair-minded Secretary of the Navy, Josephus Daniels, who was sympathetically inclined to help the suffering people of the Holy Land—Jews, Christians and Moslems—but he feared that it would be impossible to send the food supplies and medicines on a Government boat, as that would establish a precedent, and other nations might ask for the same form of relief.

I then called on President Wilson and familiarized him with the tragic situation that prevailed in Palestine at the time. I told him that I had discussed the matter with Secretary Daniels and that Mr. Daniels had explained to me the difficulty of having such supplies sent on an American transport. President Wilson was moved to tears. Then he said:

"It may be that an American ship will go in that direction before long. Ask Secretary Daniels to let you know when such a ship will start for the Mediterranean, and he will arrange to have space for food supplies and medicines to be shipped to the suffering people in the Holy Land."

Within two weeks I received a telegram from Secretary Daniels notifying me that the *Vulcan* was starting for the Orient and that the Relief Committee would have space for nine hundred tons of food supplies and medicines at its disposal.

When I sent President Wilson a message of thanks, he wrote me as follows:

"Your telegram gratified and touched me very deeply. You may be sure I was exceedingly happy to do what I could to help and I was delighted to find that one of our ships was bound in that direction."

I met Woodrow Wilson many times, both as Governor of New Jersey and as President of the United States.

Discussing the literacy test for immigrants, he said to me one day: "This is an unfair and unjust test for immigrants. Criminals and charlatans, who come to these shores to carry on injurious propaganda here or to enrich themselves by questionable methods, will not be barred by the literacy test. They can all read and write. But many of those who come here to flee religious or political persecution, who have been denied the opportunity to acquire the knowledge of reading and writing, would be barred from America by this test, even though they are honest and hard-working men and women, seeking equal opportunity, eager to adapt themselves to American standards of life and ready to contribute to America's wealth."

During the early period of the World War, before the United States had entered it, President Wilson remarked to me at the White House:

"Since the Germans accuse me of being pro-Ally, and the Allies believe that I am pro-German, I know that I am pursuing the right course of neutrality—the right course for America."

In 1914, when I established *The Day*, the national Jewish daily, President Wilson sent me the following letter:

"*The White House, Washington,*
"*October 7, 1924.*

"*My dear Mr. Bernstein:*

"I am greatly interested in what you tell me of the projected daily to be entitled *The Day* and am heartily glad to know that you are to be its editor and moving spirit. I

have learned to entertain the highest esteem for you and
to believe that you are devoted sincerely not only, but in a
disinterested way, to the advancement of the highest interests of the Jewish people in America.   I congratulate them
upon having such an editor for such a paper as that which
you are planning to issue.

"Cordially and sincerely yours

"WOODROW WILSON."

The following are a few characteristic letters I received
from President Wilson:

"*The White House, Washington,*
"*March 18, 1915.*

"*My dear Mr. Bernstein:*

"I have your telegram of yesterday about my little essay
just republished.   I doubt my right to authorize its publication as you suggest, but would be very glad if the publishers would give their consent.

"If you should publish it, pray let me know.   There is a
passage which ought to be changed.   I had not read the
essay since it was first published many years ago in the
Century Magazine.

"Cordially and sincerely yours,

"WOODROW WILSON."

"*The White House, Washington,*
"*June 16, 1916.*

"*My dear Mr. Bernstein:*

"Your letter of June twelfth is appreciated and has had
my careful consideration.   I hope sincerely that the plank
which is to be inserted in our platform will seem to you to

speak the right doctrine. It certainly seems to me to do so. One has to be very careful nowadays not to commit the governing party of the country to any course of action which might interfere with, rather than set forward, its hopes in this matter by seeming to foreshadow a course which would irritate, rather than help.

"Sincerely yours
"Woodrow Wilson."

"*The White House, Washington,*
"*Shadow Lawn, September 20, 1916.*

"*My dear Mr. Bernstein:*
"Your plan for a special issue of your magazine has interested me very much and I avail myself of the opportunity to express my deep interest in the work you are doing for the Jews of America. I hope that they feel, as I am sure you do, that America is a real home in which all forces work together for justice and fair dealing, and I am sure that I need not assure you or them of my genuine interest in my fellow-citizens of Hebrew extraction. No man who knows the history of America, or, indeed, of the world, could fail to appreciate their notable contributions to industry, philanthropy, intellectual development, and political liberty.

"Cordially and sincerely yours
"Woodrow Wilson."